INHERITING GANDHI

INFLUENCES, ACTIVISMS

Edited by

Satishchandra Kumar

Kanchana Mahadevan

Meher Bhoot

Rajesh Kharat

Foreword by
Akeel Bilgrami

Afterword by
Neera Chandhoke

SPEAKING
TIGER

in association with

University of Mumbai

SPEAKING TIGER BOOKS LLP
125A, Ground Floor, Shahpur Jat, near Asiad Village,
New Delhi 110049

First published by Speaking Tiger Books 2022

ISBN: 978-93-5447-271-8
eISBN: 978-93-5447-270-1

10 9 8 7 6 5 4 3 2 1

Meher Bhoot is Associate Professor and Head at the Department of German, University of Mumbai. Her areas of specialization are German Literature with a focus on Literature of the German Minorities, Postcolonial Studies and Culture Studies, and her areas of interest are European Cultural History and European History of Art. She is an active member of the German Institute's Partnership with the Universities of Göttingen and Freiburg in Germany. Under the aegis of this partnership she has been a Guest Professor at the Department of Intercultural German Studies, University of Göttingen. She is a DAAD Fellow since 2004 and has also been a recipient of the Rotary Cultural and Ambassadorial Scholarship (1997-98). She is also the Member Secretary of the Women's Development Cell and member of the Internal Committee at the University of Mumbai. Apart from articles published, some of her co-edited volumes include *Revisiting Günter Grass, Voices from India and Germany, Interkulturelle Momente, Einfach menschlich.* She has also co-edited textbooks for short courses for teaching Marathi to non-native speakers.

Rajesh Kharat is Founder Director, School of International Relations and Strategic Studies, University of Mumbai and Dean, Faculty of Humanities, University of Mumbai (on Deputation), and Professor and former Chairperson, Centre for South Asian Studies, School of International Studies, JNU, New Delhi. He has an MA in Political Science from the University of Poona, and has completed his M.Phil and PhD from CSAS, SIS, JNU, New Delhi. He began his teaching career at the University of Mumbai in 1991 and taught at JNU for 30 years. He has published five books and more than 30 research articles in international and national journals and edited volumes on various themes of contemporary South Asia.

Satishchandra Kumar is Professor and Head of the Department of Applied Psychology & Counselling Centre at the University of Mumbai. He is also the Coordinator of the Mahatma Gandhi Peace Centre. He is the recipient of the Summer Fellowship from the Albert Ellis Institute, New York. He was awarded a Research Fellowship by the Indian Council of Social Science Research (ICSSR), New Delhi. He has published in international peer-reviewed journals like *Journal of Personality and Social Psychology, Psychological Science, British Journal of Guidance and Counselling,* and also contributed to the Sage volume of

Eminent Indian Psychologists: 100 Years of Psychology in India. He has published five books and more than 40 research papers in national and international journals, and many students have done doctorate degrees under his guidance. His area of research is Industrial/Organizational Psychology, which includes positive psychology, engagement at the workplace, stress and coping at the workplace. He is also a member of many academic bodies and regularly advises corporates. He is also the co-editor of *Sambhashan*, the journal of the University of Mumbai.

Kanchana Mahadevan is Professor and Head at the Department of Philosophy, University of Mumbai. She teaches and researches in feminist philosophy, continental thought, critical theory and political philosophy. She also works in the interdisciplinary areas of aesthetics and film. Her book *Between Femininity and Feminism: Colonial and Postcolonial Perspectives on Care* examines the relevance of Western feminist philosophy in the Indian context, while bringing Western feminism into dialogue with its Indian counterpart. Her publications on Ambedkar explore his rearticulation of democracy from the Indian perspective. In her recently published research papers on care ethics, she has engaged with its critical potential in relation to health work and the cosmopolitan character of care. She is specifically interested in exploring the comparative and decolonizing dimensions of philosophy. She is currently working on a monograph on the relationship between the secular and the post-secular in the context of gender.

CONTENTS

Part Two: ACTIVISMS

ACKNOWLEDGEMENTS

The editors of this book are obliged to the University of Mumbai for encouraging the journal *Sambhashan* without which this book would not have been possible. We thank the authors in this book for their illuminating contributions, despite their difficult schedules. We owe a debt of gratitude to the peer reviewers, advisory committee members, board of consulting editors and assistant editors of our online journal *Sambhashan* for their help and suggestions. We thank Ravi Singh and his team for their support and assistance.

FOREWORD

Gandhi In His Time and Ours: Some Reflections on Secularism and Multiculturalism

Akeel Bilgrami

Reflections on Secularism

It is widely known that Gandhi, for most of the long period of the freedom movement that he led, was indifferent to the claims of what has come to be called 'secularism'. In fact, 'secularism' was not a concept that was much wielded by him or by Nehru[1] till the 1940s, when the acrimonies around an impending threat of partition inevitably made the rhetoric of secularism

---

[1] This striking fact about Nehru is not always plain to us because Nehru is so often—and correctly—seen as the great proponent of Indian modernity. But it is easily explained, if we keep in mind an elementary distinction between secularism and secular*ization*. 'Secularization' is the name for an ideational and social transformation in the modern period in Europe, a transformation that Weber prominently theorized, stressing loss of belief in religious doctrine (loss of belief in God, in the myths of creation, etc.) as well as a decline in religious rituals and practises (decline in church, mosque and temple attendance, giving up on pious habits of dress and diet, etc.). By contrast, secularism, also originating conceptually in Europe in the modern period, is not a name for process of transformation in society and ideas, but rather the name for a much more specific doctrine in which institutions of the law and the state are viewed as being required to be steered away from the direct control and influence of religion. Nehru and Gandhi had fundamental differences on the matter of secular*ization*. Nehru's entire temperament and set of mind was highly secularized, constantly lauding scientific rationality and descrying superstition as irrational, whereas Gandhi was an avowedly religious man, though his religiosity (for all his perverse self-description as a 'sanatani') was well-known to be highly maverick. He also openly wished to preserve many aspects of India's religious traditions of belief and practise. However, on the matter

surface. A little later, during the Constituent Assembly debates, though issues around secularism were, of course, discussed, it is also widely known that the term made no entry into the Constitution till the mid-1970s. After Gandhi's death, in the decade immediately following independence, the term secularism was mostly wielded in narrow legal contexts of the reform of Hindu law. *What accounts for this relative absence and, at best, narrow and limited relevance of a concept in all those decades?* A concept which we have now, since the 1980s, come to see as urgently and centrally relevant and which, given its urgent and central relevance now, is responsible for our sometimes assuming, with a distorting backwards projection, as always having been present and viewed as central in those earlier decades.

I will try to answer the question that I have italicized above by focusing initially on Gandhi, since it is Gandhi who is the subject of this book. The beginnings of an answer lie in a conviction that Gandhi repeatedly asserted, viz., that Indian history and society and culture were characterized by an unselfconscious pluralism for centuries.[2] (I will be relying heavily throughout this essay on the central significance of this idea of an 'unselfconscious pluralism' in Gandhi's thinking.) How does this conviction explain Gandhi's relative neglect of the concept

---

of secular*ism*, all through the years in which they worked together, neither of them placed secularism on the centre-stage in their rhetoric or in their political platforms and pronouncements. This, as I said, is a striking thing to note, given how much we associate Nehru with secularism in the period after Gandhi died. (See also my next footnote). For more detailed discussion of the distinction between secularism and secularization, see my essays, 'Gandhi, Nehru, and the Contexts of Indian Secularism' in *The Oxford Handbook of Indian Philosophy*, edited by Jonardon Ganeri (Oxford University Press, 2017) and 'Indian Secularism and Art in a time of "Crisis"' in Tapati Guha-Thakurta and Vazira Zamindar (eds.) *How Secular is Art?* (Oxford University Press, forthcoming).

[2] As even a cursory glance at Nehru's *The Discovery of India* reveals, Nehru wholeheartedly shared this conviction. He shared with Gandhi too the account of the differences between nationalism in Europe and

of secularism in the entire period of his involvement in and leadership of the cause of Indian independence? Here, we need to look at some basic developments in Europe in the modern period and Gandhi's attitudes towards them.

It is widely known that secularism had its origins in European modernity.[3] A very rough and crude sketch of its genealogy, omitting a great deal of varied regional differentiation and detail, could be said to go like this. In the seventeenth century, with the rise of the new sciences, old forms of legitimacy for state power that owed to theology (for instance, as in the divine right of the monarch who personified the state) lapsed; and a new justification was sought, no longer in theology, but rather in what we might call 'political *psychology*'. At the same time, two developments after the Westphalian peace were of obvious and related significance: scattered locations of power were integrated in an *increasingly centralized form of state* that was to claim sovereignty over the populations of a new form of entity that was emerging, *the nation*—so closely did these develop together that it is completely routine now for us to describe them with a hyphen, the nation-state, an undecouplable jointness. And so, the political psychology that was now to legitimize state power, so conceived in its fusion with the nation, created a *feeling* in the populace for the first half of this hyphenated conjunction (the nation), thereby bestowing legitimacy on the second. Later, such a feeling came to be theorized under the now utterly familiar label 'nationalism'.

It was the *method* by which this feeling was generated in

Indian nationalism that I am about to give and the implications of that difference for their common stance on secularism's non-relevance for India in those decades of the national movement.

[3] Even if secularization (for the distinction between secularization and secularism, see footnote 1) and, more generally, what has come to be labelled 'modernity' emerged in variegated forms on a vaster globally connected canvas than Europe, there can be little doubt that secularism as an explicit doctrine had its conceptual origins in post-Westphalian Europe.

the populace, however, that created the conditions that laid the seed or, perhaps I should say the need, for secularist doctrine. The method adopted all over Europe was to identify an *external* enemy *within* the nation (the Jews, the Irish, the Catholics in Protestant countries, the Protestants in Catholic countries...), to despise and subjugate it, and to claim that the nation is 'ours', not 'theirs'. With the rise of numerical and statistical forms of discourse in the study of society, notions of 'majority' and 'minority' were coined and this method, in particular, came to be called 'majoritarianism'; and since the majorities and minorities in question were often defined in religious terms, it came even more specifically to be called 'religious majoritarianism'. Now, unsurprisingly, there were minoritarian backlashes to this religious majoritarianism. And it was the violence of the civil strife of such conflicts that led many to believe that, though the fault-line started with religious majoritarianism, it was religion *itself*, that is, *all* religion, which must now be ushered out of the orbit of the polity. Thus it was that secularism first emerged—*a doctrine formulated to repair a certain damage* that had its origins in the nation-building exercises that followed upon new ways of seeking legitimacy for state power.

Gandhi's simple and firm conviction, which he frequently articulated from very early on, was that this damage had never occurred in India and so the doctrine had no relevance for Indian society.

The conviction, in full dress, was this: For centuries, Indian civilization has been characterized by, as I put it earlier, an *unselfconscious pluralism* where cultures, traditions, practises lived side by side, at once heterogeneous and yet without any of the kind of 'psychology' which characterized the nationalisms that drove the genealogy of secularism in Europe. Thus, no *self-conscious* doctrine such as secularism was needed to correct the loss of such an unselfconscious pluralism since no nationalism of the European sort had occurred in India to undermine it. Indeed, Gandhi declared that Indian nationalism would precisely be defined in contrast with Europe's, it would consist rather in a replaying or a re-presenting of this longstanding pluralism in the vast field of anti-imperialist mobilizations that he sought to generate, a movement accommodating all of the heterogeneity of people and cultures and symbols and traditions.[4]

The question that has dogged scholars for a very long time is the extent to which he (and the Congress party which he gradually came to dominate) succeeded in doing so. And one obvious reason for this is that, in a sense, the very fact of partition suggests that he had *not* succeeded since the main and largest religious population that was intended to be part of this pluralist inclusiveness of the national movement was the Muslims, and partition precisely seems to reflect the failure to make Muslims feel included in the movement and the nation that the movement was seeking to create. Whole books (and some rather good ones) have been written to diagnose this failure, so it would be foolish of me to attempt any diagnosis myself in the few pages that I have here. But I do, in my closing remarks in this essay, want to say something very brief and preliminary about it, from the perspective of Gandhi's own conviction, whose implications for secularism in our own times I will first explore now.

---

[4] When I was presenting some of these ideas in a lecture recently, Tapati Guha-Thakurta asked a sharp question during the discussion: Was Gandhi himself formulating a *self-conscious* pluralism when he sought a national movement that re-played and re-presented the unselfconscious pluralism of Indian society and its historical past? Though this is a sharp observation, as I said, I am disinclined to think that terms like plural*ism* (self-conscious or unselfconscious) are appropriately descriptive of phenomena like movements. They apply rather to societies and to polities. We can, of course, talk of a plural*ist* mobilization as what Gandhi was seeking, but that just shows that there is a connotational gap between the sub-cognates 'ism' and 'ist'—the latter is a casual adjective applicable more widely than the former which is a noun indicating a doctrine or a (relatively) abiding social formation and thus more restricted in application. But see my discussion further below on a self-conscious 'ism' and doctrine that does attempt to formalize an unselfconscious pluralism.

One thing to note is that, if what I have said captures Gandhi's very general ground for finding secularism beside the point for the society in which he lived and worked, that very ground has a clear implication for future times. That ground, as I said, declares that since secularism was needed to correct a certain damage caused by certain forms of nationalism in Europe, and since that nationalism and that damage had not occurred in India, adopting secularism for India would be slavish mimicry of one's colonial masters. This implies that were the conditions of that damage that was the soil and source of secularism in Europe to be replicated elsewhere, Gandhi would not see an adoption of secularism as an uncritical imitation of a European doctrine. *So, I put it forward as an obvious further inference that since something very close to that very same damage had begun to lay its roots in India from the late 1980s, Gandhi would be the first to say that secularism's relevance should rightly now have come into focus.* To put it differently, our obsessive focus on secularism in the last few decades is quite in accord with Gandhi's relative indifference to secularism, once we understand what ground and conviction and argument lay behind that indifference. Moreover, it is also implied by his argument, that it is not our secularist concerns now that amount to a cognitive slavery to Europe, but the form of nationalism which prompts them and which has arisen with such increasing force since the 1980s that is the slavish mimicry of Europe.

Many might be sceptical of the inference I have made and italicized in the last paragraph and view it as being unfaithful to Gandhi's conception of politics and society and religion. I suspect a great deal of such scepticism owes to a conflation of the distinction between secularism with secularization (see footnote 1 for that crucial distinction). Gandhi's avowed religiosity cannot be denied, but that is not the subject of my inference. That has to do with secularization, whereas my inference is strictly and only about secularism.

A familiar and a quite different objection to what I have been saying so far comes from those who think Gandhi was wrong *in the first place* to think that secularism was not relevant in the period in which he lived and worked because it is quite wrong to think that the European forms of nationalism and the damage they caused only emerged in India as late as in the 1980s when, as a matter of fact, that nationalism and that damage have been with us from much earlier on—and here what is standardly cited is the cultural side of Tilak's nationalism, Savarkar's work *Hindutva*, the formation of the RSS, and the non-negligible voice of the Mahasabhite element in the Congress itself from as early as the 1920s.

Such an objection, which is quite insistently and frequently made, has two closely related shortcomings.

First, it fails to see that in the trajectory of nationalism, though there are always bound to be different strands that are in play at any given time, usually, at any given time, one of these strands tends to be dominant and the others much more marginal. In India, there is no doubt that there was a strand of Hindu nationalism that conceived its ideas and strategized them quite closely along the lines that I have attributed to the nationalisms of Europe and it surfaced in some of the figures I have mentioned above more explicitly than others, especially and most explicitly in Savarkar. There was also the more Left, class-based, strand of nationalism under Communist leadership, supported as well by the more radical side of the Congress, with Nehru himself as part of this strand for a few years in the 1930s; and then there was a somewhat different Ambedkarite strand that stressed essential links between certain forms of social transformation and the anti-imperialist struggle for an independent nation. But there is also no doubt that the Gandhi-Nehru strand in Congress nationalism was far more central to the anti-imperialist struggle than these other strands.[5] It dominated

---

[5] For an interesting study of these strands, viewed as what she labels 'historiographical narratives', and exploring the possibilities of political

the discourse, it dominated decisions about the adoption of both long-term strategy and short-term tactics, and, though it did not wholly silence the other strands, it did considerably marginalize them through the three full decades of mobilization.

Once we acknowledge this, we are led directly by it to a second shortcoming in this objection. We need to make a theoretical distinction, in the study of the past's relation to the present, between roots and antecedents. Something can be an antecedent of relatively entrenched present tendencies without being its root. The strand of Hindu nationalism that we noted in the roll call of past spokesmen and organizations I mentioned above were certainly antecedents of contemporary Hindu nationalism, but they were not the root. To be a root we have to demonstrate an organic causal path from the root to the contemporary flowering, but nobody has demonstrated anything like that causal pathway from these early figures to the rise of the BJP in the electoral field a few decades ago nor to the phenomenon of Hindutva domination we now are witnessing in the era of Narendra Modi. They were merely antecedents.

If some event(s) or development in the past is called an 'antecedent' at a later time, it may be because we observe that certain issues remain unresolved at the earlier time. But it would still be a kind of 'revivalism' to invoke them at a later time. That is quite different from having the phenomena at the later time be causally shaped by the earlier event(s) or foretold by earlier events. Since, as I said, Hindu nationalist voices were not completely silenced, there no doubt were unresolved issues in the period of the national movement. Who could deny that? But the roots of Hindutva nationalism were laid in the late 1970s and 1980s and from these, one *can* demonstrate determinable

---

praxis in alliance through political integration of one another, depending on which narrative is dominant and needs to be resisted, see Anagha Ingole's forthcoming *Religion in Indian Nationalisms: Genealogies and Possibilities of Integration.*

causal pathways and narratives to the phenomenon we have been landed with in contemporary India. I cannot now spell out what these are in any detail, so let me just mention only two factors (there are a range of others) and that too in the briefest terms (there is much more that can be elaborated than what I will say) just so as to give a very rough sense of what I mean by roots in contrast with the idea of antecedents.

The most obvious factor is the development of a caste-based electoral politics that emerged in the aftermath of the Mandal Commission report, which exposed how deeply divided Hindu society was. It was to suppress and extinguish this exposure that a fiercely determined Hindutva campaign was generated by upper-caste Hindus both in the parliamentary field via the consolidation of the Bharatiya Janata Party (BJP), which was formed earlier in 1980, as well as on the socio-cultural front by the VHP (Vishwa Hindu Parishad), building on the slow grassroots work that the RSS (Rashtriya Swayamsevak Sangh) had been doing all along. This attempt to *unify* Hindus, as a way of denying their exposed caste divisions by the newly emerging politics of the 1980s, was done by the zealous and conscientious cultivation of a European form of nationalism: finding an *external* enemy to subjugate and hate, and declaring the nation to be 'ours' (i.e., all Hindus as united against the external enemy, rather than divided by caste), not 'theirs'. These efforts became the roots of what we are witnessing now.

A second factor that may plausibly be thought of as laying the very early roots of the BJP's parliamentary build-up of strength happened a little earlier when the Hindu Right, it has to be admitted, gained some moral high ground by showing courage in its opposition to the Emergency; courage that was manifestly not shown by the Centre-Left which was much more powerful then and which lay down like a doormat while Indira Gandhi and her son stamped on the hard-won liberties in independent India. This moral high ground laid the initial roots for the Hindu Right's respectability in the parliamentary field, which then made possible its subsequent gains in that field via the growing success of the BJP, a success that its predecessor, the Jan Sangh, had never attained earlier in electoral politics.

All these can plausibly be called the roots of the more pervasive flowering of current European-style Hindu nationalism we have been landed with in our present moment. As I said, for Gandhi the refusal of secularism is grounded in his conviction that the legacies of India's long history of an unselfconscious pluralism were not undermined by any such nationalism in the decades of the national movement for Indian independence, during which Hindu nationalist voices were marginal and laid no deep roots (as they later came to have). And my claim is that, given the very nature of Gandhi's argument, once those roots *did* lay down several decades later and Hindu nationalism has flowered from them, he would allow the inference I am making. In other words, it would be *his* position that secularism is rightly seen by us to be relevant and central for our time. We should not be misled to conflate his refusal of secular*ization* in his hopes for Indian society and culture, to think that this inference about secular*ism*'s contemporary aptness is illicit.

Reflections on Multiculturalism and Its Distinctness from Secularism

A question arises, however, and a very good one, about why it is that secularism and not some other doctrine more in line with the unselfconscious pluralism that Gandhi so admired in India's past, is more apt—from Gandhi's point of view—as a repair to the damages visited by contemporary Hindu nationalism on that pluralism. The way I had put Gandhi's argument for the inaptness of secularism in India for *his* time, was to say that he thought adopting a *self-conscious* doctrine such as secularism would be a slavish mimicry of Europe since its *unselfconscious* pluralism had not been undermined by the sort of nationalism typical of European modernity. But we know from *recent* European history that there are *other* self-conscious political doctrines which have been articulated there, distinct from secularism, such as 'multiculturalism'. Multiculturalism, unlike secularism, might in fact (in a way that I will explain in a moment), even be thought of as a *self-conscious version of the unselfconscious pluralism* that Gandhi had made so central to his argument that we have been discussing. So, if some self-conscious doctrine or other is needed to address the undoing of India's unselfconscious pluralism by the emergence of a European-style nationalism in India in recent decades, might it not have seemed to Gandhi that multiculturalism is more apt than secularism?

We need some basic historical background before we can answer this question, or even properly understand it. The political ideal and doctrine of multiculturalism was also forged first in Europe—though considerably after secularism—in the second half of the last century, under rather specific conditions;[6] it then spread to the United States and, with an especially lively intensity, to Canada, and eventually to the Antipodes, when those specific European conditions were replicated (or approximated) in those countries. What were these conditions under which the doctrine was forged in European nations?

The multiculturalist ideal was motivated by the need to address specific *post-migratory* scenarios of an extended period after the Second World War, when European nations were reconstructing their war-torn economies and had invited labour from their erstwhile colonies to cope with labour shortages

---

[6] I'm not for a moment suggesting that 'multiculturalism' as a casual descriptive phrase has and can be applied to many societies all over the world well before the doctrine was formulated under the specific conditions in Europe that I am about to mention. That description of many societies is, in part, what Gandhi had in mind to convey in his claims about unselfconscious pluralism. By the term multiculturalism, I am only talking of a particular self-consciously formulated doctrine that is widely current in political theory. It is this which was first formulated explicitly in Europe in those conditions.

as a result of the loss of manpower in the large number of deaths and casualties during the war. (In the case of Turkish immigrants in Germany, it was not migration from erstwhile colonies, as for instance Britain's from South Asia or France's from the Maghreb, but rather an outcome of longstanding ties, constructed first in treaties between Prussia and the Ottoman Empire, then an alliance through the First World War, and then later through co-operation on a range of subsequent economic investments and construction projects, culminating in the 'Labour Recruitment Agreement' in the 1960s that invited sizable immigration from Turkey into Germany). It was in the crucible of the racial and cultural and religious hostilities that these migrant communities faced in European nations over the next few decades and their own increasingly resentful reactions to these hostilities, that the idea of multiculturalism gradually emerged. One salient reason for it emerging is that secularism began to be considered too blunt an instrument to deal with the special claims of suffering minorities. As I expounded earlier, secularism was a response not just to religious majoritarianism, but to religious majoritarianism that had prompted religious minoritarian backlashes to it, creating a great deal of civil strife between religious populations. As a result, secularism's response was to say that even though the fault-line *began* with majoritarianism, the strife between religions that it generated, warranted a doctrine that steers *all* religion, both majority and minority religions, out of the orbit of the polity. Thus, secularism did not seek to address religious majoritarianism by addressing the plight of minorities *in any direct way*. It addressed that plight only highly indirectly, by seeking to usher out religion itself from the direct influence of the state, and thereby undercutting the dominance of the majority religion in the political sphere. And the migrant communities in post-war Europe felt that such a doctrine did not speak enough, and directly enough, to their subordinated experience, *as minorities*; that is, it did not speak enough to their identification as suffering minorities for whom their religious culture provided a sense of dignity and autonomy in the face of the deep hostilities they faced in the societies in which they had landed as labourers with their families. This well-motivated identification could only be gratified, they argued, if the polity was revised to give them more autonomy to live by the practises and customs of their religious cultures. Thus, what multiculturalism, unlike secularism, was seeking is a *self-conscious* version of the unselfconscious pluralism that was said to exist *before* notions of majority and minority even emerged, when all cultures and religions were said to have lived side by side, an ideal that nationalism based on majoritarian religions and cultures had undermined in Europe in the kind of narrative I briefly presented above.

One way to put the point of this multiculturalism as it emerged in a period when the notion of majority and minority *are* much in play in one's understanding of societies and polities, is that it frankly seeks to present an ideal that denies that there are any majorities (except in a trivial numerical sense that should not be given any political significance or substance). All religions and cultures, including secularized culture, should be treated as minorities, even the numerically larger ones. Or to put it somewhat differently (and better), in terms of the rhetoric of 'hospitality' in the writings of some recent European philosophers,[7] the multiculturalist wishes to address the issues raised in this post migratory scenario by saying 'everyone is a guest, there are no host communities'. No one lands, by migration, in an already existing social contract and willy-nilly acquiesces in it. The whole social contract must be renewed, with 'host' and 'guest' both viewed as fresh and equal contractors. (A vivid, even if somewhat trivial, analogy might be found in the fact that today you will find someone who is 'hosting' a dinner party at

---

[7] See Emmanuel Levinas, *Totality and Infinity: An Essay on Exteriority* (Martinus Nijhoff, 1979) and Jacques Derrida, 'Hospitality' in *Angelaki. Journal of the Theoretical Humanities*, 2000, vol. 5, no. 3.

her home having to ask her dinner 'guests' if she may light a cigarette and smoke it *in her own home!*) Such a doctrine, as I said, is properly called an articulation of a *self-conscious* version of earlier unselfconscious pluralisms. And the question I am posing is: Given Gandhi's avowed admiration for the latter, wouldn't it seem, from his point of view, that since multiculturalism is closer to this admired ideal, *it*, rather than secularism, should be the self-consciously doctrinal repair for the damages wrought by a European style of nationalism that the dominant Hindutva tendencies present in India today?

One further clarification—analyzing the (more or less exact) differences between secularism and multiculturalism—is needed before we can finally say something about this question. I have only spoken about these doctrines genealogically so far, and not analytically. I have only expounded what prompted the rise of secularism and multiculturalism in different periods of European history, without making any effort to give them an analytical characterization.

The trouble with secularism has always been that its analysis has been characterized by slogans and metaphors that are highly misleading and confusing. In the rhetoric that surrounds the term in the West, there is a longstanding metaphor that has become a mantra and tends to stand in as a definition: the wall of separation between Church and State. But since, in India, the term 'secularism' came to be widely used after independence in the context of the reform of existing religions, this metaphor turns out to be extremely misleading. In fact it amounts to a paradox: how could a state, in the name of secularism, propose reforms in the laws of a religion, without perforating the very wall of separation that defines secularism?

This sort of difficulty has led philosophers like Amartya Sen (and Radhakrishnan before him) to argue that secularism in India has never really taken a Western form, has never really appealed to the metaphor of separation, and is in fact to be defined quite differently as a kind of *neutrality between different religions.*[8] I have argued elsewhere at length that this is neither theoretically sound nor even accurate as a characterization of Indian secularism.[9] It is quite true that many spoke of the importance of maintaining such a neutrality between religions both in the colonial administration and in the Congress party through the long freedom movement,[10] but it was never offered as a *definition* of secularism. What was it intended as, then, if not a definition or analysis of secularism? I will answer this question after saying something brief by way of defining (or analyzing) secularism.

There is no doubt that the metaphor of a wall of separation is a confusing and misleading characterization of secularism, *but the thought that underlies* that confused metaphorical formulation can be perfectly soundly articulated as a theoretical analysis or definition of Indian secularism that fits its practise as well, without any mention of the offending metaphor.

The secularism implicit in India's pronouncements as well

---

[8] In an address, given to the Indian History Congress in December 2014, I mentioned Sen as a prominent early proponent of this view, and Irfan Habib alerted me during the discussion to the fact that Radhakrishnan was in fact the first to assert it as a characterization of secularism). See Sarvepalli Radhakrishnan, *The Recovery of Faith* (Harper Brothers, USA, 1955). The most explicit version of Sen's articulation of it may be found in his essay 'Secularism and its Discontents' in the anthology *Secularism and its Critics*, ed. Rajeev Bhargava (OUP India, 2000). In the West, Charles Taylor too has long been seeking to 're-define' secularism along these neutralist lines as well. For an extensive criticism of Taylor on this topic, see Chapter 1 of my *Secularism, Identity, and Enchantment* (Harvard University Press, 2014). See also further below in the present essay for a diagnosis of why Taylor seeks such a re-definition.

[9] See my 'Gandhi, Nehru, and the Contexts of Indian Secularism' (for reference details, see footnote 1).

[10] Just to give one example, it is explicitly articulated in the Karachi Resolution of the Congress Party, 1931 but, as I said, it was not there, or anywhere else, declared to be a characterization or definition of 'secularism', merely a general bit of political wisdom.

as practise consisted of *three* commitments with relatively clear relations between them. There are, to begin with, two ground floor commitments: 1) a commitment to freedom of religion (of both religious belief and practise) and 2) a commitment to certain fundamental constitutional rights that *neither mention religion nor opposition to religion.* These latter are the basic ideals that a society, in its polity, seeks to live up to, and will bring the resources of the state to do so. Free speech and gender equality are familiar examples of such ideals that do not make any mention of religion. With these two initial commitments (to freedom of religion and to general constitutional principles, often in the form of rights, that make no mention of religion or opposition to religion) in place, the articulation of secularism proceeds to a third, higher-order commitment, a *meta*-commitment, that is to say a commitment *about* these first two commitments. This third commitment 3) declares a *lexicographical ordering* which has it that were there to be a clash between the deliverances of commitment 1, i.e., the commitment to freedom of religion, and commitment 2, i.e., the basic ideals enshrined in rights that neither mention religion nor opposition to religion, *then the latter must be placed first.*

That's it. That is the definition of secularism with no muddled rhetoric of 'separation', yet capturing the underlying thought which that metaphor was confusedly intending to convey. Examples to illustrate the ways in which secularism, so understood, is manifested can be multiplied. Here are just two familiar sorts of example. The first commitment, to freedom of religious belief and practise, may yield a demand by a religious group that some book, which it perceives as having committed blasphemy, should be banned. If there is, among the laws and rights that the second commitment in the definition mentions, a right to free expression and speech, then the lexicographical priority places the latter first, i.e., it disallows the demand. That is a plainly secularist outcome. Similarly, all of the reforms of

Hindu personal law in India were also exemplifications of this conception of secularism.

And so now, the remaining question is: If this is the right definition or characterization of the secularism that India adopted rather than the idea of a state's neutrality between religions, how does the idea of neutrality between religions fit in with this definition?

The answer is that the idea of such neutrality is not a competing definition but rather a constraint (a side-constraint) on *how we must apply* the only definition of secularism there is—the lexicographical ordering one I gave above. When applying such a lexicographical ordering, we must do so even-handedly and equally with all religions, without favouring one religion over another. It is this side-constraint on the *application* of the lexicographical ordering that was violated in Britain when Christianity was favoured over Islam in the differential responses to Kazantzakis's novel, *The Last Temptation of Christ* (which was banned as a result of Mary Whitehouse's campaign) and to Rushdie's *The Satanic Verses* (which was never banned). As is well known, this side-constraint of even-handed application of the lexicographical ordering notion of Indian secularism was also put into abeyance (I have taken care to use the term 'abeyance' for a reason, as we shall see in a moment) when Muslim personal law remained concessively unreformed, despite its counterpart in Hindu law having been subjected to reform. This concession, as we well know, remains a matter of continuing contention and has been the subject of much commentary. Some have read it as a *minority right* formulation of the Constitution. If it is read that way, then that would be a repudiation, an exception to or partial cancellation of the lexicographical ordering notion of secularism that I am saying India adopted. But this reading is wrong. It was always intended as a kind of *affirmative action* concession, *not* a minority right one, and like all such concessions, a *temporary* one (thus the use of 'abeyance' above), explicitly formulated as holding *only until such time* as when Muslims as a minority regain their psychological and cultural confidence which was undermined by the trauma of the partition's effects (massive loss of numbers both from the migration to Pakistan and the violence around partition, the loss of zamindari, even, in a public educational sense, the loss of their language, Urdu) and which all affirmative action policies are devised to help regain. It is this confidence, once regained, that would allow them to accept what was always eventually intended, despite the concession: the state's reform of their personal and family laws in accord with the lexicographical ordering characterization of secularism, giving priority to gender equality principles in the Constitution over the freedom to practise and live by one's own religious personal laws.

The difference between secularism, so characterized, and multiculturalism, whose genealogy I briefly presented earlier, is that the latter, as I said there, is a self-conscious effort at retrieving what was once an unselfconscious pluralism—a self-conscious version of it, which ensures the pluralism through the legal and constitutional codes of a polity, just the sort of thing whose *absence* marks the *unselfconscious* version of it. These Constitutional and legal structures would be substantially different from those of secularism in the lexicographical sense that was adopted by India after independence and never overturned, not even, as I am arguing, by the concession to Muslims of their personal laws, if that concession is correctly understood as being undertaken in the spirit of affirmative action. Multiculturalist Constitutional and legal structures would have to define themselves by contrast with this secularism, insisting that all religions and communities in a polity are really minorities, whose cultures and religious beliefs and practises be permitted an autonomy that is far greater than what is allowed in the first of the trio of commitments that define the lexicographical ideal of secularism that was adopted. In this lexicographical ordering ideal, the second and third commitments *substantially constrain* the autonomy granted by the first commitment to religious and cultural practises of various groups. By contrast, multiculturalism, as it distinguishes itself from secularism, seeks a far wider autonomy and latitude for the practises and internal cultural governance (by their own norms) of religious groups. Nothing short of that wider autonomy will revive in a self-consciously formalized (Constitutional and legal) political framework, the informal pluralism of the past.

This is a clear difference between the two doctrines and only confusion follows if one does not observe and maintain that difference. This has not stopped philosophers, however, from willfully seeking to deny the difference. The reasons for this are political, not theoretical. Multiculturalism is a doctrine that has generated much opposition in European and other Western nations and what is interesting is that it has not just been opposed by right-wing nationalist majoritarian groups. It has also been opposed quite vociferously by *secularists*. As a result, a prominent theorist of multiculturalism, Charles Taylor, realizing that secularism has become a stick with which to beat multiculturalism, has tried to take away that stick by *re-defining* secularism itself *as a kind of multiculturalism* and he does this by saying something very similar to what Radhakrishnan and Sen had said in their so-called idea of peculiar and unique 'Indian Secularism'—a neutrality and impartiality that the state must show towards all the different religions.[11] Though this move may be politically well-intentioned, it is, in my view, theoretically

---

[11] 'Taylor adds something explicitly that is only implicitly assumed by Sen and Radhakrishnan, that secularism is not just neutrality between religions but also irreligious people. See Charles Taylor, 'Why We Need a Radical Redefinition of Secularism' in Jonathan Van Antwerpen and Eduardo Mendieta (ed.), *The Power of Religion in the Public Sphere*, Columbia University Press, 2011. I should say here that Taylor's work on secularism, as can be found in this paper, (and of which I am being critical here) is to be distinguished from his remarkable work on secular*ization*, which can be found in his large and highly instructive book, *A Secular Age* (Harvard University Press, 2014).

not well-motivated. You can't just upend and redefine terms and concepts for your political ends. The more intellectually honest political response is to say that secularism, the only secularism there is (as defined by the lexicographical ideal), *sometimes does bad things* (as when it is used as a *tribal weapon* by the majorities of host nations to beat up multiculturalism, which seeks to give substantial cultural autonomy to minorities[12]) and so there are some contexts in which one should, therefore, *oppose* secularism. (In India, Ashis Nandy and Partha Chatterjee, for instance, have, in some of their writings, had the boldness to be critical of secularism and to say it does bad things.[13])

---

[12] Of course, if the cultural autonomy sought leads to practises that do clash with the host nation's most fundamental laws, such as free speech for instance, there will be conflict over serious issues. The point, however, is that even on these issues, multiculturalism takes the view that migrant communities have landed in a host society with an ongoing social contract, which needs to be renewed by the participatory voices of the migrants, presenting their point of view. It is through extended engagement with them, involving democratic deliberation, equal and open debate without majoritarian domination of the debate, that a new social contract should be constructed. Much of this may involve each side presenting what I have, in my past work (following Bernard Williams) called 'internal reasoning' to the other, trying to persuade them to come around to one's values by appealing to some of *their own* values which seem to support it. There is much scope for this sort of sensitive engagement since a community's value commitments may often be in internal tension or conflict. All this form of engagement requires a set of attitudes that are quite different from the ones displayed by host nations, who show little sensitivity and simply take the attitude, 'You've come here, just suck it up and get used to our laws.' And, in any case, very often their appeal to secularism is really not even over constitutionally significant matters and borders on demands for a state-enforced secularization that would exclude a wide range of cultural manifestations of migrant religions, ranging from dress (the hijab) to architectural styles (the minaret).

[13] See, Ashis Nandy, 'An Anti-Secularist Manifesto', *India International Centre Quarterly*, special issue on Secularism in Crisis, Spring 1995 vol. 22, no. 1 and Partha Chatterjee, 'Secularism and Toleration' in *Economic and Political Weekly*, 9 July, 1994, vol. 29. Chatterjee's paper is strictly about secularism.

But this does not often happen. Certain words like 'secularism' ('democracy' is another) have become 'hurrah' words. No side in a dispute wants to give them up. I don't see that Taylor's willful shift in nomenclature here is any more plausible or theoretically well-motivated or intellectually respectable than the Soviet Union declaring that its own polity was a democracy, a 'people's democracy', simply because 'democracy' was a 'hurrah' term that all sides (both sides in the Cold War) want to use to describe their own position. Communist intellectuals, no doubt, had many very serious and convincing criticisms to make of the democracies that arose in Europe, which were grounded in capitalist economic formations, and which were then diffused by settler colonialisms to other parts of the temperate belt. But nothing in those criticisms justifies their own self-description of their own polities as 'democratic'. It would have been far better for them to have pointed out that the West's own notion of democracy had a procedural and a substantive side and that Western nations had ignored the latter and sought only to implement the former; better, that is, than pretending that the Soviet Union had offered an alternative and superior notion of democracy, which it was seeking to implement. It is no different with 'secularism', which cannot, as I said, be redefined at will without becoming an arbitrary stipulation; and the detailed developments in India since 1947 cannot correctly be read as supporting any such re-definition of the term. So also, if one is rightly and plausibly criticizing colonial theoretical ideals (that grew in distant contexts and conditions) as they strain to influence one's own political theorizing and policy-making in one's own part of the world, it is far better to say, as Gandhi

---

Nandy's essay, despite its title, covers a wider ground and speaks to issues not just about secularism but also to issues that would fall under what I have insisted (in footnote 1) is better described as 'secularization'. Though I applaud their writings for this boldness and intellectually more honest attitude, I have in some of my writings registered disagreements with and made criticisms of one or other detail in these essays.

did, that secularism is *irrelevant* in India (unless, of course, it becomes relevant), than to redefine secularism so that 'we have all along had *our own* notion of secularism'. No clarity, nor any real theoretical illumination comes from these strained stipulative moves; only conceptual clutter and confusion.

Concluding Reflections on Gandhi's Time and Ours

My dialectic so far has been to present the grounds on which Gandhi did not see any relevance for secularism in India *in his time*, and to argue that that *those very grounds* suggest an inference to the conclusion that it *is* relevant *in our time*. For him, it was irrelevant in his time on the grounds that the genealogy of secularism made it necessary as a form of redemption for the corruption of society's unselfconscious pluralism (something that Gandhi admired greatly) by nation-building exercises, as in Europe, and since that form of nation-building had no echo in India in his time, whose unselfconscious pluralism had not been corrupted, there was nothing for secularism to redeem. And my argument has been that this ground suggests an inference: if there is a replication of that corruption elsewhere, as there is in India in the last few decades, there is something for secularism to redeem in India in our time. Having made this inference, on his behalf, I then posed the question, which I have yet to address: Given the fact that a different doctrine and ideal has emerged— multiculturalism—which is much closer than secularism to the unselfconscious pluralism that Gandhi admired, indeed is a sort of self-conscious version of that pluralism, shouldn't the more appropriate inference be that what is relevant and needed in India today is the ideal of multiculturalism rather than secularism? And now that I've spelt out what roughly is the distinction between these two ideals, we are in a better position to finally address this question.

My own instinct is to say that Gandhi, who had a very real sense of what is and is not feasible in activist politics, would eschew any dogmatically simple answer to this question. And even putting aside speculation about what Gandhi would say or do, there really is no single and direct answer to such a question because so much turns on questions of strategy and tactic that should be determined by one or other of the contingencies one is faced with at one or other time and context. Gandhi would not have thought of this as a *theoretical* comparison between two doctrines so as to decide which is the better ideal, secularism or multiculturalism, but rather as a question of which is feasibly pursuable in which contingent circumstances and context; and for that one needs to first record the differences and changes of context and circumstance.

I have said that European-style nationalism, one in which an external enemy is named within one's territorial boundaries and despised and suppressed, first laid its *roots* in India (even if there were earlier *antecedents*) less than half a century ago. In the last roughly two decades, and especially in the last seven years or so, the roots have flowered crucially on two fronts: both politically in the gaining of seats and governmental power by the BJP and also ideologically in the Hindutva outlook taking hold of the mentality of many segments of the nation's populace. So, first of all, there is a distinction to be drawn between the earlier phase of laid roots and the later phase of flowering. And the complexity that this adds is that different answers to our question may be warranted, given the differences in the circumstances of the earlier and later phases.

The 'external enemy within', in this form of nationalism, as we well know, is the Muslim. Let us look, then, at the possibilities from the point of view of Muslims. What is possible can't be considered independently of their point of view, and their point of view turns on the subjectivities that they have formed in their past and present.

So, to begin with, let us ask, how did Muslims figure in Gandhi's claims for an unselfconscious pluralism in India's past?

The first thing to note is that Islam arrived in India from its classical origins in the Arabian lands via travels through Persia and Turkey and Central Asia and Afghanistan, acquiring a variety of accretions at each stage; and, having arrived, accrued even greater variety through its regional dispersal (Punjabi, Bengali, Hindustani, Malayali, Tamil, Gujarati, Oriya...) and through a highly differentiated set of spiritual traditions of worship and scholarship that developed over some centuries. To name just a very miscellaneous few, there were figures of influence such as Shah Wali Allah Dehlawi of the Naqshbandi tradition located in the courtly ethos of princes; there was the more populist Chishti Sufi tradition consolidated by Nizamuddin Awliya and Amir Khusrau and later by poets like Bulleh Shah, Mir, and Dard; there was the reformist strain of Sir Syed Ahmad Khan; there was Maulavi Chiragh Ali, the Shia thinker Ameer Ali, the novelist Nazir Ahmad, Shibli Nomani of the Nadwatul Ulema, the famous Deoband school providing neo-traditional learning, the even more orthodox Ahl-i-Hadith school favouring strict Hanafi law; down to the more relaxed Barelwi tradition stressing very local customary practises; the Ahmadiyyas who claimed that their leader Mirza Ghulam Ahmad was all at once the Muslim Mahdi, the Christian Messiah and the avatar of Krishna; and in the twentieth century, the poet Muhammad Iqbal and the refined and learned Maulana Azad representing in the last few decades of his life the 'composite culture' of Hindus and Muslims.

I have given this roll-call of remarkable accumulation of accretions that characterize Indian Islam not only to point out what is often said—that Islam is many things in India, not one—but also to point to the vast conceptual distance of the *content* of the Islam that laid these diverse roots in India from the originary Islam of the Arabian lands. *It is this Islam which is an essential part of the mix that Gandhi was speaking of when he spoke of India's unselfconscious pluralism.* A vital heartbeat in such a form of pluralism is an Islam deracinated from its distant origins, gradually and variegatedly home-grown in the centuries-long exposure to Hindu civilization and, therefore, continuous in a myriad ways with Hindu culture. As a result, any effort to assert a fundamentalism of faith by any group (Maulana Maududi and his following in the Jamaat-i-Islami, for instance) could only do so by a *second deracination*, a deracination from these homegrown roots and their broad and entrenched range of practises, and by invoking in its place an Islam which—from the point of view of this pervasive and rooted Islam—is pure artifice, the rootless construct of a bookish, normative, deferential gaze upon some claims to an originary Islam of 7th century Arabia. This is the Islam that turns its back on Gandhi's understanding of an unselfconscious pluralism in India's part, and is familiarly discussed under the summarizing label, 'Muslim fundamentalism'.

Let us turn now to more recent times.

It is widely known to all who have the capacity for honest perception ever since the hideous events of 2002 in Gujarat and now the illegal interventions in Kashmir and the parliamentary enactment of the Citizens Amendment Bill (as well as the constant impending threat of the implementation of the National Register of Citizens), not to mention the brutality of authoritarian state violence against honourable dissent, that the current Prime Minister and Home Minister of India are men of ruthless anti-democratic tendency, presiding over a government that is dismantling the achievements (however partial and however qualified) built up over a half century of Constitutional construction, democratic legislation and institution-building. But these events of more recent years had their slow build-up since the 1980s when Hindutva first emerged as a serious force in Indian public life and politics, and the effect it had on Muslims *in that earlier period* was far less devastating than it has been in the last decade. Proof of this lies in the fact that in the aftermath of the destruction of the Ayodhya mosque, Muslims showed some real agency and fought back. It is this agency that was (until winter before last) withdrawn for about a decade as Muslims sank into an understandable funk under the repeatedly stunning blows dealt by the fascist complexion that Hindutva acquired with the political rise of Mr. Modi and Mr. Shah.[14] What is more, it does seem as if the state's authoritarianism seeks and gets considerable sanction from a growing and widely spreading ideological embrace of Hindutva on the part of ordinary Hindus in a wide range of classes and most especially in the influential middle classes whose ranks have somewhat swelled in the recent decades of lopsided neo-liberal forms of economic growth and whose control of such institutions as the media and education perpetuates the appeal of this populist nationalist ideology. Nothing like this phenomenon existed in the earlier phase when the BJP was first gaining ascendancy in the electoral field.

It is for this reason that my instinct is to give differential answers to the question I have posed about whether, from Gandhi's point of view, multiculturalism is not a better strategy of repair against European-style Hindu nationalism than secularism. The ideal of multiculturalism might well have been a feasible ideal for Muslims to demand in that earlier phase. In that phase, as I said, Muslims showed some real agency and confidence in the responses they made in the face of a rising Hindutva. In fact, some of the responses (for instance, soon after the Babri Masjid's destruction) were deplorably violent and, even when they were not, some of it was voiced by leaders and organizations that sought to combat Hindu fundamentalism with fundamentalist Islamist claims, denying, as I said, what Islam had come to be over centuries in the deep roots it laid in India. But, despite these disturbing tendencies, the point is that they

---

[14] It is interesting that Dalits, even in the face of actual and threatened violence, have not shown the same funk in this same period and have, in fact, from time to time showed bursts of impressive resistance. However, it is also interesting and worth diagnosing, how much of the agency they show in such resistance is restricted to movements and protests in the long middle period of the electoral clock. At the actual time of elections, they have sometimes in some regions allowed themselves to be persuaded to vote for the BJP in the hope of gaining one or other advantage that the BJP claims to offer.

showed agency and there was at least scope for internal debate and for claiming that the rise of Hindutva was precisely because India had adopted secularism rather than multiculturalism. Such debate and argument might have been used to develop a basis for steering the energies and engagement that Muslims were showing towards a set of demands for a multicultural society in which they would have a sort of autonomy that the Hindutva vision, and even the secularist vision, would seek to deny them. But in the later phase when a Hindu nationalist government holds an opposition-free sway at the centre and exercises its authority as relentlessly as it has been doing and, as I said, with considerable and growing support for its nationalist vision in the Hindu populations among whom Muslims have to live, the idea that such a multiculturalist demand for Muslim autonomy could be successfully made seems to be a sheer fantasy. Perhaps it would still be possible if there was a weakening of the centre and a federal devolving of political power, which recent electoral losses by the BJP may hold out some promise for. That may eventually allow for regional Muslim voices to make some demands for the sort of autonomy that multiculturalism seeks, at least in states where there is less Hindutva domination. But all that requires large transformations in the nature of the Indian state and the structure of the polity and such transformations, even if they were to occur, would do so gradually and very likely in fits and starts and with great unevenness.

That still leaves Muslims with the question about what the best strategy for them is now, in the face of the odds they face in a polity and society so heavily dominated, as it is, by Hindutva populist sentiment and a government determined to undermine the equal citizenship status of over a tenth of its population that is comprised of Muslims. In these present circumstances, the tools for pursuing multicultural demands for autonomy are not in hand, and if there is any inspiration to be had from Gandhi, it is not from his feeling for India's unselfconsciously pluralist past, but rather the canny pragmatism he showed through his many campaigns which often seized whatever tools that seemed to him be most effectively at hand. The tools at hand in the immediate present are the principles that are *already there* in the *secularist* formulations of citizenship and the freedoms and equalities that citizens were intended to enjoy by those formulations. The Muslim youth and women and their many supporters in the squares and the maidans last winter understood this very well. They were, shrewdly and sensibly, simply demanding the implementation of the Constitution, nothing more. They were not seeking to pursue a vastly ambitious vision of a multicultural India with wider cultural autonomy for Muslims and all religious groups. If they had any such fantasy, their demands and their strategy were not invoking it, but seeking out what is immediately possible, the recovery of what was actually in hand—a Constitution that guaranteed equal *secular* citizenship.

Having said that, a very noticeable thing in their remarkable campaigns, however, is that their rhetoric, their slogans, their posters, and their habits of public address quite generally, were deeply and precisely *unselfconsciously pluralist*, richly appealing to the poetry, the art, and popular religion of the past in all its diversity, just as Gandhi's many mass mobilizations did. And yet, uniquely, and departing from Gandhi, the jouissance of this pluralist mayhem was all in the service of demands for *the abstractions and rights and laws enshrined in the Constitution*. This was a fascinating mix of two seemingly discrepant things. On the one hand, elements of everyday, popular, often religious, pluralist culture invested in the *means*. But, on the other hand, these were means for an *end* that was a highly abstract liberal code of modern citizenship. This is an innovation, which is unprecedented in the mobilizations of the past. No prominent Indian leader had achieved such an integrated mix. Gandhi, who almost single-handedly tapped the appeal of popular religion to generate the most prodigious of political mobilizations for some thirty consecutive years, as is well known, showed a studied indifference to the codes and rights that defined citizenship. He openly said at times, that he did not think that the heterogeneity of the people of India (in which he even sometimes included what he idealized naively as the more pure *non*-hierarchical differentiations allowed by the swadharma ideal of caste that, he insisted, were only later corrupted by developments that introduced hierarchy) should be undermined by making ordinary people over into some abstract, homogenous, codified form of being called 'citizens'. Nehru too had no inkling of how this integration might be made. The Nehru who wrote with deep affection in *The Discovery of India* of the *unselfconscious* religious pluralism in Indian history entirely shifted gears when he articulated a very *self-conscious* set of secularist principles which characterized the Constitutional provisions that would, for instance, go into the formulation of the Hindu Code Bill. Nehru recognized the honour and worth in each, but in his thought these moved in different gears. Ambedkar too had no integrating vision that joined the long egalitarian, anti-caste pluralist traditions of popular religion going back to the early Varkaris and such figures as Kabir with his own remarkable innovations in Constitutional affirmative action to empower the deprived castes. In fact, I suspect that is why he was partly suspicious of the eventual efficacy of the anti-caste Bhakti ideals.

The *integration* of the young activists that winter, of which I am speaking is, thus, simply without precedent. It was devised spontaneously, without the eminence of great leaders to shape it. It might fairly be said that these young women and men and the urban intelligentsia of large and small towns in India, though they were brilliantly effective activists, were much more than activists. They were, without any theoretical vanguard, fashioning through their struggles a *theoretical* framework that brings together practises *and* abstractions; and thereby instructing us into *the habits and dispositions* of democracy, which the Constitution's abstractly formulated laws and principles always had as their deeper underlying historical and philosophical source and which were always formulated with a view to producing a cultivation and enactment of these habits and dispositions in the citizens of the future to whom they applied.

In this mobilization, it is well known that Muslims were a driving force in the activism and, given their particular *integrated* mix of elements that I am emphasizing, any Muslim voice that spoke with a fundamentalist strain sounded shrill and jarring and immediately invited an internal correction. That is no small achievement. In this Muslim agency, Hindu fundamentalism was being opposed once again by Muslims *qua Muslims*, not merely Muslims qua abstract citizens—but they were doing so by an insistent signing onto an abstract Constitutional commitment to a secularist ideal of citizenship dictated to them from the point of view of reasons that flow from their own understanding of themselves *as Muslims*. That is no small achievement either—it exposes how confused we were to think, as we have for so long, that secularism must be something we must sign onto on wholly and only secular grounds.

We can see through the filter of these contemporary mass mobilizations with the complexity that I am ascribing to their political stances, a retrospective illumination of a historical point of some importance. So, let me finally turn to the question that I had promised I would close with. From the very outset I had said that Gandhi sought to generate a nationalism that replayed India's unselfconscious cultural pluralism and that would therefore be inclusive of Muslims (a claim that has been denied from time to time—Perry Anderson's careless invective being a conspicuous recent example—but is not, I believe, plausibly deniable[15]), whose self-understanding, as I have tried to convey, was itself formed by this pluralism as it took root in a place at which they had arrived by a path of accretions that had already gradually deracinated them from their originary faith. But I also said that it must, at the same time, be granted

---

[15] See Perry Anderson, 'Gandhi Centre Stage', *London Review of Books*, July 2012, vol. 34, no.13.

that the very fact of partition amounted to a failure of that Gandhian inclusive nationalist aspiration, a failure that Gandhi himself frequently asserted in the last years of his life, especially during the violence he so courageously sought to stem and heal in the immediate surround of partition. I then said that we have long and incessantly reflected on this failure and sought a diagnosis for it. And though obviously, I cannot provide any such diagnosis in a paper that is already too long and would in any case take a book's length to provide, some of what I have described in the extraordinary mobilizations of Muslim students and women and a wide range of others who stood and sat with them in those winter months demanding their citizens' rights, point to a general and rough direction of diagnosis.

What is very striking is that whenever Muslims were included in the struggle for independence *in mass movements*—in the way that they were last winter as well—their involvement was wholeheartedly nationalist and anti-imperialist and was *not* sectarian or communal. This is what Gandhi understood very well. It was, in fact, Gandhi's deepest and most fundamental contribution to Indian politics. The Khilafat movement that Gandhi launched, even though it mobilized the mass of Muslims *qua Muslims*, and even though it did eccentrically appeal to an obscure Muslim cause related to the end of the Ottoman Empire, was not only through and through a nationalist and non-sectarian mobilization, it had dynamic effects in many regions of the country that made Muslims more progressive than they ever had been, both on gender issues and on issues of political economy that affected the peasantry.[16] In fact, the later more purely class struggle of the 1930s, over which the Congress did not always have control, could not have been possible without the antecedent inspirations of the Khilafat and non-cooperation mobilizations.

---

[16] For some detail on this wider dynamic and progressive effects of the Khilafat movement, see my essay in the *Oxford Companion to Indian Philosophy* ed. Jonardon Ganeri (reference provided in footnote 1).

The effects of the Khilafat movement on Muslim consciousness had subsided by 1927-28 and there followed a decade in which Muslims were included in Indian nationalism by a quite different understanding of democratic inclusion, not via mass mobilizations but more formal negotiations by their leaders with the Hindu leaders of the Congress in round table conferences and other such fora. In these more formal efforts at inclusion, the Muslim leaders always felt alienated and dominated by their Hindu counterparts. So much so, that Nehru explicitly declared in the late 1930s that it was a wholly wrong method of inclusive nationalism and one would have to return to a mass movement to include Muslims in the nationalist cause. It was with such a declared understanding that the Muslim Mass Contact Campaign was launched by the Congress under the leadership of the left-leaning Muslim leader K.M. Ashraf, and it was through these campaigns that a wide range of Muslims were brought again into the anti-imperialist nationalist campaign—the Khudai Khidmatgars (who though they had been involved earlier too, really came into their own during this period), the Aligarh academics, many of the Deobandi leaders. The campaign was shorter lived than the Khilafat movement and never really reached deep into the peasantry as the earlier campaign had. Still, these points, I believe, bring out something that the recent campaigns in the squares and maidans are retrospectively making clear. The failure of partition was the failure of formal methods of inclusion through negotiations between leaders. While ordinary Muslims had a genuinely participatory role, *qua* Muslims, in mass mobilizations, they never felt the tug of a sectarian or communal or separatist aspiration. In a sense, then, the failure of Gandhi's nationalism lay in the fact that, for crucial and extended moments, it was not always sufficiently Gandhian in its commitment to mass politics.

INTRODUCTION

Satishchandra Kumar, Kanchana Mahadevan, Meher Bhoot, Rajesh Kharat

Sambhashan, the University of Mumbai's online interdisciplinary journal collaborated with the Mahatma Gandhi Peace Center, University of Mumbai for its October 2020 and November 2020 issues dedicated to Mohandas Karamchand Gandhi's 151st birth anniversary. The present book, *Inheriting Gandhi: Influences, Activisms* is an outcome of this collaboration, with an additional set of papers. The essays in this book reveal that despite being routinely invoked and referenced, Gandhi's relevance in the contemporary context continues to be strong and spirited. His journey poses several questions that are germane to the contemporary world, some of which include: How can non-violence speak to recent upheavals of race, caste and gender across the globe? How can the values of Gandhi influence the feeling of oneness and compassion in a situation like the Covid-19 pandemic? The essays in this book invoke Gandhi for integrating the theoretical and the practical, while at the same time engaging in self-doubt on practise. Gandhi is remembered as a symbol of peace and compassion for the human race. This is especially so in the context of the contemporary predicament with violence, where every person could embrace Gandhi's ideologies to overcome this hostile situation. In our attempts to unfold ways to save this world, we need to hold peace in our minds and compassion for everyone residing in it. The principles of Mahatma Gandhi are eternal and reflect his relevance in the twenty-first century—in this time of uncertainty, grief and pain caused by the social, political and economic structures humanity has built.

Gandhi presents an enormous hermeneutic challenge in the

twenty-first century. Much ink has been spent on discussing his relevance and significance in the course of reading his texts and engaging with the applications of his thoughts in diverse domains. Gandhi has his zealous admirers. Martin Luther King professed to be inspired by the Gandhian ideals of non-violence after spending a night in Mani Bhavan in erstwhile Bombay in the year 1959 (Frayer, 2019). Yet, years later Obadele Kambon has critiqued Gandhi's problematic relationship to race (Kambon, 2018). Gandhi's critics have posed questions regarding his relation to caste following B.R. Ambedkar, or nationalism following Rabindranath Tagore. These criticisms reveal that influences are not simply hand-me-downs; they are rather reflections to engage with. These complex and conflictual perspectives show that one cannot adopt a reductionist and uncritical attitude in the continuous attempt to rethink Gandhi.

Gandhi's speeches and writings are not simply theoretical speculations or utopian ideals. They are rooted in praxis that transform individual, groups, organizations, institutions, and society through practises that nurture unity, cohesiveness and solidarities. Gandhi immersed himself in practising his experiments and counsels at the personal level. Therefore, it can be said that Gandhi had explored the practise first with himself, and understood the practise before he brought it into the public sphere. Non-violent resistance is explicit in his satyagraha, which is also a mode of building communities that anchor the individual. The individual and the community have a reciprocal relationship where they develop through each other. It is in this sense that Gandhi has spurred activist cultures, cooperative societies, indigenous educational frameworks, village communities and non-corporate economies, to name a few. As Ramachandra Guha notes, Gandhi continued to inspire activist cultures in post-independent India, 'For example, the Chipko Movement of the 1970s…was a non-violent protest against deforestation and its leaders called themselves Gandhians' (Kaushik, 2018). Another movement after independence led by Gandhian Acharya Vinoba Bhave was the famous Bhoodan Movement (Land Gift Movement). However, one cannot claim with Guha that Gandhi was village-centric (Kaushik, 2018) in the sense of valorizing villages ahistorically. Gandhi travelled to remote villages. The village for Gandhi is a symbol of peaceful coexistence and interdependence. It is from this point of view that in 1936 Gandhi claimed India 'to be found not in its few cities but its 7,00,000 villages' (Joshi 2002, 11). He urged city dwellers to leave their exploitative life-style that used the resources of the villages, without contributing to them meaningfully. Thus, the problem for Gandhi is the 'town-dweller' who '…has generally exploited the villager' (Joshi 2002, 11). It is the exploitative relationship based on the privileged position of the city vis-à-vis the village that concerned Gandhi. A change in this respect required transforming lifestyles of consumption. Gandhi believed that village life—in the ideal sense—could be a guide for forming communities of interdependence. Progress could be made if the basics of cooperation were followed. Gandhi's ideal village was both self-sufficient and interdependent. His discussion with Shri Krishna Das reveals a stoic cosmopolitan perspective on the symbiotic relationship between the village and the domains outside it. 'Our outlook must be that we would serve the village first, then the neighbourhood, then the district and thereafter the province' (Joshi 2002, 6).

This volume comprises two sections, reflecting Mahatma Gandhi's relevance in the twenty-first century; the first section, 'Influences', has five articles, while section two on 'Activisms' contains nine articles. The essays in both sections highlight Gandhi's impact on other eminent figures, while at the same time bringing out the potential for activism in Gandhi's life and writings. The foreword, 'Gandhi in his Times and Ours' is written by Akeel Bilgrami, distinguished philosopher and Gandhi scholar. It introduces the concepts of secularism and multiculturalism in a Gandhian context. It maps the emergence and relevance of these distinctive concepts in Indian society from the pre-independence era to modern times. The essays in the first section show Gandhi's tremendous influence across the length and breadth of not only the country but also the diaspora in south East Asia, the Indian sub-continent, the African continent and across the world. Two of the essays in this section are from thinkers in the diaspora. Nandini Patel, who has to her credit a wide array of research focusing mainly on democratic institutions, tries to highlight the impact Gandhi made on the African American civil rights movement, and the African liberation movement. She also throws light on Gandhi's contribution towards a developmental model based on socialism defined as 'Sarvodaya', meaning the upliftment of all towards self-development. Rajendrakumar Dabee examines how Gandhi's charismatic presence in Mauritius ignited fiery revolutions in the small British colony of the Indian Ocean that transformed the lives and thoughts of Indian labourers culminating in Independence in 1968. Zubin Mulla, who has corporate experience and has worked with manufacturing and service organizations, reflects his research interest in transformation leadership. He uses Gandhi's life as one of the best examples of transforming, focusing initially on Gandhi's early life from his birth in 1869 until 1914 when he left South Africa and later on Gandhi's work in India from 1914 to 1948 when he inspired and mobilized the Indian people to participate in the freedom struggle. Vinay Lal explores the impact of the ideas of Mahatma Gandhi on healthcare systems, the role of doctors and nurses in the development of society, especially at a time when the entire world is trying to recover from the COVID-19 pandemic. Lal illuminates an aspect of Gandhi that has not received much attention, namely his relationship to nursing. This is particularly significant given Gandhi's appreciation of Florence Nightingale. Karen Gabriel brings out Gandhi's role in the colonized impacting the colonizer by reconstructing notions of masculinity and femininity. She argues that Gandhi tied the public political dimension with the intimate through a dual notion of swaraj (self-rule) as both self-control and liberation from the logic of the empire. She develops her account of Gandhi's primordial influence in the context of the much neglected phenomenon of the colonial encounter. Gandhian activism in her view covered both the personal and the political to reshape sexuality and gender.

The second section engages with the innovative ways in which each author dwelled upon the Gandhian activism which continued to develop his thought. These articles reveal how, since Gandhi himself practised what he preached and first experimented with the self, those who adopt his vision have a bigger responsibility in integrating the world of theory and practise. They have a responsibility to Gandhi, to themselves and to their communities. Moreover, this responsibility is also one of the ways of critically evaluating Gandhi. On this note, Saurabh Chaturvedi, Niharika Ravi, Sheetal Ravi and Ravi Narayanan focus on the complex terrain of village life as a vibrant work in progress that is related to the worlds around it. The essays by Anita Patil-Deshmukh, Fauziya Patel, Faraz Khan and Sandhya Mehta bring out the manner in which Gandhian thought has influenced the formation of communities, some of which are creative, as well as civil society institutions such as Mani Bhavan. The paper by Aparna Phadke reveals that peace for Gandhi is not simply the absence of violence, but a proactive condition of creating the spaces for interactive living. They argue that by embodying the interconnectedness of life and living beings, peace integrates the individual, families and community along the lines of Sarvodaya. In sum they argue for a broader interpretation of Gandhi's notion of village republics than that of isolationism or solipsism. The reflections by Virendra Kumar and Suchita Krishnaprasad show that Gandhi's contemporary relevance has 'straddled' not just two centuries as Anthony Parel notes (Parel, 2002, 19), but three. They bring out the specific ways in which Gandhi speaks to the present context of violence and pandemics in ways that can heal. Sybil Thomas's paper reveals how teacher education evolves to fulfil the objective of higher education. Her article explores Gandhi's ideas of education where the values of freedom, equality, justice, and brotherhood are instruments of social transformation. She further seeks to address whether his thoughts and philosophies are relevant even today in a neoliberal, post-colonial era after 73 years of independence.

Finally, in the epilogue Neera Chandhoke argues for Gandhi's impact on civil society activism in postcolonial contexts through his notions of non-violence and solidarity. She argues for his continuing relevance in movements of resistance that seek to forge relationships of solidarity, what she terms people-to-people relationships, committed to peaceful coexistence. The essays in this volume go to show that even in the twenty-first century, Gandhi's relationship to those who reference him in his endeavours to bridge theory and practise—and who are thereby his contemporaries—continues to be marked by what Parel has termed dialogue, critique and indifference. These essays reveal that for Gandhi civil society and cultures of resistance are crucial to democracies. For Gandhian praxis draws upon the power of civil society, as the space of the individual and community.

References

Frayer, Lauren. 2019. Gandhi is deeply revered, but his attitudes on race and sex are under scrutiny. *NPR.* https://www.npr.org/2019/10/02/766083651/ (Accessed on September 5, 2020).

Gandhi, M.K. 1925. Young India. *The Collected Works of Mahatma Gandhi* (Electronic edition) vol. 33 pp. 133–134.

Gandhi, M.K. 2010. *Hind Swaraj: A Critical Edition*, ed. Sudesh Sharma and Tridip Suhrud. Hyderabad: Orient Blackswan.

Joshi, Divya. 2002. *Gandhiji on Villages*. Mumbai: Mani Bhavan Gandhi Sangrahalaya.

Kambon, Obadele. 2018. Ram Guha is wrong. Gandhi went from a racist young man to a racist middle-aged man. *The Print*, December 24. https://theprintin/oppinion/ramchandra-guha-is-wrong-a-middle-aged-gandhi-was-racist-and-no-mahatma/168222/ (Accessed on December 20, 2020).

Kaushik, Tushar. 2018. Mahatma Gandhi inspired environmental activism. *New Indian Express*, June 18. https://www.newsindianexpress.com/cities/bengaluru/2018/jun/18/mahatma-gandhi-inspired-environmental-activism-says-ramchandra-guha-1829680.html (Accessed on October 18, 2020).

Parel, Anthony. 2002. Mahatma Gandhi and His Contemporaries: An Overview. In *Mahatma Gandhi and His Contemporaries* ed. Bindu Puri. Shimla: Indian Institute of Advanced Study.

Part One

INFLUENCES

REFLECTIONS ON GANDHI AND THE BLACK LIBERATION STRUGGLE

Nandini Patel

On the occasion of the Gandhi centenary in 1969, the renowned African scholar Ali Mazrui (1970) wrote, 'In the history of African nationalism and black political militancy, Mahatma Gandhi has been an important intellectual influence. Tributes were paid to Gandhi by black admirers as well as by others. But how much relevance does Gandhi retain for black aspirations? The Gandhi centenary calls for a revaluation in historical perspective, against the background of new forms of radicalism in Africa and the US at the present time.'

Ironically, on the 150th birth anniversary of Mahatma Gandhi, the same questions are being echoed about the relevance of Gandhi today, not only in the context of the United States and Africa but in many other parts of the world including India. Over the last five decades, radicalism has deepened further and physical and verbal violence over issues of race, religion and caste has become the norm. In such an environment, the call for a reassessment of Gandhi from a historical perspective, to revisit the impression of Gandhi's philosophy and approach on African independence and the American civil rights movement is imminent.

Gandhi repeatedly emphasized the interconnection between Indian and African freedom. In his Message to the American Negro (1929), he wrote, 'Let not the 12 million Negroes be ashamed of the fact that they are the grandchildren of slaves. There is no dishonour in being slaves. There is dishonour in being slave-owners. But let us not think of honour or dishonour in connection with the past. Let us realise that the future is with those who would be truthful, pure and loving. For, as the old wise men have said, truth ever is, untruth never was. Love alone binds and truth and love accrue only to the truly humble.' Gandhian values of truth, non-violence and social justice, resonating with black theological principles, were a strong source of connection between Gandhi and the black movement.

Gandhi's direct personal engagement with the African-American civil rights leaders such as Du Bois, Howard Thurman, James Lawson, Martin Luther King Jr., amongst others, built a strong bond of mutual respect and empathy. Rev. Lawson, a theologian and civil rights leader who spent three years in India studying peace and nonviolence, said, 'Gandhi brought together and synthesised elements whose spirit existed around the world.' Howard Thurman, mentor of King Jr., visited India in 1936 and met Gandhi. Gandhi said to him, 'It may be through the Negroes that the unadulterated message of nonviolence will be delivered to the world.' And in 1959 Martin Luther King Jr. visited India, and upon return said, 'We were looked upon as brothers with the color of our skins as something of an asset. But the strongest bond of fraternity was the common cause of minority and colonial peoples in America, Africa and Asia struggling to throw off racialism and imperialism.'

The deep-rooted connection between the African American and the Indian struggles was reflected as the city of Philadelphia celebrated the 150th anniversary of Gandhi by passing a resolution urging people to 'honour the legacy of Gandhi and unite in mutual love to achieve peace and justice.' This was a real tribute to Gandhi, much needed in today's world.

Anil Nauriya (2006), who has written extensively on Gandhi, observes that the relationship between Gandhi, Africa and its leaders was mutually productive and symbiotic; a connection which has often been under-analyzed. Nauriya contends that Gandhi himself is largely responsible for this omission. He said little of his discussions with African leaders of his time. He wrote in *Harijan* (July 1, 1939): 'I yield to no one in my regard for the

Zulus, the Bantus and the other races of South Africa. I used to enjoy intimate relations with many of them. I had the privilege of often advising them.' Who did he advise, and what was his advice? We do not know from his writings. It may be that he was concerned that the racist rulers would use any publicity to those discussions to allege a conspiracy against the racist order, contends Nauriya (2006).

Gandhi's Africa connection is not only confined to his nonviolent experiment of freedom struggle in South Africa but also his involvement with West African leaders in the nationalist movement. There was a growing realization of the fact that colonial rule was a negation of civilization and had to be fought. The message cabled by the National Council of Nigeria and the Cameroons (NCNC) on Gandhi's death expressed the sentiments of all African nationalists, for whom Gandhi was the 'bearer of the torch of liberty of oppressed peoples and whose life had been "an inspiration to colonials everywhere".'

In Africa, the freedom struggle of Kwame Nkrumah of Gold Coast, today's Ghana, adopted the strategy of 'Positive Action'. In his autobiography, Nkrumah describes the strategy as one to pressure the British authorities to grant concessions gradually to the nationalist movement. Nkrumah described 'Positive Action as the adoption of all legitimate and constitutional means by which we could attack the forces of imperialism in the country. The weapons were legitimate political agitation, newspaper and educational campaign and, as a last resort, the constitutional application of strikes, boycotts and non-cooperation based on the principle of absolute nonviolence, as used by Gandhi in India.'

The influence of Gandhi in Africa extended beyond political liberation and embraced economic justice and social equality. The cocoa farmers' strike in Ghana is a case in point. The farmers adopted a boycott of foreign goods and mass action through strikes. The protest was against the value accorded to cocoa which, according to the farmers, was below its real value. The protest gathered momentum with thousands of native cocoa producers holding meetings at various cocoa-producing districts, discussing ways and means of defending themselves against imperialist oppression. The strike, coupled with the boycott, drew the entire country into action. George Padmore (real name Malcome Ivan Meredith Nurse) a Trinidad-born leading Pan-Africanist, journalist and author commenting on the cocoa farmers' strike and boycott of British goods in the Gold Coast described it as 'symptomatic of the New Africa, which is gradually becoming conscious of its strength, and is learning to use Gandhi's well-known technique, the boycott, with effect.' The motor transport workers and dockers refused to handle the goods of foreign firms, and a nationwide boycott of British commodities was proclaimed. The entire economic life of one of West Africa's richest colonies was at a standstill.

In Nigeria there was Mallam Aminu Kano, leader of a socialist movement in the northern part of the country in opposition to British rule. Kano took several initiatives for grassroots democracy, land and social reform, supporting peasants' co-operatives and advocating gender equality. In his method of mobilizing the people, he followed a style that connected him closely with the people—talk to the people in simple, clear language; live, eat and clothe yourself in the same way as the ordinary people; be accessible to all, high and low, educated and illiterate; and above all be morally upright, honest, sincere and truthful to the cause of the people. He was called the 'Gandhi of Nigeria'. The name of Aminu Kano is associated with high ideals and moral purpose. Chinua Achebe, the noted Nigerian scholar, wrote 'Gandhi was real; Aminu Kano was real. They were not angels in heaven; they were human like the rest of us in India and Nigeria. Therefore, after their example, no one who reduces the high purpose of politics which they exemplified down to a swinish scramble can hope to do so without bringing a terrible judgement on himself.'

As rightly observed by Pankaj Mishra (2018), 'Those who criticise Gandhi as a "racist" based on remarks he made in South Africa tend to completely ignore the African-American

encounter with Gandhi and certainly do not appreciate its depth.'
In the US, when the Black Lives Matter protests spread, statues
of prominent figures have been defaced or brought down for
their racist pasts. It is unfortunate that amidst this, some have
also pointed fingers at M. K. Gandhi. In Blantyre, Malawi, there
was strong agitation by some young people against a proposed
statue of Gandhi. These acts could be nothing but reaction
misguided by half-truths and emotions relegating objective facts
to the background.

Gandhi was a complex man and had his flaws. His philosophy
of nonviolence has not always worked. But whether he is revered
or condemned, Gandhi's political philosophy and his ideas have
prevailed to provoke thinkers and guide activists for well over
a century, not least in Africa. They shall undoubtedly continue
to do so for centuries to come, even where the oppressors and
the oppressed have the same colour of skin.

References

Du Bois, W. E. B. (William Edward Burghardt). 1868-1963. Gandhi and
American Negroes. July 1957. W. E. B. Du Bois Papers (MS 312). Special
Collections and University Archives, University of Massachusetts Amherst
Libraries.

Gandhi, M.K. 1929. Message to the American Negro. http://www.mkgandhi.
org/letters/unstates/amer_negro.htm

King Jr., Martin Luther. India Trip February 3, 1959 to March 18, 1959.
Martin Luther King Jr. Research & Education Institute Paper 5:233. https://
kinginstitute.stanford.edu/encyclopedia/india-trip

Mazrui, Ali A. 1970. Black Militancy and Gandhi's Centenary. *The Indian
Journal of Political Science* 31 no.2 (April-June 1970), pp. 99-112.

Mishra, Pankaj. 2018. Gandhi for the Post Truth Age. Newyorker.com/
magazine2018/10/22

Nauriya, Anil. 2006. The African Element in Gandhi. National Gandhi
Museum.

The Wire. 2016. Gandhi and West Africa: Exploring the Affinities. November
5. https://thewire.in/history/gandhi-west-africa-exploring-affinities

POLITICAL EMPOWERMENT, SOCIO-RELIGIOUS AWAKENING AND CULTURAL REVIVAL

Mahatma Gandhi's Contribution towards Emancipation of People of Indian Origins in Mauritius

Rajendrakumar Dabee

Introduction

'Generations to come will scarce believe that such a one as this ever in flesh and blood walked upon this earth.'

—Albert Einstein

The above statement by the father of the Theory of Relativity is clichéd, yet so true! Gandhi's charisma and influence as a global figure may lead to the belief, especially among post World War II generations, that the Mahatma may not have existed, so superhuman does his stature seem. Wherever Gandhi set foot, he was, directly and indirectly, the catalyst of change. By extension, one can also assert that even seven decades after his untimely death, he still casts his influence over humanity through his religious beliefs, philosophy of life and political ideology, inspiring leaders to adopt his methodologies in their fight against all forms of injustice and oppression.[17] Mauritius is one of the few countries in the world to have had the privilege of being blessed by his presence and thus to have been directly and indirectly impacted by the life and message of the votary of

---

[17] Nelson Mandela, Martin Luther King, Barack Obama, Al Gore, John Lennon, Aung San Suu Kyi, etc. ('Famous Personalities Influenced by Gandhi', *Hindustan Times* 9.09.2009)

peace. His landmark visit at the turn of the 20th century was so powerful an event that the waves of transformation that arose are still felt in contemporary Mauritian society. At their peak, these waves freed indentured *coolies* from the disguised slavery they were subject to, lifted them towards political freedom, swept away colonialism and heralded an era of peace and harmony in the small island nation. This essay examines three dimensions of the relationship between the Apostle of Non-violence and Mauritius: the point of impact when Gandhi made his memorable visit, the aftershocks it generated as it inspired many Mauritians to struggle for their emancipation, culminating in the independence of the country in 1968, and the continuing influence he still commands.

The *Atithi*[18] Whose Visit Changed Destiny

It was a twist of fate that in 1901, barrister Gandhi, then 39 years old, had to make an unexpected transit via Mauritius. The steamer 'SS Nowshera', in which he was traveling from Natal to Bombay, had to make a halt at the harbour of Port Louis. The ship was anchored from the end of October to mid-November,[19] providing a unique opportunity for both the illustrious visitor and the islanders to acquaint themselves with each other.[20] Gandhi was aware through one of his lieutenants in South Africa that there were a substantial number of people from India settled on the island.[21] On the other hand, news of his successful achievements in South Africa having preceded him, the honour of receiving such a distinguished figure was a

---

[18] Meaning 'an unexpected guest.' In Hindu tradition, an *atithi* is considered as equal to god—*atithi devo bhava.*

[19] Pahlad Ramsurrun in *Mahatma Gandhi and his Impact on Mauritius* situates the date as the 29th while Prof. Basdeo Bissoondoyal thinks it was the 30th.

[20] *The Standard*, a local newspaper edited in English-French. (*Mauritius Times* 31.10.2014)

[21] In his 'Satyagraha in South Africa,' Gandhi writes amply on Thambi Naidoo.

golden occasion not to be missed by the islanders. He was offered
lavish receptions and was treated with the highest reverence by
the locals. While there are controversies over the length of his
stay in the country, claims ranging between 10 and 21 days,[22]
and the places he visited around the island as there was also
an epidemic prevailing at that time, the profound marks he left
on the minds and hearts of the people who met with him are
undeniably true. (Ranjan 2003, 77). Among his hosts were the
Governor General, Sir Charles Bruce (Gandhi 1968, 252),[23] and
local businessmen—essentially Soortee (Surat) Muslims who
originated from Gujarat .[24] Receptions were held in his honour
in Port Louis, on the eve of his departure[25] and at Curepipe,
a town in the centre of the island.[26] Being a renowned man of
law, Gandhi was most naturally introduced to his counterparts
of the profession and was received at the Supreme Court amidst
members of the Bar. The countrymen who hosted him, on the
other hand, opened his eyes to the realities of the colony and

---

[22] While Pahlad Ramsurrun in his work entitled *Mahatma Gandhi and His
Impact on Mauritius* calculates 21 days, Prof. Basdeo Bissoondoyal in his
'Mahatma Gandhi and Mauritius' counts 18. Another historian, N. Napal
counts 14 days while Gandhi himself states that 'the long halt' lasted about
10 days (*Le Mauricien* 2011). There was even controversy regarding the year,
with some claiming that he came as early as 1893 (*ibid*).

[23] In his autobiography he writes, 'So I sailed for home. Mauritius was one
of the ports of call, and as the boat made a long halt there, I went ashore
and acquainted myself fairly well with the local conditions. For one night
I was the guest of Sir Charles Bruce, the Governor of the Colony.'

[24] In a letter to Dr. K. Hazareesingh, dated 26.5.1936, Gandhi confirmed
his visit and mentioned that 'I stayed in the house of some Muslim friends'
who were Ajum Goolam Hossen and Ibrahim Sulleiman Atchia. The latter
provided lodging and transportation facilities to the esteemed guests (Kalla
2011, 1-3).

[25] On the 13th of November 1901 by the Surtee Sunnee Vohra community
(Kalla 2011, 1-3).

[26] According to G.M.D Atchia's credible eye-witness account (*Le Mauricien*
2011).

the issues facing Indians who had migrated there. He was deeply moved by the woeful plight of the indentured labourers called *girmitya*,[27] bound by engagements they had ignorantly and innocently signed on to. Though he appreciated the beauty of the island in the manner of Mark Twain by visiting natural spots, ('Gandhi's Visit to Mauritius—Mauritius Times' n.d.) Gandhi developed a greater affection and thereafter, a deeper interest in the welfare of his compatriots settled there.

On the eve of his departure for India, while addressing the enthusiastic audience[28] gathered to bid farewell to their celebrated guest, Gandhi expressed his concerns regarding the future of the Indians who, despite their significant number and excellent entrepreneurial skills, were not adequately represented in the socio-economic and political affairs of the colony. According to Deolall Thacoor, author of *Mahatma Gandhi in Mauritius* (1971), Gandhi made a seminal observation during that speech. According to him, the only way to freedom from socio-political segregation and economic exclusion was through education (Mahesh 2019). These words seem to have sunk so deeply in the psyche of the Indo-Mauritians that even in the 21st century, parents of Indo-Mauritian origins echo them to their children. It is undoubtable that the political empowerment and economic prosperity now enjoyed by their descendants are the fruits of the seeds Gandhi sowed more than a century earlier.[29] It is true, as claimed by some, that even before the visit, some Indians had achieved success in upward social mobility but these were exceptions. However, he is known to have personally encouraged some to engage themselves, though without much

---

[27] From 'agreement' referring to the contract signed by them.

[28] Hosted by the Surtee Vohra community where there were about 200 (Kalla 2011, 1-3).

[29] Ministers, magistrates, doctors, and other important posts are mostly occupied by the great-grandchildren of the indentured labourers who sacrificed their lives and invested intensely in educating their children.

success.[30] Gandhi's words instead seemed to have touched the minds of listeners and galvanized their resolve (*Le Mauricien* 2017).[31]

Aftermath of the Visit: Manilal Doctor's Structuration

Education was not only the door out of misery but also the key to self-determination and self-government for the indentured labourers and the first waves of Gandhi's catalysing visit began to make themselves felt with the emergence of individuals who we venture to call Gandhians. Ramkelawon Boodhun was the first lawyer of Indian roots who had met Gandhi while studying in London. The latter strongly advised him to return to his motherland in order to serve his community ('Mahatma Gandhi and Mauritius', *L'Express Mu* n.d.). Pandit Sahadeo, regarded as one of the founders of the Mauritian Labour Party, inspired by Gandhian philosophy, literally adopted his methods: wearing the topi and khadi. He is also known to have opened an ashram for the elderly, bearing the name of Gandhi. ('The Struggle of Pandit Sahadeo,' *L'Express Mu* n.d.) The Bissoondoyal brothers were among the most ardent Gandhians. Both Sookdeo and Basdeo were highly active, especially in the arena of politics. Sookdeo was the founder of the Independent Forward Bloc (IFB), a political party with strong Hindu rhetoric and was openly pro-independence. He served as MP on several occasions and was at the Ministry of Cooperatives during the post-independence era. His source of inspiration was his elder brother, Basdeo, the

---

[30] 'GOOLAM MAHOMED ISSAC' *Le Mauricien* n.d. 'Cassam Ajum Piperdy and Goolam Mahomed Issac were the first two Surtees to follow Gandhi's advice' according to 'Goolam Mahomed Issac (1872-1927)' in *Surtee Soonee Mussulman Society Centenary Celebration (1897-1997) Souvenir Magazine.* 'He (Piperdy) failed of election securing 595 out of the 2347 votes that were cast, but Gandhi's wish was fulfilled: a start had been made'(S. Bissoondoyal 1963).

[31] For instance, Dr. Hassen Sakir was elected to the Municipal Council of Port Louis in 1896.

'Gandhian Missionary' who applied the Mahatma's principles to the letter, emulating his strategies in the Mauritian context.

A prolific writer, historian, poet and philosopher, Prof. Basdeo Bissoondoyal stands as a towering figure in the history of Mauritius, being one of the architects of its independence. His countless works, written in Hindi, English and French, reached readers far and wide. At a time when access to education was limited, 'Pandit Basdeo,' as he was lovingly referred to, made public addresses in Hindi. His rhetoric was fundamentally religious and exhibited deep influences of Swami Dayananda and the Arya Samaj. His *darshan* of Gandhi as a student at D.A.V. College, Lahore, in 1934, was a turning point in his life. The last words of his autobiography place Gandhi as the 'greatest visitor Mauritius had had' (B. Bissoondoyal 1984, 191).

Basdeo Bissoondoyal's life is an open confession of allegiance to Vedic philosophy and the greatness of Hindu thought, taught by S. Radhakrishnan, H.C. Mookerjee and P.R. Sen (B. Bissoondoyal 1984, 68). It is within the walls of the Lahore College and in a climate suffused with Gandhian ideologies that the foundations of Gandhism in Mauritius were laid in the mind of the youthful Indo-Mauritian. He was reminded of the similar state of affairs in his homeland. It can be said that the undergraduate Basdeo was initiated into Gandhism in India itself as he participated in debate competitions. One such debate was entitled 'Patriotism is not enough,' where he referred to Mahatma Gandhi's view that 'Patriotism would be enriched with internationalism' (B. Bissoondoyal 1984, 75). In a subsequent debate, he ventured to speak on the 'weapon' called 'non-co-operation,' through which the Congress could achieve its goals. While his fearlessness in publicly speaking out against the Empire and his clear eloquence won him several prizes in his fatherland, yet it is in his motherland that he endured their harsh consequences.[32]

---

[32] He was jailed thrice between 1943 and 1944.

However, before dealing *in extenso* the Gandhian philosophy in Mauritius which reached its height under the Bissoondoyal brothers, its infancy needs to be highlighted since it delineates the conditions which made it favourable for the latter to emerge. Gandhi's words were not blanket statements made to please his hosts and audience at a reception in his honour. They were genuinely felt and expressed out of compassion and concern for his Indian brothers and sisters (Ramnauth 1981, 115).[33] Not more than a month following his historic visit, at the 17th Indian National Congress, he highlighted the contribution of Indians in Mauritius, Fiji and other colonies, towards the prosperity of the Empire (Mahesh 2019).

> Gentlemen, I appear before you not as a delegate, but more as a petitioner on behalf of the hundred thousand British Indians in South Africa, and probably also of the future emigrants...The traders have gone in their thousands to different parts of the world, to South Africa, Zanzibar, Mauritius, Fiji, Singapore... Gentlemen, if some of the distinguished Indians I see before me to-night were to go to South Africa, inspired with that noble spirit, our grievances must be removed.[34]

Moreover, it was at his personal behest that Manilal Maganlal Doctor[35] came to Mauritius in 1907. The latter was, like Gandhi, a lawyer by profession, and came from Burma (Joshi 1990, 76). He was highly instrumental in widening the field of activities of a branch of the Arya Samaj opened in the capital, though neither Swami Dayananda nor his famous *Satyārthaprakāśa* were

---

[33] Deolall Thacoor states in *Mahatma Gandhi and Mauritius* that his (Gandhi's) words 'came out of his heart and fell as nectar on the famished ears of the audience.'

[34] Deolall Thacoor, *Mahatma Gandhi in Mauritius* (Port Louis, Mauritius: The Royal Printing, 1970, pp 210-211 in Ramnauth 1981, 114-115).

[35] 'Doctor' was an epithet he inherited from his father. His actual name was Manilal Maganlal Shah and he hailed from Gujarat. The proximity with Gandhi was not simply professional.

unknown to the Hindus.[36] Since then, the Arya Samaj has been the platform par excellence for the application of Gandhism. With the association of the Bissoondoyal brothers three decades later, the Samaj played a crucial role in educating, empowering and ultimately liberating Hindus (Ranjan 2003).

A Gandhian at heart, Manilal Doctor rightly diagnosed the legal and political lacunae which the Indians faced in the country. He started his mission of awakening Indians to the need for education and made their case in India for the indenture system to be ultimately discontinued. Until 1911, the year he left the island, Manilal Doctor worked ceaselessly for the upliftment of Indo-Mauritians, sending regular reports to the Mahatma. The latter, while corresponding with his political mentor Prof. Gokhale, expresses in flowery terms the excellent work being accomplished by his envoy:

> Mr. Manilal Doctor has, as you are aware, done very good public work in Mauritius and gained the affection of the poor Indians there to whom he became a friend in need (Mahesh 2019).

Subsequently Doctor fought for the cause of indentured labourers in Fiji where, like in Mauritius, his dedication and leadership disturbed the colonial government (Tinker 1974)[37] and in both countries he is held in high esteem by their descendants. In Mauritius, 11th October is celebrated as Manilal Day, being the date on which he set foot on the island. Incidentally, the abolition of indentureship did not come from Indo-Mauritians but from Indians who made public outcries against their compatriots' inhumane ordeals[38] and Manilal Doctor can to a large extent be given credit for this (Nilay 2003). His application of Gandhian

---

[36] They were introduced in the previous century by one Sepoy.

[37] Wherever he went, Doctor challenged a biased justice system, completely bent in favour of the plantocracy.

[38] There were several visitors from India since the beginning of indentureship.

techniques of satyagraha and passive resistance[39] to fight against an oppressive system[40] were later emulated by his successors in the Arya Samaj, namely Pandit Kashinath Kistoe and others. True to Gandhi's parting wish in 1901, Manilal Doctor had laid the foundations for the liberation of Indo-Mauritians in three vital areas: education, economics and politics. To educate them he started newspapers like *The Hindustani* and founded the Young Men Hindu Association to boost the morale of Hindus ('Manilal Doctor' *Mauritius Times* n.d.). He died in 1956, after tumultuous years of providing legal services to the causes of his countrymen. In Mauritius, many public places bear his name and busts have been erected, the most ironical being one in the *Jardin de Compagnie des Indes* in Port Louis, in the midst of those colonial rulers whom he confronted in the courts (Tinker 1974b).

Education As the Gateway to Empowerment

The two decades that followed the ground-breaking work of Manilal Doctor saw the gradual rise in the financial standards of the people of Indian Origin (PIOs) and along with it, greater assertions of their right to self-determination. The introduction of the *morcellement* system whereby sugar estate owners could sell their lands allowed PIOs to acquire property and thus liberate themselves from the shackles of indenture contracts. This process also generated conditions conducive for the formation of villages. According to Richard Allen, already between 1864 to 1900, Indo-Mauritians had bought lands evaluated at more than 24 million rupees. An astronomical figure for that time,

---

[39] In Mauritius, he refused to remove his shoes and turban at the command of the Chief Judge.

[40] U. Bissoondoyal in Indian Overseas—*The Mauritian Experience*, p.337, quotes Raj Mathur's *Indian and Politics, 1834-1934*: 'according to the colonial secretary, Manilal had sought to instil into the minds of PIOs, ideas and grievances which did not exist before, apart from bringing to light well-grounded grievances.'

bearing in mind that the average wage paid was Rs.10 per month! The degree of sacrifice that they must have borne is thought-provoking. By 1921, twenty years after Gandhi's visit, 93% of the planters were PIOs who occupied 35% of the agricultural land.[41] In addition, thanks to the intervention of anti-indenture campaigners like Kunwar Maharajsing (Joshi 1990), the system was abolished by 1922 and a new Labour Law enacted which gave greater rights to *coolies* (Ranjan 2003,52). Maharajsing also emphasized the need to study the Indian languages, which later became a strategic tool for their rise to power.

The real liberation of the Indian immigrants started after the literacy movement (Ranjan 2003, 42). Mahatma Gandhi, learned lawyer and wise sage that he was, had understood that the emancipation of the PIOs lay in mass education and this was the front where the fiercest struggles took place. Both the colonizer and the colonized had understood that education was the best weapon to break bondage to life-long servitude for the latter or, for the former, to strengthen it. The British colonizers had greater affinity with the French plantocracy who controlled the economy. The whole state apparatus was therefore geared towards promoting a system of education that further enslaved and re-enforced the spirit of dependency in labourers. The latter on the other hand, ignorant and illiterate, had at their disposal nothing of the sort, except their cultural heritage[42] from which Gandhi derived his own convictions. It is this spirit of Gandhism bequeathed to them by Manilal Doctor and perpetuated by the subsequent Arya Samajist leaders that ultimately led to their emancipation. Gandhi's own success with his various Civil Disobedience campaigns in India was a source of inspiration to many in the island, and especially to one youth by the name

---

[41] Richard B. Allen, *Indian Immigrant and the Beginning of the Grant Morcellement*, 1860-1885 in Bissondoyal ed. *Indian Overseas*, Moka-Mauritius, MGI Publication, 1987 (cited in Nilay 2003, 34).

[42] They brought with them popular religious works like the *Ramcaritmanas* and the *Bhagavadgītā*.

of Basdeo. After the departure of Manilal Doctor, the flag of Gandhism could not be carried much further (Tinker 1974, 223)[43] until Bissoondoyal returned (B. Bissoondoyal 1984, 29).[44]

Although it is true that there was an educational system set in place by the colonial government, as well as private institutions, there was deep distrust among the immigrants about their real motives. They suspected a hidden proselytizing agenda. Moreover, poverty was an important factor deterring parents from sending their children to schools. Doing so meant sacrificing pairs of hands that could have helped earn more money for the family. This could be perhaps why Gandhi exhorted them to make this enormous sacrifice, a long-term investment in the future generations. Despite the records of the Education Department showing a school population of 50 percent (*Le Mauricien* 2017) Indian-origin children, the overall majority of the population, did not send their children to schools. Moreover, the following table on the percentage of professionalization among PIOs is quite informative:

TABLE 1: Percentage of Professionalization of PIOs

Year	%PIO	%Professional	%Civil Service
1851	43	4	27
1901	70	23	28
1952	67	27	53

Source: Ranjan 2003, 41.

There is a noticeably sharp rise in both the percentage of professionals and those joining the civil service, especially after 1901, the year Gandhi visited Mauritius.

---

[43] He writes in the introductory paragraph: 'This is the statue of Manilal Doctor, who—in the absence of any alternative candidates—has been raised up as the champion of the Indians of Mauritius.'

[44] 'When nobody could come out to Mauritius to allow me to take a subordinate place I had to take the lead.'

Gandhian Philosophy in Action: Bissoondoyals' Consolidation of Doctor's Achievement

The departure of Manilal Doctor created a vacuum of leadership that was difficult to fill. The educated professionals could not rally the people behind them with the same fervour as Doctor, owing perhaps to their European education and pro-Western cultural influences. R.K. Boodhun, Rajkoomar Gujadhur and others tried to carry further the Arya Samaj with a series of activities. Gujadhur started a newspaper in 1923 called *The Mauritius Mitra* which unfortunately could not muster a sustainable following. The intricate relationship between education and politics and their mutual dependence became a crucial issue for the Indo-Mauritians. Realizing perhaps the prophetic utterance of Gandhi at the beginning of the 20th century (B. Bissoondoyal 1984, 83),[45] the need of the time was to find that the Messiah would take the boat of the PIOs fate to its destination. The Bissoondoyal brothers came forward to steer this boat, applying to the best of their abilities the teachings and philosophy of Mahatma Gandhi. They initiated in the process what was referred to as the Hindu Cultural Revival Movement (Boudet 2011, 1-3).

Their motto was simple: endow Hindus with self-respect, self-pride and self-confidence so that they could free themselves from colonization (B. Bissoondoyal 1984, 56). These notions echo Gandhi's ideas of swaraj. And the key to that was education of the masses coupled with a passive resistance and non-co-operation movement. Laws were passed which did not allow illiterate voters to cast the ballot and despite their overwhelming majority, only a handful of them could vote. As a result, PIOs were always underrepresented in the legislative council. With a government policy of education not in their interest, the Bissoondoyal brothers decided to take matters into their hands.

Satya and Ahimsa are cornerstones of Gandhi's socio-

---

[45] 'Mahatma Gandhi told his countrymen in 1901 that a preacher was in great demand in Mauritius.'

religious and political philosophies which his votaries emulated in spirit and action. These were manifest in the Bissoondoyals, winning the elder brother the title of 'Gandhian Missionary'. The violent riots that took place in 1913 witnessed by Basdeo were a reminder of the desolation that violence can bring (Boudet 2011, 1-3). The different methods of passive resistance patiently developed, practically experimented with and lucidly documented by Mahatma Gandhi in his famous autobiography were re-enacted in the Mauritian context. When Basdeo Bissoondoyal returned to his native country in 1939, he was appalled at the dire conditions people of his community were living in. Saddened by the absence of strong leadership, he felt compelled to enter the political arena. He was clearly guided by Gandhian values when he stated:

> To remind the work of Gandhi is to put it in mind of an ideal soldier, a true servant of the people, an original and fearless thinker and a bugbear of all manner of tyrants [sic] (B. Bissoondoyal 1984, 57).

He started thus his career of Gandhism in the manner of his Ideal: with a public event that brought him into the limelight. Gandhi's famous march to Dandi awakened the soul of India and ultimately became the march to freedom. Similarly, the *Mahayajña* organized by Basdeo Bissoondoyal on the 12th of December 1943 was a milestone in the history of Mauritius. 60,000 Indo-Mauritians responded to his appeal and sent a clear indication of their desire for self-rule. This peaceful defiance ultimately resulted, a quarter of a century later, in independence. In 1968, Sir Seewoosagur Ramgoolam (SSR), another Gandhi-inspired child of immigrants (C. N. Boudet 2013, 1-3), became the first Prime Minister. His designation of 12th of March for this momentous day was very symbolical as it was linked with Gandhi. Moreover, the year of the birth of Mauritius as a sovereign nation coincided with the Mahatma's birth centenary. It was fastidiously celebrated in Mauritius as a reminder and an expression of gratitude of its people towards the Great Soul's priceless contribution. Commemorative stamps were issued, souvenir magazines and books were published, speeches were given (Ramnauth 1981, 119).

Much in the manner Gandhi was called 'Mahatma,' Basdeo Bissoondoyal was addressed as 'Pandit' owing to his erudition in Hindu lore and practises. His purpose was to re-establish, re-build and consolidate the confidence of the Hindus, especially the youth who 'were wandering away from the principles cherished by their forefathers' (B. Bissoondoyal 1984, 107). In his own words, he asserts that:

> The Mahayajna is a landmark in the history of the revival of Hinduism in our island home. The revival came as a necessary consequence of the Hindu Religious movement set on foot towards the close of 1939 (B. Bissoondoyal 1984, 101).

In 1940, he founded the *Jan Andolan* with the aim of materializing these goals. It was much like the Quit India campaign by Gandhi. Both challenged the Empire's supremacy. The sermons which both delivered were highly political and socially impactful. Jimmy Harmon identified four aspects to the Professor's rhetoric: language, dress-code, flag and anthems.

> Wearing *dhoti* and *kurta*, 'Gandhians in Mauritius'[46] sung the famous slogan *aum ka jhandā*[47] which meant, 'Here comes up our flag, leave off your slumber. Arise, awake, unite and forge ahead my co-religionists' (Harmon 2015, 1-3).

Prof. Basdeo had correctly understood, like Doctor who had likewise rightly discerned the implications, of Gandhi's words on the 13th of November, 1901. All three of them had realized that education was key to empowerment that could shatter the fetters of domination and exploitation. Voting required eligible ballot casters to have a minimum level of literacy in

---

[46] Ramnauth (1981, 118) also makes a similar reference.

[47] *Yahan Aum ka Jhanda Ata Hai Soney Walo Jag Chalo* (B. Bissoondoyal, 1984).

English, French and Oriental Languages (OL), in order to elect their candidates. Despite attempts to thwart the project, the Bissoondoyals, with a regiment of 800 volunteers of the *Jan Andolan*, carried out massive educational campaigns, especially in villages.[48] Indo-Mauritians learned basic Hindi, Urdu, Tamil, Gujarati, Marathi and Telugu, enabling the electorate to inflate seven-fold.[49] If Mauritius is one of the rare countries in the world where all these languages are formally included in the National Curriculum, it is probably owing to the efforts of Prof. Basdeo Bissoondoyal and his followers in the 1940s. Newspapers in OL were also encouraged.[50] Similar to *Young India, Harijan* and other publications by Mahatma Gandhi, local newspapers carried further the agenda of the Indo-Mauritians towards auto-determination. While there were 6 Hindi newspapers before 1948, 5 more came up before 1968 and 4 post-independence (Ranjan 2003, 77). The result was astounding: for the first time in history, an overwhelming majority of elected candidates were non-whites, amongst whom were Sookdeo Bissoondoyal and many other Hindus. It was the first step towards political freedom.

The ruling government, seeing the role education could play in immigrant emancipation, devised a plan to deter Indo-Mauritians. In 1941, the Director of Education, M.E.F Ward recommended the discontinuation of OL teaching in public schools.[51] Two years later, the Director got an opportunity to taste the Gandhian technique of non-co-operation when 300 OL teachers belonging to state-funded schools staged a walkout

---

[48] Moheeputh, Anand, *The Political Emancipation of the Indo-Mauritian*, n.5, pp. 310-320 (cited in Ranjan 2003, 80).

[49] The number jumped from a meagre 11,445 to a whopping 72,000.

[50] *The Hindustani, The Indo-Mauritian, People of Indian Origin Times, The Mauritius Mitra, Aryoday, Janata, Mazdoor, Nav Jeewan* and *Samajwad* are some examples.

[51] Ranjan (2013, 80) referring to K. Hazareesingh's *Selected Speeches of Sir Seewoosagar Ramgoolam*, (London: Macmillan, 1979, pp. 11-16).

during his speech.[52] Until the 1948 elections, OL suffered from Ward's recommendations. Yet, even then, the struggle did not lose its momentum. Access to education was facilitated by socio-religious and cultural centres called *Baithkā*, *Gītāmandalī* and *Rāmāyana Mandali* where afternoon classes were carried out. Matters improved in the 1950s when SSR, appointed as the liaison officer for education, initiated the teaching of OL at a national level in primary schools. The battle for education was therefore a crucial one in the war waged by PIOs against the tyrannical rule of colonizers. Its immediate outcome was an emboldened Hindu community, proud of its culture and traditions, with a sense of empowerment that led to political sovereignty.[53]

While PIOs had become politically empowered through education, freedom was not won and only complete and unconditional freedom from colonial rule would guarantee that they were masters of their own fate. The Bissoondoyal brothers stood as valiant Gandhian soldiers of Truth and Non-violence. The *Jan Andolan* was essentially a Hindu Cultural Revival Movement, not a political body. The terrible riots that took place in 1943[54] which resulted in several deaths, compelled his brother Sookdeo three years later to resign from his job as teacher and join politics. In 1958, he created the Independent Forward Bloc (IFB), a political party with a clearly Hindu agenda and an anti-colonial bias. Despite the lateness in its formation, the IFB was able to get 6 out of 40 of its candidates elected during the elections held in 1959, including Sookdeo Bissoondoyal himself

---

[52] Ramyead, Lutchmee Prasad, *Indian Languages in Mauritius: A Perspective*, No.5. pp 140-177 cited in Ranjan (2003, 80).

[53] Mathur and Sydney Selvon, *A Concise History of Mauritius*, pp. 38-342 cited in Ranjan (2003, 81).

[54] Owing to abuse and exploitation by estate owners, some *coolies* voiced their dissatisfaction at a place called Belle Vue Harel, in the north. They were brutally suppressed on 27th September 1943 with a toll of 4 dead and 17 injured. Anjalay Coopen, a pregnant woman, was martyred in the process.

(Ranjan 2003, 91). The older Mauritius Labour Party was more successful, under the leadership of SSR. Sookdeo was a Gandhian who fought for his community and PIOs with much valour, politically supplementing the latter's campaign to re-instil pride and confidence on Hinduism. In 1954, as a Member of Legislative Council, he tabled a motion that demanded the state provide equal consideration to all religions practised in the country alongside Christianity (Ranjan 2003, 79). Despite persecution, imprisonment and physical assault, he faithfully stood with Basdeo, confident of his Gandhian ideology (B. Bissoondoyal 1984, 129). Upon his death in 1977, his brother recalled his contribution towards the independence of Mauritius, that 'was achieved without the necessity of shedding a single drop of blood. Sookdeo was a Gandhian, as *The Times of London* put it in 1973' (B. Bissoondoyal 1984, 155).

Conclusion: The Continuing Ripples of Gandhi's Impact on Mauritius

> The people of Mauritius should be grateful to Professor B. Bissoondoyal, M.A., who with patience, diligently unearthed the hidden historical treasure which lay covered under thick layers of dust of ignorance and lost in the dark abyss of Time.
>
> —Deolall Thacoor[55]

The Bissoondoyal brothers stand as the representatives of a generation of Indo-Mauritians whose forefathers, brought under the inhumane indenture system as *coolie* PIOs, had heeded Gandhi's visionary message. Despite their gloomy living conditions, the ephemeral passage of the Mahatma through their midst was enough to spark a glimmer of hope. They nurtured this hope by offering unimaginable sacrifices until it became a fire that ushered in an era of revolutionary transformations. By educating their children, they enabled them to overcome

---

[55] Ramnauth (1981, ii).

misery, both physical and moral. The confidence thus acquired paved the way for political assertion and with enhanced political power, these children today enjoy the status of being proud citizens of a sovereign nation. Non-violent satyagrahas and other successful Gandhian approaches won even the admiration of Franco-Mauritians like Dr. Maurice Curé and France Boyer de la Giroday (Ramnauth 1981).

In gratitude for his immense contribution in shaping its people's fortune, Bapuji is remembered in many ways and at many places across Mauritius. In memory of his coming to the island, *āgaman divas* is celebrated. Along with the peaceful observance of Gandhi Jayanti, his falling to martyrdom too, is solemnly observed as *balidan diwas* (Ramnauth 1981, 120).[56] His life and achievements, his philosophy of Satya and Ahimsa, his educational, social, economic and political ideologies are topics of study in primary, secondary and tertiary education institutions.[57] Public places bearing the Gandhi patronym are legion, from streets and lanes to schools, institutions, homes and orphanages. His statues and busts can be seen prominently at important locations around the island while his universal prayer[58] is recited daily by thousands of students in all schools bearing his name (Ramnauth 1981). Pictures of him are reverentially hung along with those of Swami Dayananda, *pitris* and *devatas* in many Hindu homes. While these are tangible, the intangible legacy of Mahatma Gandhi can be seen in the daily lives of hundreds of thousands of Mauritians, Hindus and non-Hindus alike, who practise his principles and observe his values, making

---

[56] France Boyer, a sincere Christian, once wrote in *La Vie Catholigue*, a Christian Weekly in Mauritius: 'If Gandhi had met Christ the latter would have loved him' (10.11.1968).

[57] For instance, Gandhi as a topic in Hinduism is examined at O and A Level examinations by Cambridge International Examinations (CIE), Gandhian Philosophy is a module taught at Diploma, B.A and M.A level courses in Indian Philosophy at the Mahatma Gandhi Institute.

[58] *Grant me, O master…*

the country a reference of peaceful co-existence. For, it is worth remembering that Gandhi never hinted at any form of exclusion in his speech. In his own words:

Indian community should rise but not to battle against the Government, but to claim its rights and its place under the sun and under the flag of freedom (Tiwari 2019) .

Interestingly, he was also aware of the success of the transformative process his methods had brought in Mauritius. When communal clashes between Hindus and Muslims caused thousands of deaths in India, Gandhi reminded his countrymen how these two communities were living in harmony in Mauritius and collaborating in their struggles against exploitation and injustice. Gandhi and Mauritius share in this manner, a relation of mutual influence.

References

Bissoondoyal, Basdeo. 1984. *Life in Greater India*. Bombay: Bharatiya Vidya Bhavan.

Bissoondoyal, S. 1963. *A Concise History of Mauritius*. Bharatiya Vidya Bhavan. https://books.google.mu/books?id=V4QcAAAAMAAJ.

Boudet, Catherine. 2011. Basdeo Bissoondoyal (1906-1991) et Son Époque, Prélude à Un Éveil Socio-Politique. *ODI-Mauritius Conference* 1–3. Port Louis.

Boudet, Catherine Nadia. 2013. Nationalisme, Décolonisation et Consociation à l'île Maurice: L'émergence d'un Mauricianisme Stratégique (1945–1967). *Canadian Journal of African Studies / Revue Canadienne Des Études Africaines* 47 (3): 385–403. https://doi.org/10.1080/00083968.2014.892434.

Hindustan Times. n.d. Famous Personalities Influenced by Gandhi. Accessed September 22, 2020. https://www.hindustantimes.com/world/famous-personalities-influenced-by-gandhi/story-wly3FKFBeobO1g4k7ZOCLK.html.

Gandhi, Mohandas Karamchand. 1968. *An Autobiography Or The Story of My Experiments with Truth*. Edited by Mahadev Desai and Shriman Narayan. Ahmedabad: Navajivan Publishing House. https://www.mkgandhi.org/ebks/An-Autobiography.pdf.

Harmon, Jimmy. 2015. Basdeo Bissoondoyal (1906-1991), Sermons of Liberation. *Aapravasi Ghat Trust Fund Newsletter* No. 12: 1–3.

Joshi, P.K. 1990. Study in Indo Mauritius Relations 1970–1990. PhD diss., Chhatrapati Sahuji Maharaj University. http://hdl.handle.net/10603/270382.

Kalla, Abdool Cader. 2011. Gandhiji's Hosts in Mauritius, 'Diasporic' Trajectories. *Le Mauricien*, December 8, 2011. https://www.academia.edu/8058251/Gandhijis_hosts_in_Mauritius.

Le Mauricien. 2017. M. K. Gandhi Visited Mauritius in 1901 with His Whole Family (II). October 3, 2017. https://www.lemauricien.com/le-mauricien/m-k-gandhi-visited-mauritius-1901-his-whole-family-ii/160595/.

Le Mauricien. n.d. GOOLAM MAHOMED ISSAC (1872-1927): Précurseur de l'engagement Indo-Mauricien En Politique. Accessed September 21, 2020. https://www.lemauricien.com/actualites/magazine/goolam-mahomed-issac-1872-1927-precurseur-lengagement-indo-mauricien-en-politique/124581/.

Le Mauricien. 2011. HISTOIRE: Un Survol Chronologique de La Visite de Gandhi à Maurice. October 31, 2011. https://www.lemauricien.com/actualites/magazine/histoire-survol-chronologique-la-visite-gandhi-à-maurice/135307/.

Le Mauricien. n.d. M.K. GANDHI: Disciples Du Mahatma. Accessed September 22, 2020. https://www.lemauricien.com/actualites/societe/mk-gandhi-disciples-du-mahatma/107091/.

L'Express. n.d. Mahatma Gandhi and Mauritius. Accessed July 31, 2020a. https://www.lexpress.mu/article/mahatma-gandhi-and-mauritius.

L'Express. n.d. Mahatma Gandhi and Mauritius. Accessed September 16, 2020b. https://www.lexpress.mu/article/mahatma-gandhi-and-mauritius.

L'Express. n.d. The Struggle of Pandit Sahadeo. Accessed September 22, 2020. https://www.lexpress.mu/article/struggle-pandit-sahadeo.

Mahesh, Supraja. 2019. Mahatma Gandhi's Little-Known Mauritius Trip and Its Link to India's Partition. *The New Indian Express*, October 1. https://www.newindianexpress.com/nation/2019/oct/01/mahatma-gandhis-little-known-mauritius-trip-and-its-link to-indias-partition-2041895.html.

'Gandhi's Visit to Mauritius—Mauritius Times.' n.d. Accessed September 16, 2020. http://www.mauritiustimes.com/mt/mt-60-years-10/.

Mauritius Times. n.d. Manilal Doctor—A Man of the People. Accessed September 25, 2020. http://www.mauritiustimes.com/mt/satyendra-peerthum-12/.

Ramnauth, Dev. 1981. The Spiritual Element in the Educational Philosophy of Mahatma Gandhi. PhD diss., Maharaja Sayajirao University of Baroda. http://hdl.handle.net/10603/58100.

Ranjan, Nilay. 2003. Political Assertion and Ascendancy to Power of People of Indian Origin in Mauritius (1948-98) : Success and Challenges. PhD diss., Jawaharlal Nehru University. http://hdl.handle.net/10603/16648.

Tinker, Hugh. 1974. Odd Man Out: The Loneliness of the Indian Colonial Politician—the Career of Manilal Doctor. *The Journal of Imperial and Commonwealth History* 2 (2): 226–43. https://doi.org/10.1080/03086537408582406.

Tiwari, Savita. 2019. How Mahatma Gandhi Played a Role in the Independence of Mauritius. *Organiser.* https://www.organiser.org/Encyc/2019/10/2/Mahatma-Gandhi-role-in-Independence-of-Mauritius.html.

FASHIONING HEROES OUT OF CLAY

Gandhi As an Exemplar of Moral Leadership

Zubin R. Mulla

'Gandhiji, it has been well said, could fashion heroes out of common clay. His first and, undoubtedly, his most successful experiment was with himself.'

—(Upadhyaya 1965, 6)

Mohandas K. Gandhi is undoubtedly one of the best exemplars of leadership. Gandhi not only inspired millions of Indians during his life (Burns 1978), he created followers who were also leaders and who became the makers of modern India (Erikson 1993). His ideas of love and non-violence inspired leaders across the world such as W. E. B. Du Bois and Martin Luther King Jr. in the American civil rights movement, South Africa's Nelson Mandela, Tibet's Dalai Lama, Zambia's Kenneth Kuanda and Myanmar's Aung San Suu Kyi (Wolpert 2001). So powerful was his influence that within thirty-seven years of India's independence, forty-four nations were freed from the British Empire (Gonsalves 2012).

Gandhi's contribution is also unique because he gave new meaning to ancient Indian thoughts and philosophies. By harnessing traditional Indian beliefs to address contemporary challenges, Gandhi added a new freshness and vigour to Indian thought and the Indian nation (Rudolph & Rudolph 1967). He opposed European colonialism, rejected materialism, championed civil rights, and evolved a philosophy of non-violent protest which could embarrass the oppressor while demonstrating the moral superiority of the protestor (Hardiman 2003). His impact on individual transformation, political action, and social change is unmatched in recent human history.

In this essay, I explore James MacGregor Burns's concept

of moral leadership and show how Gandhi represents a good example of it. Historical figures are good subjects to study leadership since their actions and outcomes achieved are established by historical record (Bligh & Robinson 2010). Prior studies (e.g., Bligh & Kohles 2009; Gardner & Cleavenger 1998) have highlighted aspects of leadership theories using examples from history. Drawing on the moral leadership exhibited by Gandhi, we get an understanding of how we can evolve to being better leaders in organizations and society.

Moral Leadership

Leadership is one of the most misunderstood terms in the social sciences. It is a word used by laypersons and scholars alike. Each one of us has our own implicit understanding of what it means to be a good leader. Shaped by our early experiences with individuals in authority, we enact behaviour that we observe in powerful individuals around us and call it leadership. But leadership is much more than simply imitating those in power.

According to American historian and political scientist James MacGregor Burns, our obsession with individual leaders and their personalities has prevented us from understanding leadership. His 1978 book, *Leadership*, is the cornerstone in leadership studies and hundreds of leadership programmemes in business and government.

Burns distinguishes between power and leadership, both of which are relationships amongst individuals and not absolutes. Power is the ability of one individual to influence change in the behaviour of another individual. Power is a relationship because the power that one individual has with respect to another is a function of the motives and resources of both the individuals and the context within which they operate. Leadership is a special kind of power which is exercised when the wielder of power considers the needs of the recipient of power. In other words, leaders do not ignore followers' motives, instead they seek to arouse, engage and satisfy the motives of followers.

Burns further distinguishes between two kinds of leadership—transactional and transforming. Transactional leadership occurs when leaders exchange valued resources with followers in return for specific actions. While this kind of leadership is commonly observed in corporations and public life it is far less potent than transforming leadership. Transforming leaders not only recognize and exploit existing needs of potential followers; they look for potential motives and higher needs in followers and thereby raise the awareness of their followers to higher levels of conduct and morality. By engaging the full person of the follower in the task of achieving higher goals, they completely transform their followers. As followers are transformed into their higher selves, leaders too need to shift to still higher levels of motivation and morality. Hence, transforming leadership is a dynamic relationship in which both leaders and followers evolve such that *followers* become *leaders* and *transforming leaders* become *moral leaders* (Burns, 1978).

Moral leadership has three characteristics—first, leaders and the led have a relationship beyond power which involves mutual needs, aspirations, and values; second, followers voluntarily choose to respond to leaders among other viable alternatives; and third, leaders take responsibility for bringing about the economic, social, and political change that they commit to. Moral leadership is not about preaching or ensuring social conformity. 'Moral leadership emerges from, and always returns to, the fundamental wants and needs, aspirations, and values of the followers (Burns 1978, 4).' Moral leadership is a process 'wherein individuals take a moral stance on an issue, convince others to do the same, and together spur change in a moral system' (Solinger, Jansen & Cornelissen 2020, 504).

The test of effective moral leadership is the transformation of individuals into their better selves and an enduring legacy which can serve as a driver of social change (Burns 1978). When leaders fail to transform others, they merely display individual heroism which does not lead to any permanent social change.

Also, in the absence of a sustainable ideology or worldview which the followers can adopt to change themselves, the impact of heroes is temporary.

Burns (1978) gives leadership a normative dimension which is often missing in political science and management (Dalton 1993; Fu et al. 2010; Hoch et al. 2016). The leader is essentially an educator who not only raises the awareness of human needs but also suggests the means to gratify or transcend them. This process of gratification and transcendence of human needs raises individuals to higher levels of motivation and morality. This is exactly what Gandhi did—swaraj (self-rule) was a vision symbolizing several individual, social, and political needs and satyagraha (non-violent resistance) was the path through which swaraj was to be sought. Gandhi's distinctive achievement was not just his idealism but his ability to apply it in practise (Dalton 1993).

In the next few sections, I describe some of Gandhi's developmental experiences which shaped his personality and reinforced his values. Next, I describe specific elements of moral leadership which are exemplified in Gandhi's public life. After that, I provide examples of the kind of massive transformation he shaped in the lives of millions of people worldwide. Finally, I discuss his enduring legacy which continues to inspire people across the world.

Gandhi's Developmental Experiences

Gandhi was born in the town of Porbandar into the bania (trader) caste and an upper middle-class family. His mother, who was an orthodox Hindu and who followed strict religious vows involving self-control through fasting, was a strong role model. His emphasis on ahimsa or strict non-violence can also be traced to his mother's faith. There is nothing notable in his childhood and adolescence which could explain the greatness of the leader that emerged (Burns 1978; Easwaran 2000). Among the few incidents described by Gandhi which helped shape his sense of self and purpose are—leaving his ailing father to go to his wife's bed, violating religious sanctions by eating meat, and visiting a brothel (Burns 1978; Erikson 1993).

As a young man of 19 and a law student in London, he admired the British Empire and took great pains to become the perfect English gentleman. When Gandhi was a 22-year-old law student in London, he was asked why he came to England. To that question, he answered emphatically—'Ambition!' (Erikson 1993). Later the ambition of this young lawyer was to be rudely challenged during a train to Pretoria when a European co-passenger had him thrown out of a first-class compartment despite him having a ticket. This led to a lot of turmoil and reflection and perhaps sowed the seeds for the changes in his personality that were to follow (Erikson 1993; Mehta 1977).

Gandhi's years in South Africa shaped his personality and political strategy (Guha 2013). Drawing on Indian and Western ideas, Gandhi created a philosophy as well as an effective programme of action (Gardner 1993). Gandhi's deepest Indian influences were the Bhagawad Gita, the Isa Upanishad, and his spiritual mentor, Srimad Rajchandra. Among Western thinkers, Gandhi was influenced by Plato, Thoreau, Emerson, Tolstoy and Ruskin. His political mentors were Dadabhai Naoroji and Gopal Krishna Gokhale—two cosmopolitan leaders (Guha 2013; Patel 2020; Weber 2005).

From 1894 until 1906, Gandhi and his compatriots had relied on letters, articles, and petitions to fight racial injustice in South Africa. Since 1896 the idea of passive resistance was visible in Gandhi's writings. But his first act of moral leadership occurred on September 11, 1906 at the Empire Theatre in Johannesburg. The hall was filled with 3,000 Indians from all over Transvaal to protest the discriminatory 'Asiatic Ordinance' which required every Indian to carry a registration certificate or face arrest. In this meeting, Gandhi made them all take an oath to struggle non-violently against injustice (Erikson, 1993). This was the first time he had communicated his technique which he would later call satyagraha—the power born of truth and love or non-violence.[59]

In 1914, at the age of 45 after the successful conclusion of a civil disobedience campaign in South Africa and return to India, Gandhi changed his dress dramatically and started dressing like a common Indian. He also rejected aspects of Western civilization and had lost his faith in the British system of law and justice (Dalton 1993).

After returning to India, on advice of his mentor Gopal Krishna Gokhale, Gandhi toured the nation but did not make any public speeches or political statements. In 1916, he made a provocative speech at Benaras. In 1917, he led a farmers' revolt in Champaran. One of the most pivotal experiences in his political career occurred in 1919 when he was leading a strike in a textile mill in Ahmedabad. Gandhi was leading the negotiations on behalf of the workers' union with the proprietor (who also happened to be a family friend of Gandhi). After days of stalled negotiations, he discovered the fast as an instrument of moral coercion almost by accident when mill workers accused him of eating sumptuous food while they starved (Dalton 1993; Gardner 1993).

Gandhi's early experiences in South Africa and India had helped him to forge his ideology to a large extent. In 1920, the death of Bal Gangadhar Tilak created a void, which Gandhi filled

---

[59] Though some authors (e.g., Livingston 2017) claim that Gandhi was influenced by Henry David Thoreau's (1849) idea of civil disobedience, according to Guha (2013), this is unlikely since Gandhi had not read Thoreau before the meeting on September 11, 1906. Spodek (1971) suggests that it is more likely that Gandhi got the idea for his unique protest from a custom called *risaamanu* in Kathiawad where he spent his childhood. *Risaamanu* was a temporary severing of relations from someone who was otherwise closely related. It was a peaceful means of protest employed by people against the arbitrary actions of the state. It involved fasting and sitting in public, thereby evoking public sympathy for one's cause and playing on the emotions of one's antagonist.

as the leader of the Congress-led Indian freedom movement (Guha 2018). In the next few sections, I explore the specific elements of Gandhi's moral leadership which enabled him to mobilize and transform the Indian people in the service of their nation.

Elements of Moral Leadership

Moral leadership empowers followers to look beyond their everyday wants, needs, and expectations and pursue higher values, thereby producing social change that satisfies authentic human needs. Gandhi's relationship with his associates and large masses of Indians is an excellent example of moral leadership. Gandhi's public life illustrates four elements of moral leadership. First, the leader is a credible role model. Through personal conduct comprising of authenticity, integrity, and a sense of purpose, the leader attracts the attention of potential followers. Next, by empathetically listening to followers' wants and needs, the leader crafts an idealized vision of the future along with a practical road map for achievement of the idealized vision. Third, the leader does not merely remain a role model but actively engages the followers in confronting their own internal conflicts and sacrificing themselves in achieving the vision. Finally, the leader emphasizes moral means and does not compromise even when the group's immediate goals are in jeopardy.

Being a Credible Role Model

Charisma is defined as a special magnetic charm or appeal which can inspire loyalty or enthusiasm for a person (Merriam-Webster 2020). Though Gandhi was physically unimpressive and a poor orator, he was highly charismatic due to his personal conduct, the content of his communication (Bligh & Robinson 2010), and his pleasing personality (Brown 2018). One of his greatest assets was his sense of humour. He used humour to diffuse tough situations and welcomed it when the joke was on him (Guha 2018).

In India, clothing is an important identifier of an individual's caste and social status. Through his simple dress and ascetic lifestyle, Gandhi re-created himself in the image of India's poorest people (Wolpert 2001) and this brought him closer to the masses. His use of a simple loin cloth made of khadi (homespun cotton) symbolized his renunciation of his birth caste and class. It also challenged British imperialism and Western civilization and promoted an alternative social and economic vision for India (Gonsalves 2012).

In all aspects of his public life he consistently demonstrated congruence between his thoughts, words, and actions and thereby was a symbol of integrity and authenticity (Erhard & Jensen 2011). Through his daily actions, Gandhi provided his followers with a symbol of moral living, a template of how to live so as not to be dysfunctional for the self, society and the planet (Weber 2005). Gandhi was a prototypical Indian and someone who was also willing to sacrifice his life for the larger cause. Both factors enhanced his appeal to the Indian masses (van Knippenberg & van Knippenberg 2005).

Gandhi also expressed the common Indian belief that by controlling one's impulses one could acquire control over one's environment. He sought to free himself from anger, greed, lust and self-interest. When faced with helplessness to deal with external events, he would assume that this was because of a moral lapse on his part and hence engage in more serious austerities to purify himself. This 'self-suffering courage' which could control and transform one's circumstances appealed to the Indian people (Rudolph & Rudolph 1967, 32-33).

Crafting an Idealized Vision and a Practical Ideology

Leadership begins with change and the driver for change is human wants. But simply satisfying people's 'wants' is not leadership.

Instead, the essential task of leadership is to discern the genuine *needs* underlying the stated *wants* of people. Like parents raising children, leaders legitimize some of their followers' wants as genuine needs and veto the others. Leaders listen to the wants of their followers and respond to them as legitimate needs, articulating them as values. Followers' needs are thus transformed by leaders into aspirations, purposeful expectations, and political demands (Burns 2003). This process—'leading by being led'—is one in which leaders and followers move toward progressively higher needs until they reach their fullest potential as human beings (Burns 1978, 143).

Gandhi's technique of satyagraha or non-violent resistance was developed during his time in South Africa as a response to his South African adversaries Alfred Milner and Jan Smuts (Guha 2013). The term satyagraha literally means to seize, grasp, or to go towards the truth. However, since it is impossible for one to grasp the complete truth, one is not competent to punish a fellow human being, which leads to the second Gandhian principle of ahimsa or non-violence (Bondurant 1958). Satyagraha was free of internal violence in the form of any kind of ill will, enmity, or anger against one's adversary (Dalton 1993). Gandhi's principle of ahimsa was like the Christian concept of agape or unconditional love and goodwill towards all beings (Mele 2012). The third Gandhian principle was that of tapasya or self-suffering, often expressed in the form of asceticism or fasting which was a tool of moral purification and moral persuasion. The three elements of satyagraha—truth, non-violence and self-suffering were developed into a technique and practise of social and political action (Bondurant 1958) in response to the needs of the Indian people in South Africa.

Satyagraha was a technique ideally suited for the needs of the Indian people at that time. Indians having been subject to foreign rule for centuries had begun to feel that they lacked valour and moral worth. Addressing this impotence and its associated lack of moral worthiness was the crying need of

India which was satisfied by satyagraha. There were several instances of extremists using violence against the British. This provided a kind of heroic leadership on which the masses projected their frustrations and aggression and sought a kind of symbolic release from their misery (Burns 1978). However, heroic leadership does not engage individuals and symbolism alone cannot meet authentic needs. Though stories of heroes confronting the British provided some solace, they did not substantively transform individuals. Through satyagraha, Gandhi 'turned the moral tables on the English definition of courage by suggesting that aggression was the path to mastery of those without self-control, non-violent resistance the path of those with self-control' (Rudolph & Rudolph 1967, 31).

The practise of satyagraha was to be deployed in the pursuit of a deeper purpose, which Gandhi articulated in 1932: 'The purpose of life is undoubtedly to know oneself. We cannot do it unless we learn to identify ourselves with all that lives. The sum-total of that life is God. Hence the necessity of realizing God living within every one of us. The instrument of this knowledge is boundless selfless service' (Desai 1932, 184).

Gandhi's vision was inclusive, which not only included the people of India but all of humanity in an undivided whole. Despite the fact that some individuals (such as the British Empire) had succumbed to greed and were oppressing the Indian people, he still saw a divine spark in them and hence he sought to win them over through non-violent means (Gonsalves 2012). Gandhi had an ecosystem perspective (Crocker et al. 2006) in which he recognized the essential interconnectedness of all beings. This led him to the realization that only by striving for the wellbeing of all can one achieve one's own wellbeing (Easwaran 2000).

Gandhi's vision of swaraj meant 'disciplined rule from within' (Gandhi 1931). He articulated his vision in the form of a word picture which he called, the 'square of swaraj', having four corners—political independence, economic independence, social independence, and moral independence (Gonsalves 2012, xxviii). In this manner, Gandhi's concept of swaraj was able to harmonize individual freedom with social harmony (Pantham 1983) and create a vision which was inclusive yet politically practical (Dalton 1993). Swaraj was a combination of freedom from racial oppression with inward liberation, a transformation of society and self. Hence, the struggle was not just political but also personal (Burns 2003). Gandhi summed up his entire ideology in the statement, 'Real swaraj is self-rule or self-control. The way to it is satyagraha; the power of truth and love' (Gandhi 1909).

Engaging People in Achieving the Vision

Gandhi always maintained that swaraj was not something that would miraculously arrive, it could only come to be as the result of arduous self-effort by every Indian. He connected easily with individuals of different social groups in India, South Africa, and in Britain. Unlike prior political leaders in the Indian freedom movement, he could reach out to the masses across the length and breadth of India by being one of them in clothes and speech (Dalton 1993). This connection with people helped him to arrive at practical approaches by which the common people could strive towards the vision of swaraj. Two of these approaches were satyagraha and the swadeshi movement.

Satyagraha was not just a means of political action; it was a complete system of self-development and growth aimed at addressing the fundamental need of a human being to become a better person. Satyagraha meant to rid oneself of anger and hatred so that the force of non-violence will flow. It was about overcoming fear to create love (Dalton 1993). To make this system accessible to the common man, Gandhi worked out an elaborate set of rules or guidelines for the seeker to follow. The follower of satyagraha seeks to establish the contested truth in a social system through three steps: first, by persuading and reasoning with opponents while being open to their persuasions; second, by appealing to the opponents through self-suffering; finally, by non-cooperation and civil disobedience (Pantham 1983).

The ideology of satyagraha was made practical by allowing different individuals of diverse temperaments to participate in the struggle. For those who could, Gandhi invited them to join the Congress and throw themselves into the movement. For others, Gandhi suggested that they give up their government jobs or stop sending their children to government-run schools and universities. Those who had titles and honours from the British government were urged to surrender them. People were urged to boycott government functions and British courts (Guha 2018). Finally, for all the others there was the practise of swadeshi, i.e., the boycott of British cloth and the use of Indian-made goods, specifically homespun cotton. In this manner, Gandhi provided every person with a range of options through which they could engage in the larger movement. By doing this, Gandhi provided an opportunity for common people to participate in a national movement.

Providing the common people with a choice to participate in the freedom movement was a crucial aspect of Gandhi's influence. When individuals are faced with a choice between doing some small yet inconvenient action for the good of the group versus continuing with the comfort of the status quo, they are forced to confront their values and beliefs. When faced with conflicting courses of action, individuals discover their true beliefs and choose their identities. It is these difficult choices which form the basis for an authentic and enduring transformation of individuals (Burns 1978).

An excellent example of setting the stage for value conflict and transformation of a large number of people was the Salt March. On March 12, 1930, Gandhi embarked on a long march to gather salt from the seashore and thereby defy the government's monopoly on its collection. Over twenty-four days, across two hundred miles, Gandhi led thousands of men, women, and children in a celebration of non-violent action against the mighty

British Empire (Burns 2003). At the culmination of the Salt March when the marchers reached Dandi, Gandhi addressed a crowd of more than 50,000 people (Dalton 1993).

The Salt March and the subsequent challenge to the salt monopoly provided an opportunity for several groups of Indians who were not included in the freedom movement earlier such as poor peasants, women, and students from across the country, to participate in the movement. Individuals could participate either by joining the march themselves or by providing hospitality and shelter to the marchers when they passed by their homes or camped in their villages during the twenty-four days. Gandhi dramatized the issue as a 'nonviolent struggle of right against might' to seize the moral high ground. After Gandhi made salt, all over the country people started making their own salt. As a result of this, the British imprisoned 60,000 Indians (Dalton 1993). As an instrument of mass transformation, the Salt March had served its purpose.

Gandhi also used structural mechanisms or self-imposed rules to enforce his ideals. For example, in Noakhali in 1947, he told women in the village of Chandipur to invite a person belonging to the scheduled caste to touch the food or water before they consumed it. Similarly, towards the end of his life, he decided that he would not be present or give his blessings for any wedding unless one of the parties belonged to a scheduled caste (Gandhi, R. 2015).

Gandhi's influence over the poor peasants in India was substantial. By 1921, many Indians had assimilated the message of swaraj as personal, social, and political revolution and self-purification. People understood swaraj as demanding changes in their personal behaviour including family planning and diet. For example, in Gorakhpur district, an entire village had altered its eating habits by giving up meat and fish as a step towards swaraj (Dalton 1993).

Ensuring Ethical Means to Achieve Ends

A common dilemma faced by leaders is the use of unethical or questionable means to achieve desired ends. At one extreme the philosophy of political realism recommends that a leader must not be concerned with the ethics of means but must only strive for achieving and retaining power at all costs (Alinsky 1971; Machiavelli 1976). Psychological experiments have shown that when individuals provide advice from a distance, they are idealistic, i.e., they prioritize principles and values over practical considerations. However, when asked to make a choice as an individual experiencing the dilemma, people were likely to adopt a pragmatic approach, prioritizing practical considerations over principles and values (Danziger, Montal & Barkan 2012).

The metaphor of 'dirty hands' presumes that being a good person is often incompatible with being a good leader (Griffin 1989; Walzer 1973). Some may even suggest that 'to discard one's own principles for a larger good beyond oneself is an even greater act than that of attaining the same good by being within one's principles because it involves contesting an internal turmoil and a discomfort of conscience.'[60]

Gandhi's view on the ethics of means and ends are explained in *Hind Swaraj*. According to Gandhi (1909) the means are indistinguishable from the ends and both means and ends form a continuum. Hence, immoral acts by moral leaders as reformers may 'taint and pervert the ends' and must be avoided at all costs (Burns 1978, 170). Gandhi (1909) argued that ends and means are as closely related as the tree which grows out of the seed.

According to the traditional Indian notion, the self is a spiritual entity connected to a universal natural order and a responsible bearer of a divine legacy. Hence, any unethical act would contaminate the divinity and character of the self (Shweder et al. 1997). At a more temporal level, unethical actions

---

[60] Ishma Raina suggested this to me in an assignment that she submitted for her course work.

by the leader or followers undermine the main objective of the transformation; i.e., the transformation of individuals into their higher selves.

There are several examples when Gandhi shunned immoral means even when a lot was at stake. In 1915, a family, considered 'untouchable' by the residents of the ashram, asked to stay in the ashram. The ashram experiment was only three months old and this created a commotion amongst the residents. Yet Gandhi persisted. When agitating farmers in Kheda had stopped paying their dues, a social organization offered to pay the dues on their behalf. However, Gandhi refused it on the grounds that the purpose of the satyagraha was to 'make people fearless and free' (Guha 2018, 69-70).

On April 13, 1919, the Jalianwala Bagh massacre cemented his resolve to fight against the British Empire. Contrary to several other freedom fighters who demanded 'an eye for an eye,' Gandhi said that if the Indians responded with violence then they too would descend to the level of their tormentors. Instead, they (the Indians) ought to respond to the violence of the British with non-violence—including forgiveness and non-cooperation.

In 1921 when the Prince of Wales was arriving, Gandhi planned a massive bonfire of foreign clothes. There was violence on the streets between those who were celebrating the prince's arrival and those who were protesting. Gandhi went on a fast to protest against the violence by his own supporters (Guha 2018).

On February 4, 1922, in Chauri Chaura in Gorakhpur, U.P., a police station was burnt, and 23 policemen were killed. A few days later, in the Congress Working Committee meeting, Gandhi passed a resolution to suspend civil disobedience, despite pressure from all his associates (Guha 2018).

Gandhi showed by personal example that a lifelong career in politics and public life is perfectly compatible with integrity and spiritual growth (Dalton 1993). The more important lesson is that moral leaders must recognize that the goal of transforming people is not less important than the goal of achieving the group's objective. Moreover, merely achieving a temporal goal while the individuals who achieve it have lost their character is of no meaning.

Transforming People and Society

The ultimate test of moral leadership is the achievement of actual social change in the direction of higher values (Burns 1978). In Gandhi's time, most Indians were illiterate and there were hardly any means of mass communication, yet Gandhi effectively mobilized a large following (Bligh & Robinson 2010; Suedfeld, Cross & Brcic 2011). When Gandhi arrived in India in 1915, he was the only Indian who consciously wished to involve all Indians irrespective of their religion, caste, and occupation in a national movement. For example, he was able to make several groups including prosperous communities such as the politically conservative merchants in Transvaal (Guha 2013) and the Parsis in India look beyond their immediate material well-being towards larger moral and political issues such as national freedom (Patel 2018). By 1920, Gandhi had created a genuinely national movement into which numerous others who were earlier active only in their own linguistic/cultural regions participated enthusiastically (Gandhi, R. 2015).

Gandhi left behind a generation of tall leaders committed to his cause across several continents: Jawaharlal Nehru, Vallabhbai Patel, Vinoba Bhave, Jayprakash Narayan, C. Rajagopalachari, Rajendra Prasad, Khan Abdul Ghafar Khan, and Maulana Azad in the Indian subcontinent; Martin Luther King Jr. in America; Albert Luthuli, Kwame Nkrumah, Julius Nyerere, Kenneth Kaunda, Nelson Mandela in Africa (Weber 2005); and Joseph Jean Lanza Del Vaso in Europe (Hardiman 2003).

Each one of these stalwarts is a story of deep transformation after being introduced to Gandhian ideas. Jawaharlal Nehru, who loved wearing expensive clothes, playing polo, and skiing in the Alps was completely transformed after he met Gandhi and immersed himself in the freedom movement (Easwaran 2000). Rajendra Prasad was a lawyer who gave up his profession to join the non-cooperation movement in 1920. Even as free India's first president, he lived a simple life and lived true to Gandhi's ideals (Weber 2005). Vallabhbhai Patel had just returned from England and was a pipe-smoking Westernised lawyer who was cynical of 'Mahatmas' and Gandhi's methods. However, in 1917 after Gandhi's success in Champaran against the British, Patel began to follow Gandhi. Soon Patel was a devoted follower of Gandhi, indispensable to the freedom movement, and to the subsequent unification and administration of the nation (Krishna 2005).

Gandhi was able to bring out the best from his followers by revealing qualities that even they did not know they possessed. Dwarkanath Harkare was one of the marchers who accompanied Gandhi from his ashram to the seashore at Dandi in 1930. In his youth he had been involved in terrorism and had contempt for non-violence. Later when he joined Sabarmati Ashram and observed Gandhi, he changed. He was influenced by Gandhi's identification with the poor, his simple lifestyle, and his fearlessness when he once calmly handled poisonous snakes (Dalton 1993).

According to Easwaran (2000), several men, women, and even children were transformed by Gandhi and merely meeting him was 'to run the risk of being turned into a hero' (64). Gandhi had high expectations of his associates while simultaneously showing great concern for their welfare. This significantly contributed to their growth. His power over them was so much that their identities merged with his and they would sacrifice everything to help realize their mutual ideals (Gardner 1993).

Harold Laski, an eminent English political theorist, observed in the *Daily Herald* on September 11, 1931 when Gandhi arrived in London for the last time: 'No living man has, either by precept or example, influenced so vast a number of people in so direct and profound a way' (cited in Dalton 1993).

Gandhi's Enduring Legacy

Even before Gandhi, leaders like Bal Gangadhar Tilak and Dadabhai Naoroji had used the term swaraj, but when they used it, they meant only political autonomy. Gandhi gave swaraj a whole new meaning as self-rule and self-restraint. In other words, the goal was not just political freedom but freedom from illusion, ignorance, and other forms of human bondage which came through self-discipline and self-control (Dalton 1993).

In India, Gandhi inspired Vinoba Bhave and Jayaprakash Narayan who then led large social movements in India's villages which transformed the lives of millions (Wolpert 2001). Gandhi's influence was clearly visible in the Sarvodaya and Bhoodan movements of the 1950s and 1960s, the Chipko movement in 1973, and more recent movements by Baba Amte, Medha Patkar, and Anna Hazare (Gandhi, T. A. 2012; Hardiman 2003).

Gandhi's message resonated not just with Indians but with tens of millions around the world who found an antidote to the ills of materialism and violence (Lal 2008) as well as a challenge to European imperialism and racism (Hardiman 2003, 285). His innovative approach to change outlived him and inspired Martin Luther King Jr. and other leaders of the American Civil Rights movement (Hardiman 2003; Livingston 2017).

Gandhi's contribution extended far beyond politics; he made Indians self-reliant and generated a sense of Indianness beyond social, regional, religious, and economic differences among the people of India (Brown 2018). Many decades after his death, Gandhi is still revered as the father of the Indian nation. His ideas have survived despite attacks from the political left and the political right (Guha 2013). Gandhi's greatest contribution was to help India 'acquire a national coherence and identity, to become a nation, by showing Indians a way to courage, self-respect, and political potency' (Rudolph & Rudolph 1967, 64-65).

Gandhi's ideology that 'the cure for the ills that afflicted state or society lay in changing men's inner environment, their hearts and minds, not their laws and institutions' (Rudolph & Rudolph 1967, 82) lives on. The statement in the Preamble to the Constitution of UNESCO—'since wars begin in the minds of men, it is in the minds of men that the defences of peace must be constructed' (UNESCO 2020) resonates with Gandhi's ideals. His example is still relevant for today and continues to inspire and guide human rights and peace movements and political activists throughout the world (Brown & Parel 2011; Gandhi R. 2015).

Perhaps the most profound and striking aspect of Gandhi's life and leadership is the ability to combine the Biblical injunction of 'love thy neighbour' with an active political life (Guha 2013). Gandhi was able to see the close link between politics and moral development. He realized that in ignoring citizens' moral and religious concerns, we merely suppress disagreements (Sandel 2009). Instead he vigorously engaged with moral and religious convictions and invited all others to do so as well.

In his autobiography Gandhi states: 'my devotion to Truth has drawn me into the field of politics; and I can say without the slightest hesitation, and yet in all humility, that those who say that religion has nothing to do with politics do not know what religion means' (Gandhi 1927/2009, 455). As a result of this, he not only inspired three hundred million people to revolt and shake the foundations of the British Empire, but he also introduced into human politics a strong religious and moral impetus (Rolland 1924/2008).

Conclusion

The distinctive element of James MacGregor Burns's (1978) theory of moral leadership is that it describes the process of mutual engagement and moral elevation of leaders and followers as they strive towards achieving real and enduring social change. Moral leaders are powerful role models, and they provide a road map by which ordinary individuals can transform themselves into their 'better selves' (1978, 461). Gandhi exemplified truth, universal love, and non-violence for his followers. He provided an inclusive vision of swaraj and a practical ideology of satyagraha which could 'fashion heroes out of clay' (Upadhyaya 1965, 6)—transforming several people in his lifetime and continuing to inspire change across the world.

(Acknowledgement: I thank Dinyar Patel for his valuable feedback on an earlier version of this paper.)

References

Alinsky, S. D. 1971. *Rules for Radicals: A Pragmatic Primer for Realistic Radicals*. Vantage Books.

Bligh, M. C.,& Kohles, J. C. 2009. The Enduring Allure of charisma: How Barack Obama won the historic 2008 presidential election. *The Leadership Quarterly*, 20 (3): 483–492.

Bligh, M. C. & Robinson, J. L. 2010. Was Gandhi 'Charismatic'? Exploring the rhetorical leadership of Mahatma Gandhi. *The Leadership Quarterly*, 21(5): 844–855.

Bondurant, J. V. 1958. *Conquest of Violence: The Gandhian Philosophy of Conflict*. Princeton, NJ: Princeton University Press.

Brown, J. M. 2018. Gandhi: A man for our times? *Journal for the Study of Religion,* 31(1): 96–111.

Brown, J. M. & Parel, A. 2011. *The Cambridge Companion to Gandhi (Cambridge Companions to Religion)*. Cambridge: Cambridge University Press.

Burns, J. M. 1978. *Leadership*. New York: Harper Torchbooks.

Burns, J. M. 2003. *Leaders Who Changed the World*. New Delhi: Penguin Viking.

Crocker, J., Nuer, N., Olivier, M.-A. & Cohen, S. 2006. *Egosystem and Ecosystem: Two motivational orientations for the self*. Unpublished manuscript.

Dalton, D. 1993. *Mahatma Gandhi: Nonviolent Power in Action*. New York: Columbia University Press.

Danziger, S., Montal, R. & Barkan, R. 2012. Idealistic Advice and Pragmatic Choice: A psychological distance account. *Journal of Personality and Social Psychology*, 102(6): 1105–1117.

Desai, M. 1932. *The Diary of Mahadev Desai, Volume 1*. Ahmedabad: Navjivan Publishing House. https://www.gandhiheritageportal.org/fundamentalworkdetail/the-diary-of-mahadev-desai-vol-I#page/204/mode/2up (Accessed on October 30, 2020 at 1041 hours.)

Easwaran, E. 2000. *Gandhi: The Man.* Mumbai: Jaico.

Erhard, W. & Jensen, M. C. 2011. The Three Foundations of a Great Life, Great Leadership, and a Great Organization. *Harvard Business School, Organizations and Markets Research Papers,* 11–122.

Erikson, E. H. 1993. *Gandhi's Truth: On the origins of militant nonviolence.* New York: W. W. Norton & Company.

Fu, P. P., Tsui, A. S., Liu, J. & Li, L. 2010. Pursuit of Whose Happiness? Executive Leaders' Transformational Behaviors and Personal Values. *Administrative Science Quarterly,* 55 (2): 222–254.

Gandhi, M. K. 1909. *Hind Swaraj or Indian Home Rule.* Ahmedabad: Navajivan Publishing House.

Gandhi, M. K. 1931. *Complete Works of Mahatma Gandhi,* Volume 51, p. 220. https://www.gandhiashramsevagram.org/gandhi-literature/mahatma-gandhi-collected-works-volume-51.pdf (Accessed on November 16, 2020 at 1441 hours).

Gandhi, M. K. (1927) 2009. *My Experiments with Truth: An Autobiography of Mahatma Gandhi.* Translated from Gujarati by Mahadev Desai. New Delhi: General Press.

Gandhi, R. 2015. Independence and Social Justice: The Ambedkar-Gandhi Debate. *Economic and Political Weekly,* 50 (15): 35–44.

Gandhi, T. A. 2012. India's Moral Crisis: The Gandhian Answer. *ASCI Journal of Management,* 41(2): 140–150.

Gardner, H. 1993. *Creating Minds: An anatomy of creativity seen through the lives of Freud, Einstein, Picasso, Stravinsky, Eliot, Graham, and Gandhi.* New York: Basic Books.

Gardner, W. L. & Cleavenger, D. 1998. The Impression Management Strategies Associated with Transformational Leadership at the World-Class Level: A Psychohistorical Assessment. *Management Communication Quarterly,* 12 (1): 3–41.

Gonsalves, P. 2012. *Khadi: Gandhi's mega symbol of subversion.* New Delhi: Sage.

Griffin, L. 1989. The Problem of Dirty Hands. *The Journal of Religious Ethics,* 17 (1): 31–61.

Guha, R. 2013. *Gandhi Before India.* New Delhi: Penguin Random House.

Guha, R. 2018. *Gandhi: The years that changed the world (1914-1948).* New Delhi: Penguin Random House.

Hardiman, D. 2003. *Gandhi in His Time and Ours*. Ranikhet: Permanent Black.

Hoch, J. E., Bommer, W. H. & Dulebohn, J. H. 2016. Do Ethical, Authentic and Servant Leadership Explain Variance Above and Beyond Transformational Leadership? A Meta-Analysis. *Journal of Management*, 44 (2): 1–29.

Krishna, B. 2005. *Sardar Vallabhbhai Patel: India's Iron Man*. New Delhi: Rupa.

Lal, V. 2008. The Gandhi Everyone Loves to Hate. *Economic and Political Weekly*, October 4, 55–64.

Livingston, A. 2017. Fidelity to Truth: Gandhi and the Genealogy of Civil Disobedience. *Political Theory*, 46 (4): 511–536.

Machiavelli, N. 1976. *The Prince*. Translated with introduction and notes by James B. Atkinson. Indianapolis: Hackett Publishing Company.

Mehta, V. P. 1977. *Mahatma Gandhi and his Apostles*. New York: The Viking Press.

Mele, D. 2012. The Christian Notion of Αγάπη (agápē): Towards a more complete view of business ethics. In *Leadership Through the Classics*, edited by G. P. Prastacos, F. Wang, & K. E. Soderquist. New York: Springer.

Merriam-Webster. 2020. Merriam-Webster Online Dictionary. https://www.merriam-webster.com/dictionary/charisma?utm_campaign=sd&utm_medium=serp&utm_source=jsonld (Accessed on November 1, 2020 at 0924 hours.)

Pantham, T. 1983. Thinking with Mahatma Gandhi: Beyond liberal democracy. *Political Theory*, 11(2): 165–188.

Patel, D. 2018. Beyond Hindu-Muslim unity: Gandhi, the Parsis and the Prince of Wales Riots of 1921. *The Indian Economic & Social History Review*, 55 (2): 221–247.

Patel, D. 2020. *Naoroji: Pioneer of Indian Nationalism*. Cambridge: Harvard University Press.

Rolland, R. (1924) 2008. *Mahatma Gandhi: The man who became one with the universal being*. New Delhi: Prabhat.

Rudolph, S. H. & Rudolph, L. I. 1967. *Gandhi: The Traditional Roots of Charisma*. Chicago: University of Chicago Press.

Sandel, M. J. 2009. *Justice: What's the right thing to do?* London: Penguin.

Shweder, R. A., Much, N. C., Mahapatra, M. & Park, L. 1997. The 'Big Three' of morality (autonomy, community, divinity), and the 'Big Three' explanations of suffering. In *Morality and Health*, edited by A. Brandt & P. Rozin. New York: Routledge.

Solinger, O. N., Jansen, P. G. W. & Cornelissen, J. P. 2020. The Emergence of Moral Leadership. *Academy of Management Review*, 45 (3): 504–527.

Spodek, H. 1971. On the Origins of Gandhi's Political Methodology: The heritage of Kathiawad and Gujarat. *The Journal of Asian Studies*, 30 (2): 361–372.

Suedfeld, P., Cross, R. W. & Brcic, J. 2011. Two Years of Ups and Downs: Barack Obama's Patterns of Integrative Complexity, Motive Imagery, and Values. *Political Psychology*, 32 (6): 1007–1033.

Thoreau, H.D. 1849. *Resistance to Civil Government*. In *Æsthetic Papers*, edited by Elizabeth P. Peabody, pp. 189–211. Boston and New York: The Editor and G.P. Putnam.https://archive.org/stream/aestheticpapers00peabrich#page/n197/mode/2up (Accessed on October 30, 2020 at 1235 hours).

UNESCO 2020. UNESCO Constitution. http://portal.unesco.org/en/ev.php-URL_ID=15244&URL_DO=DO_TOPIC&URL_SECTION=201.html (Accessed on November 9, 2020 at 2155 hours).

Upadhyaya, J. M. 1965. *Mahatma Gandhi as a Student*. New Delhi: Ministry of Information & Broadcasting, Government of India.

van Knippenberg, B. & van Knippenberg, D. 2005. Leader Self-sacrifice and Leadership Effectiveness: The moderating role of leader prototypicality. *Journal of Applied Psychology*, 90 (1): 25–37.

Walzer, M. 1973. Political Action: The problem of dirty hands. *Philosophy & Public Affairs*, 2 (2): 160–180.

Weber, T. 2005. *Gandhi as Disciple and Mentor*. Cambridge: Cambridge University Press.

Wolpert, S. 2001. *Gandhi's Passion: The life and legacy of Mahatma Gandhi*. Oxford: Oxford University Press.

RAAG GANDHI
Musical Essence of the Mahatma

Fauziya Patel and Faraz Khan

'Music does not proceed from the throat alone. There is music of mind, of the senses and of the heart.'

—M.K. Gandhi

Introduction

Someone once asked the Mahatma, 'Mahatmaji, don't you have any liking for music?'

Gandhi replied, 'If there was no music and no laughter in me, I would have died of this crushing burden of my work.'

The Mahatma that we know as Mohandas Karamchand Gandhi has his presence engraved on every path he ever crossed, every life he touched, every community, country—to be precise, he changed the perspective of humankind and opened doors of an awakening we are still short of fully assessing and admiring. The world remembers him as a mascot of human rights, crusader of the Indian freedom struggle, the prophet of Satya and Ahimsa (Truth and Non-Violence). All these are at the core of Bapu's essence and presence; equating Gandhi with just one of these is limiting his immeasurable greatness. When you dive deep in the ocean you discover pearls, and our journey of Raag Gandhi has taken us on a path of enlightenment towards Gandhi the Artist or, more precisely, Gandhi the Musician.

Gandhi the Artist

'There are so many superstitions rife about me that it has now become almost impossible for me to overtake those who have been spreading them. As a result, my friends' only reaction is almost invariably a smile when I claim I am an artist myself' (Roy 1950, 65–66).

When one tries to trace the imprints of Gandhi the man who had an eye for beauty and aesthetics, who had an unparalleled sense of the healing touch of music (as is evident by the opening statement of the article), who wrote a prayer in prose ('Hey Namrata ke Sagar'), who wrote and translated hundreds of volumes in English and Gujarati, we discover an unexplored dimension of his personality. We come across a different man. We meet Gandhi the Artist.

Gandhi the Lyricist

In 1934, Gandhiji wrote a prose poem as an answer to a question on prayer and God with these opening lines:

> Lord of Humility,
> Dwelling in the little Pariah hut
> Help us to search for Thee throughout...

In 1969, the Government of Maharashtra released this song in Hindi to mark 100 years of Gandhiji's birth. The Hindi version goes by the name 'Hey Namrata ke Sagar' (Chandvankar 2012). This song has been the opening verse of Raag Gandhi performed by us throughout the nation in the past couple of years. This song signifies the yearning of Gandhi to strike a balance between Spirituality and Art. So we consider it to be the cornerstone of the journey of Gandhi on the path of finding the healing touch of Art that soothes one's soul, relieves us of our worldly burdens and takes us to a land where Art and Music elevates us to become one with the Almighty. By submitting oneself to the Creator we bring peace, and Gandhi chose Music as the path and medium of this submission.

Gandhi's Music (Bhajans) as a Catalyst for Religious Harmony, Compassion and Establishing Secularism

'We see Hindu and Mussalman musicians sitting cheek by jowl and partaking in musical concerts. When shall we see the same fraternal union in other affairs of our life?' (Neuman 2011).

Gandhi wondered what could be the common platform that could bring people from different strata of society together; he found his answer in music. To him music had the charm and silent power of binding the otherwise divided society. The lyrics of his favourite bhajan are a testimony to that—'Vaishnav Jan to Tene Kahiye je Peed Parayi Jane re' (One who is a devotee of Vishnu, knows the pain of others). By placing importance on this, Gandhi emphasized compassion for one's fellow humans as the only criteria to judge oneself. So, Gandhi's Music is all about establishing equality among the socially, economically and politically differing individuals and bringing harmony.

i. Africa: The Tolstoy Farm: Gandhi's tryst with the Ashram and a unique lifestyle of self-reliance, the experiment of bringing the deprived together, began with the establishment of Tolstoy Farm in 1910. Gandhiji attributed his success in the struggle against racial discrimination prevalent in South Africa to his experiments at Tolstoy Farm. It is here that he began the practise of reciting religious hymns (bhajan) in the prayer meets held at 7 pm every evening (Bhana 1975). This brings to the fore the fact that Gandhiji believed in spiritualism as a must for attaining 'cooperative commonwealth' and he chose his bhajan sandhya meet as a tool in attaining this goal.

Another noteworthy aspect of these prayer meets was that they had prayers from all religions and prayers emphasizing humanity rather than devotion to a particular religion. The idea of accommodating every religion and establishing a secular environment was an experiment that helped Gandhiji later during the freedom struggle of India.

ii. Gandhi's experiments with the violin: It is a known fact that Gandhi found solace in music; however, it is less known that he actually bought a violin and tried learning music formally (Orwell 1949). Because of the call of duty, he could not continue with it as a passion or profession. But his attempt at learning music qualifies him as an enthusiastic music lover who yearned to be a disciple of music.

iii. Gandhian Music: Gandhiji started a community life in Africa, and the Shramik Prayer was a part of it. He published a collection of hymns that were sung as 'Proverb Poems'. Along with the Pragya located in the Gita, he started singing at the time of prayer. Prayer meetings and music became a symbolic Gandhian activity both before and after independence. The songs selected for the prayer meetings were popular bhajans and nazms with musical and melodic appeal. Gandhiji himself deliberated on the raag and rendition tunes of the same (Subramanian 2020). Narayan Moreshwar Khare (1922), the music teacher and musician at the Sabarmati Ashram, compiled and published the *Ashram Bhajnawali*, the bible of Gandhian Music, reflecting the secular fabric of the prayers, raags, moods and tunes selected carefully to connect with the masses. As the life of the ashrams bloomed, so did the collection of hymns and bhajans, and in the process this gave birth to a different genre of Music-Literature that healed the distressed and helped everyone cross the class and religion divide to become one whole. Music became the thread to hold the pearls of different origins together.

Raag Gandhi: Our Journey in the World of Gandhi's Symphony

Our team started the journey of putting together a single musical show on Gandhi's 150th Birth Anniversary with the title 'BAA-BAPU 150—*Sangeet mien Gandhi*' (Gandhi in Music). This took us to libraries across Mumbai, meeting Gandhians, trying to understand the lifestyle of Gandhi Ashrams. What astonished us was the hundreds of books of poems, ghazals, bhajans and every form of literature written on the Mahatma and his ideology. It was a treasure trove. And this was meant to be, as we were destined to bring Gandhi to people again, but this time with our music. We not only found Gandhi Music, we became spellbound by the great symphony of Gandhi himself!

Literary Expedition: The first step was to look for the literature we could present and what we came across was a sea of literature in different languages, written under different genres, published in different states, even countries. Such is the legacy of Gandhi the phenomenon that countless words still fall short of comprehending completely. Mukhtar Khan did the first draft of the research for the project.

Bhajans and Nazms (Poems): Among everything we found while exploring these writings, we decided to include 'Hey Namrata ke Sagar' written by Gandhiji himself as it shows the spiritual height of a person who was a karmayogi and a leader of humanity too. 'Vaishnav Jan to', the bhajan that was part of daily prayers at his ashram, was also sung by Narayan Khare when Gandhiji ventured on the historic Dandi Yatra (Lal 2014). The ultimate definition of being human rather than just living as a human being, it is indispensable to any Gandhian bhajan sandhya. A poem written in Urdu by Allama Iqbal, 'Lab pe aati hai Dua' that gives the message of devoting one's life to learning and enlightenment and 'Allah tero Naam Ishwar tero Naam' was included to reflect the Gandhian idea of Sarvadharm Sambhav (equality of all religions). Apart from this, many devotional songs, prayers and hymns were included in various shows depending on the region of the show and the local languages at the venue.

Gandhian Principles in Music: The biggest challenge as well as inspiration was to draw a parallel to the famous Gandhi Katha popularized by the greatest storyteller on Gandhi, Shri Narayan Desai. The essence of our presentation of the principles of Gandhi were influenced greatly by the *Gandhi Katha* (Desai 2011). *Mrutyunjayi* (1969), a collection of poetic literature on Gandhi in 12 languages, edited by Bhavani Prasad Mishr, was a gem we found. A poem that gained immense popularity during this musical journey is 'Shakti Ahimsa Mein Jitni woh Nahi Shastra Hunkar Mein' (Nonviolence is a greater power than any weapon or war cry), written by Shri Poddar Ramavtar. It is a testimony to the fact that Gandhian Music is not just about the musical notes but about how it reflects and propagates Gandhian ideology. The struggles of Gandhi in personal, public and spiritual life and his determination to fight alone for the truth was presented through Gurudev's 'Ekla Chalo Re' (Keep Walking Alone). Across the spectrum of different languages and dialects, what remained constant was Gandhi the teacher who practised what he preached, come what may.

Kasturba Gandhi—A shadow that showed the path: Kasturba Gandhi, the Mahatma's soulmate, shadow, an unsung freedom fighter, the functional head of ashrams, started Satyagraha even before it was popularized by Gandhi. Gandhi believed her to be practising nonviolence in life (Basu 2011). As we were celebrating 150 years of Baa Bapu, poems and songs were written and performed to pay homage to her.

Writings Worth a Mention: Excerpts from 'Bapu', a poetic narration of Gandhi's life written by Ramdhari Singh Dinkar (1948) was used to narrate the show poetically. The literature of Sheri Bhopali, Dr. Masood Hussain, Majaz Lucknowi, Balkrishna Rao and others were used to bring balance and meaning to the musical. The writings of Hridayesh Mayank and R. K. Paliwal were presented too, and remained an unflinching support and encouragement to the idea of Raag Gandhi!

Fresh Perspective, Fresh Tunes: Bringing Gandhi to the young generation was a challenge and so we decided to use some renowned but mostly fresh literature set to tune by the young singer, composer and music director Faraz Khan, who not only composed the whole show but also presented it in his velvet voice. The audience, ranging from 5 years of age to as old as people who grew up in Gandhi's presence, were mesmerized. We started with a show that became a life mission for its crew. Delivering, spreading, professing, propagating and understanding Gandhi, to learn, unlearn and re-learn what Gandhism is through the lens of music.

Harmony of Classical and Modern Instrumentals: While keeping the traditional classical music of the Gandhian era intact the young team of teenagers and musicians in their early 20s like Shikha Srivastav (Singer), Utkarsh Jadhav (Flautist), Roshan Gayekar (Tabla), Joshua Urunkar (Guitarist) and Aman Jadhav (Synthesizer) brought a breath of fresh air to the music that could connect with and appeal to younger audiences. Through soothing tunes and some upbeat Western music, reinventing and reincarnating Gandhian Music to bring Gandhi to the next generation is another aim of our project.

Analogy of Tunes used: *Ashram Bhajnawali* (Khare 1928) has mentioned specific raags under which the rendition of bhajans are to be done. What is noteworthy here is that the tunes and raags were handpicked and for it to be authentically a musical even tunes were mentioned in writing. Raags originate from *thaats* (Manna 2016). Most of the bhajans are in Raag Khamaj, Raag Des, Raag Kaafi followed by Raag Bhairav and Bhairavi. Raag Des and Raag Khamaj are from the same *thaat* called 'Khamaj Thaat', that has the *ras* (mood) of praising. Apart from *ras* the *thaat* also represents the folk texture of presentation. Thus, the music Gandhi preferred was praising the lord, connecting people by using music close to the folk culture, thus creating connection with masses and finally serving them the message of unity, equality and humanity with the carefully picked lyrics of hymns, poems and narratives.

From Gandhi Bhajan to Gandhi *ko Gaana* (Singing Gandhi): Our experience of interactions with Gandhian Shri Sanjay Tula, Shri Kiran Chavda, Vice Chancellor of Gujarat Vidyapeeth Shri Anamikbhai Shah and our stay at Lokniketan, Ratanpur and Gandhi Ashram, Zilia, opened a new window of understanding Gandhian lifestyle, where music is a part of the daily routine. It made us realize that Gandhi is not just about a few bhajans that the world knows, there is a whole genre of music to be explored. As Shri Sanjay Tula Ji aptly said, 'Gandhi *ko Gaana*' (Singing Gandhi) is a genre, and our exploration of this genre will not be possible without these greats enlightening our path.

Raag Gandhi, Today and Tomorrow: What remains constant and fails to adapt, perishes and decays slowly but surely. Any legacy, however great it is, if not reinvented and redesigned for the next generations may become obsolete and may not be accepted at all by future generations. Gandhism is an eternally accepted lifestyle, an ideology based on *My Experiments with Truth*. The name of his autobiography, carefully chosen, evokes the idea of continuous evolution of the ways in which Gandhi can be taught in the future. Gandhi is not meant to be only in history books, he must be instrumental in understanding the present with his prism of truth and more importantly in moulding tomorrow. Keeping the essence pure, presenting it through the medium of music—what Gandhi believed to be harmony and equality—the only leveller in a world full of inequalities, is the purpose and mission of our Journey that is RAAG GANDHI.

References

Basu, Aparna. 2011. *Kasturba Gandhi*. Pune: Gandhi National Memorial Society.

Bhana, Surendra. 1975. The Tolstoy Farm: Gandhi's experiment in cooperative commonwealth. *South African Historical Journal* 7, no. 1 (November): 88-100.

Chandvankar, Suresh. 2012. Lyricist Gandhi—Revisited. *The Record News: The Journal of the Society of Indian Record Collectors,* 20–27. https://dsal.uchicago.edu/books/trn/pdfs/trn_2012.pdf

Desai, Narayan. 2011. *Gandhi Katha*. Ahmedabad Management Association.

Dinkar, Ramdhari Singh. 1948. Bapu. *Hindi Kavita* (Website). https://www.hindi-kavita.com/HindiBapuDinkar.php

Khare, Narayan Moreshwar. 1922. *Aashram Bhajnawali*. Ahmedabad: Navjeevan Prakashan Mandir

Lal, Vinay. 2014. Vaishnava Janato: Its Place in Gandhi's Life (A Short Note). *UCLA Social Sciences* (Website) http://southasia.ucla.edu/history-politics/gandhi/vaishnava-janato/

Manna, Sujata Roy. 2016. The Thaat—Ragas of North Indian Classical Music: The basic attempt to perform. *Anudhyan: An International Journal of Social Sciences (AIJSS)* 1, no.1 (February): 204–207.

Mishr, Bhavani Prasad. 1969. *Mrutyunjayi*. Kendriya Hindi Nideshalay.

Neuman, Daniel M. 2011. String Theory: A Meditation on Lives in Ethnomusicology. In *Ethnomusicological Encounters with Music and Musicians*, edited by Timothy Rice, 129–152. Los Angeles: Ashgate Publishing.

Orwell, George. 1949. Reflections on Gandhi. *The Orwell Foundation* (Website). https://www.orwellfoundation.com/the-orwell-foundation/orwell/essays-and-other-works/reflections-on-gandhi/

Roy, Dilip Kumar. 1950. *Among the Great*. Bombay: Jaico Publishing.

Subramanian, Lakshmi. 2020. *Singing Gandhi's India: Music & Sonic Nationalism*. New Delhi: Roli Books.

THE CORONAVIRUS'S WOUNDS
Gandhi on the Ethics of Nursing and Medical Care

Vinay Lal

Though Mohandas Gandhi occupies no place as such in histories of nursing in India, it should not come as a surprise to those who have reflected on his long career as perhaps the principal exponent in history of the idea of ahimsa (nonviolence) that he displayed a great affinity for nursing and thought of it as a noble way of rendering service to humankind. Gandhi's capacious understanding of ahimsa has been reduced in common thinking to his articulation of nonviolent resistance to oppression, rendered by the term satyagraha, but for Gandhi, nonviolence was a way of being in the world and the unimpeachable law of existence itself. Ahimsa is nothing but love, a mode of ministering to the soul and nursing the wounds—of others and those which are self-inflicted. Yet, Gandhi also had a withering critique of modern medicine and doctors—a critique that does not sit well with the medical profession, though it is notable that this critique did not extend to nursing, even if some of his own thoughts on nursing do not conform to the textbook prescriptions of nursing. He viewed modern medicine as animated by the evil of vivisection and plagued by the profit motive, but his critique of it has other socio-ethical, political, and philosophical dimensions that are far beyond the scope of this paper. For instance, in his 1909 treatise *Hind Swaraj or Indian Home Rule*, which is increasingly being viewed as the most fundamental expression of his ideas but still lacks the traction and recognition of his autobiography, *The Story of My Experiments with Truth* (1927/1940), his critique of the figure of the 'doctor' was fundamentally rooted in Gandhi's deep suspicion of what he calls the 'third party'

(Gandhi 1909/1939, 52–54).[61] Just as lawyers come between two adversaries and profit only themselves, and just as the British drove a wedge between Hindus and Muslims and set themselves up as transcendent peace-keepers, so the doctor appeared to Gandhi as someone who *distances* the patient from his or her own body. He imagines the circumstances under which a visit to a doctor becomes necessary: 'I have indulged in vice. I contract a disease, a doctor cures me, the odds are that I shall repeat the vice. Had the doctor not intervened, nature would have done its work, and I would have acquired mastery over myself, would have been freed from vice and would have become happy' (Gandhi 1909/1997, 63).

Happy is not what others have been with Gandhi's critique of modern medicine and its practitioners, and many have dismissed *Hind Swaraj*, and certainly his critique of railways, hospitals, and the legal profession, as an ill-informed diatribe. However, his position on modern medicine is easily mischaracterized; in accepting an invitation to inaugurate the opening of a medical college in Delhi in 1921, Gandhi offered his 'humble tribute to the spirit of research that fires the modern scientists,' while adding this proviso: 'My quarrel is not against that spirit. My complaint is against the direction that the spirit has taken. It has chiefly concerned itself with the exploration of laws and methods conducing to the merely material advancement of its clientele.' It is 'not without reluctance' that he had accepted the invitation, not only because the movement of non-cooperation that he was leading had rendered it difficult for the Viceroy to honour his word to preside over the opening, but Gandhi thought that his audience should be aware that 'I hold strange

---

[61] Chapter 12 is called 'The Condition of India: Doctors'. The edition that is most widely cited by scholars is *Hind Swaraj and Other Writings*, ed. Anthony J. Parel (Cambridge: Cambridge University Press, 1997). Chapter X, 'The Condition of India: The Hindus and the Mahomedans', references the 'third party': 'The fact is that we have become enslaved and, therefore, quarrel and like to have our quarrels decided by a third party.'

views on medicine and hospitals and have scrupulously avoided any special contact with such institutions.'[62]

And, yet, as he told a German visitor who met with him in 1937, he did 'not despise all medical treatment. I know we can learn a lot from the West about safe maternity and the care of infants.'[63] If, then, his outlook on medicine still remains unacceptable to many, on the question of nursing, however, he adopted views that may be rather more agreeable and even admirable to most people, most particularly at this time of the coronavirus pandemic when health care practitioners are being celebrated the world over as 'front line' workers who have put their lives at risk. He might have thought, incidentally, that the effortless ease with which we have all fallen into speaking of the 'front line' suggests the extent to which we have unthinkingly absorbed the vocabulary of war into our thinking, even if he would have understood the spirit in which we have all been called to recognize and applaud the altruistic behaviour of those, particularly nurses, who have become part of the corps of 'essential' workers. Indeed, it is not too much to say, as shall become apparent in due course, that he thought of nurses, not doctors, as 'essential,' and in this respect he seems to be characteristically contrarian in his thinking.

At the time that Gandhi transitioned into adulthood, one name entirely dominated the public perception of nursing, at least in the Anglophone world and the British empire: Florence Nightingale.[64] Gandhi himself penned a tribute to her in Gujarati

---

[62] 'Speech at Opening of Tibbia College', 13 February 1921, in *The Collected Works of Mahatma Gandhi* [hereafter CWMG], Vol 19, 356–58. New Delhi: Ministry of Information & Broadcasting, Publications Division; the quote is on p. 358. The entire set is available at https://www.gandhiheritageportal.org/the-collected-works-of-mahatma-gandhi

[63] This is from a conversation between a certain Captain Strunk and Gandhi (Tendulkar 1961, Vol. 4, 166).

[64] Nightingale was a recluse for the last five decades of her life, almost never leaving her home and working entirely from the confines of her bedroom.

in his newspaper, *Indian Opinion*, several years before her death in August 1910. Though it is a short piece, it is vintage Gandhi and deserving of a much lengthier commentary than what I can offer at present. Some of the language is characteristic of the writing where he speaks of those whom he views as pious and selfless: 'There were in those days very few men who considered it an act of mercy and merit to succour the wounded. It was at such a time that this lady, Florence Nightingale, came upon the scene and did good work worthy of an angel descended from heaven.' He describes how, through the selfless care of the wounded British soldiers at Scutari, Nightingale and the nurses trained under her immediately brought the mortality rate among the wounded down to 31 per cent from 42 per cent and eventually to 5 per cent. But he loses neither the opportunity to castigate the British Government which, he says, 'was *as usual* [emphasis added] not alive to the situation' when war first broke out in Crimea, nor to press forward with his own homilies on what might be viewed as the basic principles of nursing:

In her engaging biography, *Nightingale: The Extraordinary Upbringing and Curious Life of Miss Florence Nightingale* (2004), Gillian Gill writes that even the leading English politicians, among them Viceroys to India and Prime Minister William Gladstone, were by no means guaranteed admission into her foyer and had to be prepared to be 'disappointed to learn, when the appointed day arrived, that Miss Nightingale was after all too unwell, or perhaps too busy, to receive them' (2004, 423). 'Working from home,' to use a rather contemporary expression, she remained enormously influential in shaping not just the profession of nursing, but in introducing sanitary reforms within the military in England and in India, though her writings on India covered subjects such as famine, irrigation, epidemics, prisons, and health. Her writings on India encompass two massive volumes of *The Collected Works of Florence Nightingale*, ed. Gérard Vallée (2006). See Volume 8, 'Florence Nightingale on India', and Volume 9, 'Florence Nightingale on Social Change in India.' See also Elisabeth Robinson Scovil, 'The Later Activities of Florence Nightingale' (1920). It is unclear to what extent Gandhi was aware, when he wrote his piece on her in 1905, or even at a later date, of her deep involvement with reform in India.

though the results Nightingale produced were 'miraculous,' they 'can be easily visualized. If bleeding could be stopped, the wounds bandaged and the requisite diet given, the lives of many thousands would doubtless be saved. The only thing necessary was kindness and nursing, which Miss Nightingale provided' (Gandhi 1905, 62–63).

There is nothing on record to suggest that Gandhi had read Nightingale's short manual, *Notes on Nursing* (1860), but there can be little doubt that he would have been in agreement with its most fundamental propositions: 'The very elements of what constitutes good nursing are as little understood for the well as for the sick. The same laws of health or of nursing, for they are in reality the same, obtain among the well as among the sick' (Nightingale 1860/1969, 9). Nevertheless, in the matter of nursing, as in many other domains, Gandhi was essentially self-taught. When he was sixteen years old, he nursed his father who was then suffering from a fistula and was confined to bed. 'I had the duties of a nurse,' Gandhi recalled many years later in his autobiography, 'which mainly consisted in dressing the wound, giving my father his medicine, and compounding drugs whenever they had to be made up at home.' Every night, Gandhi massaged his father's legs: 'I loved to do this service. I do not remember ever having neglected it.' But then came what Gandhi himself called the 'dreadful night': overtaken by the carnal urge, Gandhi left his father's bedside to share the bed with his wife, Kasturba, to whom he was married when both were thirteen years old. He had been with her for all of five minutes when a knock came on the door: his father had expired (Gandhi 1927/1940, 21–22). In the centenary year of Gandhi's birth, in an influential book called *Gandhi's Truth: On the Origins of Militant Nonviolence* (1969), Erik H. Erikson argued controversially that the incident and Gandhi's guilt over it exercised an incalculable influence on his life. Whatever the merits of Erikson's view, Gandhi's interest in nursing can be traced to this incident. There would be other occasions, far too numerous to enumerate, where Gandhi would find the opportunity to nurture his instinct for nursing within the ambit of the larger extended family.

Gandhi found himself in Bombay in 1896, which was then being decimated by bubonic plague, and he chose to spend day and night by the bedside of his brother-in-law, who had taken seriously ill and whose wife, that is Gandhi's sister, 'was not equal to nursing him.' Gandhi could not save his life; however, as he was to write years later in his autobiography, 'my aptitude for nursing gradually developed into a passion, so much so that it often led me to neglect my work, and on occasions I engaged not only my wife but the whole household in such service' (Gandhi 1927/1940, 125–26). In 1918, when India was struck by the so-called Spanish Flu, Gandhi was taken seriously ill: some have thought that he, too, had been afflicted with that malignant influenza,[65] but the doctor declared that he was suffering from nothing more than 'a nervous breakdown due to extreme weakness' (Gandhi 1927/1940, 333–34).[66] Though Gandhi remained free of infection, his own nearness to death was brought home to him by the fact that he lost his grandson, Shantilal, as well as his daughter-in-law, Gulab, to the plague.

To the extent that scholars have paid any attention whatsoever to Gandhi's life-long passion for nursing among a wider public, the narrative generally begins with his initiative in setting up an Indian Ambulance Corps, consisting of 1,100 volunteers, during the Boer War in South Africa in 1899. We must recall that Gandhi had made South Africa his home and he spent twenty years there before returning to India for good in January 1915. The South African years are vitally important, more particularly if we consider that Gandhi had acquired experience of nursing under conditions of a pneumonic plague epidemic which somewhat resonate with the contemporary

---

[65] Laura Spinney (2017, 240–41) is clearly mistaken in supposing that Gandhi had been laid low by influenza.

[66] See also Narayan Desai (2009, 111–18).

experience of COVID-19. In 1904, as he details in his book, *Satyagraha in South Africa* (1928), which recounts the struggle waged by Indians in South Africa to oppose racism and gain political recognition, Gandhi was settled in the Johannesburg area where he had established a law practise. Early that year, he was to write, 'a virulent plague broke out among the Indians in Johannesburg. I was fully engaged in nursing the patients...' (Gandhi 1928/1950, 160). He describes his own contribution modestly; however, the *Autobiography* offers a somewhat more detailed account in two short chapters entitled 'The Black Plague-I' and 'The Black Plague-II'. Gandhi and his friends took possession of a vacant house by breaking its lock and shifted 23 Indians suffering from the scourge, nursing them through the night. The following day, the local municipality made available a vacant if dirty warehouse which they placed at Gandhi's disposal, leaving the Indians to clean the premises, haul beds into it, and turn it into a 'temporary hospital' (Gandhi 1927/1940, 216). The municipality lent the services of a nurse, whose name Gandhi did not recall years later when he wrote his books but who has since been identified as Emily Blake: she became infected and died a few days later, the only nurse to die in that outbreak.

The following year, an official account on the plague appeared under the name of the Johannesburg Plague Committee Report.[67] It suggests that neither Ms. Blake, nor any of the Indians (including Gandhi) providing care for the sick, were furnished any protective equipment or masks. The report tacitly recognizes the part played by Gandhi and Dr. William Godfrey, a physician practising in Johannesburg who had come to the aid of the Indians, in raising the alarm and preventing the plague from taking hold in other parts of the city. 'Here, the value of isolating infected persons was immediately appreciated by

---

[67] Rand Plague Committee. 1905. *Report upon the outbreak of plague on the Witwatersrand: March 18th to July 31st, 1904.* Johannesburg: Argus. https://wellcomecollection.org/works/m2ep9d5c/items

Dr. Godfrey and Mahatma Gandhi,' says a recent scholarly study of the plague commission's report, one of the very few that has ever been undertaken, 'and progress was made before municipal authorities first realized that the epidemic was fully under way' (Evans, Egan, and Hall 2018, 101). Still another research essay is yet more pronounced in underscoring Gandhi's capacious understanding of the circumstances that had no small part in precipitating the plague among indentured Indian workers, whose health in the best of conditions was feeble, and the role he played in bringing the epidemic under control. Delving into previously unexplored correspondence, the author, Tim Capon, notes that since early February 1904 Gandhi had sought to bring to the attention of Dr. Porter, Medical Officer for Health for Johannesburg, the extremely unsanitary conditions under which the Indians lived and the Municipality's gross negligence in safeguarding their health. Writing to him on February 11, Gandhi described 'the shocking state of the Indian location': 'rooms appear to be overcrowded beyond description' and the sanitary services had deteriorated. 'From what I believe,' noted Gandhi rather ominously, 'I believe the mortality in the location has increased considerably, and it seems to me that, if the present state of things continues, [an] outbreak of some epidemic disease is merely a question of time.' Capon goes so far as to say that 'Gandhi helped save not just the Indian community, but also the city itself' (Capon 2015).

Significant as Gandhi's interventions appear to have been to stem the rise of the plague in Johannesburg in 1904, his volunteer work during the Zulu Rebellion is still more remarkable for what it reveals about the ethics of Gandhi's nursing. It is necessary first to revisit his work on the battlefield in 1899 during the Boer War to which I have adverted briefly: though there is an account of this in Gandhi's own writings, the apparent anomaly of him appearing as a nurse in aid of the British is also explored in what is possibly the most exhaustive history of the Boer War, by the British historian Thomas Pakenham. 'Ahead of the field hospitals marched a strange procession,' he writes, 'two thousand volunteer stretcher-bearers, who were also political symbols...About eight hundred were members of Natal's Indian community, led by a twenty-eight-year-old barrister...Gandhi had announced in Durban that the Indian community wished to give active expression to their loyalty to the Empire; unable to fight, they would serve as stretcher-bearers. Years later, men might wonder why Mahatma Gandhi, the anti-imperialist and the arch-pacifist, had served as a non-combatant in an imperial war. At the time, it seemed natural enough to the British. Here was one of the 'subject peoples' showing the solidarity of the coloured races in the 'white man's war' (Pakenham 1979, 234). The work is described, but barely so in the two lines that he gives to it, by Gandhi himself in his autobiography. At a critical moment, despite assurances that the Ambulance Corps would not be required to serve 'within the firing line', Gandhi and the 1100 Indians, 800 of whom were still indentured, were asked if they would be willing to take the risk of removing the wounded from the line of fire. They accepted the risk without hesitation: 'During those these days we had to march from twenty to twenty-five miles a day, bearing the wounded on stretchers.' Remarkably, Gandhi rendered his assistance to the British though his own sympathies were with the Boer: as he explained in the autobiography, 'I felt that, if I demanded rights as a British citizen, it was also my duty, as such, to participate in the defence of the British Empire' (1927/1940, 156).

Less than ten years later, Gandhi again found himself raising the Natal Volunteer Ambulance Corps, occasioned by what is known as the Zulu Rebellion. The year, 1906, is recognized by scholars as a pivotal, and doubtless a transformative, moment in his life: he took a vow of celibacy and abjured all sexual relations, even with his wife, for the rest of his life—and this on the grounds that he had come to the conviction that 'procreation and the consequent care of children were inconsistent with public service' (1927/1940, 150). It is not possible at this juncture to delve into the intricacies of this decision, except to say that, oddly enough, the many scholars who have probed the subject of Gandhi's views on sexuality have not considered the manner in which the vow came to fruition when he was nursing the wounded Zulus. Two decades ago, in a lengthy paper on the politics of Gandhi's sexuality, I suggested, contrary to the (still) dominant view that Gandhi's outlook was characterized by an unhealthy and even repulsive form of sexual puritanism, that it is critical to distinguish between his repudiation of the sexual act on the one hand and, on the other hand, his love of intimacy and sexuality (Lal 2000). When he took the vow of celibacy, Gandhi did not thereby abjure touch, nor proximity to the bodies of others: both, I would argue, entirely central to his conception of nursing. Let us hear what he has to say: 'I was delighted, on reaching headquarters, to hear that our main work was to be the nursing of the wounded Zulus. The Medical Officer in charge welcomed us. He said the white people were not willing nurses for the wounded Zulus, that their wounds were festering, and that he was at his wits' end. He hailed our arrival as a godsend for these innocent people, and he equipped us with bandages, disinfectants, etc., and took us to the improvised hospital. The Zulus were delighted to see us' (1927/1940, 232).

The 'festering' wounds of which he speaks were a consequence of the floggings by which the Zulus were brow-beaten into submission. These floggings 'had caused severe sores' which had been left unattended. Their protocols of war—more precisely 'the color line' of which W. E. B. Du Bois had spoken three years ago in *The Souls of Black Folk*—prevented the British from tending to the wounded Zulus, and as we have seen, Gandhi remarks that 'white people were not willing nurses for the wounded Zulus'. So Gandhi, who had been appointed Sergeant Major of the Corps, commanded a number of men who assisted in tending to the wounded Zulus. Here he resumes his narrative: 'The white soldiers used to peep through the railings that separated us from them and tried to dissuade us from attending to the wounds. And as we would not heed them, they became enraged and poured unspeakable abuse on the Zulus.' White people were unwilling to nurse the Zulus, but their voyeurism as they 'peep' through the railings while the Indians attended to the wounded men is glaring. Sight has been privileged among the senses, at least in the Western tradition, but Gandhi's conduct points to the phenomenological importance of touch in his worldview. What is equally inescapable is the magnanimous ethics of hospitality behind the nursing of the Zulus: though Gandhi craved to be accepted as a subject of the British Empire, he plunges headlong into nursing the Empire's enemies.

So what might Gandhi have thought, then, of the present pandemic, the jeopardy in which the livelihood of hundreds of millions of people around the world has been placed, the enormous toll it has taken on human lives, and even, considering his own stated 'passion' for nursing, of the advice of scientists and doctors that each one of us should practise 'social distancing'? Before turning to this question, it is necessary to reflect on what would be obvious to most people: when Gandhi avers to his passion for nursing, or invokes the occasions when he felt called upon to nurse the ill or the wounded, he calls to mind a profession that over the course of the twentieth century became heavily feminized. The feminist critique of nursing—as a discourse, practise, and profession—has, not unreasonably, torn to shreds the assumption—one indubitably shared both by Nightingale and Gandhi—that women have a natural aptitude for nursing, or that they are by nature, disposition, and training better suited to the care of the sick than men. Feminists have put into serious question the supposition that women are especially called upon to be self-sacrificing. There is a large literature on the subject, but it suffices to introduce briefly only two considerations. First, there is no gainsaying the fact that Nightingale forcefully advocated for women as nurses rather than as doctors, but the feminist critique is perhaps not sufficiently mindful of the fact that even in mid-19th-century Britain and Europe nursing was scarcely a profession for women from respectable homes. Nursing was commonly left to those who came from impoverished families or to those engaged in prostitution. To this extent, Nightingale's endeavour was to make nursing open to respectable or educated women, introduce professional standards, furnish women with secure employment, and liberate women from the tyranny of the home. Secondly, Gandhi's own predilection for nursing can also profitably be viewed within the ambit of his larger design both of feminizing the public sphere and, in practise, controverting the assigned gender roles that his own writings appear to endorse.

The beginning point of a Gandhian view of the pandemic is perhaps to recognize that he would have been one with Nightingale in holding to the view that 'whatever a patient can do himself, it is better' (Thomas 1993, 20). He was very much his own doctor, and a theorist of a biopolitics which placed the responsibility of well-being both upon each individual and the state. He knew enough about public health, and the importance of sanitation, to discern that the advance of the plague in Johannesburg was imminent, and he was sharply critical of the local authorities, having pointed out in a 'Letter to the Johannesburg Press' on 4 April 1904 that 'but for the criminal neglect of the Johannesburg Municipality, the outbreak would never have occurred'—a statement that he stood by months later, as is revealed in a letter he addressed to the Indian Member of Parliament, Dadabhai Naoroji, on October 31 (CWMG 4, 287). It cannot be doubted that the words, 'criminal neglect', would have formed part of his indictment of how the coronavirus pandemic has been managed by most governments the world over. But on the issue of social distancing he would likely have displayed some ambivalence. While he would have been critical of the reckless disregard for the lives of others manifested in the behaviour of those who are unable to look beyond their own wants, comforts and drives, it is inconceivable that he would not have found it disconcerting and unacceptable that some are hiding behind the excuse of this pandemic to shun their neighbours, introduce new hierarchies and drive a wedge between themselves and others whom they imagine are their social inferiors. Social distancing can create its own forms of ghettoization.

Gandhi held to the view that there are laws of compensation at work in this universe, however opaque they may be to us. The comparatively clean air in the wake of the shuttering of the world economy, for instance, is perhaps a sign to human beings to be mindful of the devastation they have wrought upon planet earth. But Gandhi was not one to only philosophize: it is impossible to imagine him not present on the scene, tending to the sick and comforting members of their families. Even as his compassion was known to be boundless, nowhere more was this in evidence than in the fearless walk that he undertook through riot-torn Noakhali just months before his assassination, comforting the afflicted while accepting the taunts of some as though they were bouquets of flowers. Gandhi was also tough as nails, and I suspect that he would have punished himself to the hilt in working around the clock, organizing relief workers and cajoling people not to rely on government handouts but to make themselves useful and apply their ingenuity. Gandhi did not require a pandemic to discover, as is true of many of us, that many of those who are among the lowest paid workers are in fact the most 'essential'. His relentless critique of industrial modernity has led many people into believing that Gandhi was opposed to science, but that is far from being the case: he was a scientist in his own fashion, ceaselessly testing the truth of every proposition, but, more critically, he was opposed to scientism. While he would have respected scientific advice, I think it can safely be said that Gandhi would have also said that we cannot leave our understanding of the pandemic and its social, political and philosophical implications to the scientists alone, because the pandemonium engendered by the pandemic is ultimately a reflection of the unrest within each of us and within *homo sapiens* as a whole. Magnificent as the nurses have been in tending to the sick and the diseased, we *all* are called upon to nurse this earth back to health—something which can only begin with the recognition that, as a species, we are likely less 'essential' than we have imagined ourselves to be.

References

Capon, Tim. 2015. Plague, Gandhi and the Parliamentary Clerk's Daughter. *The Heritage Portal*, November 9, 2015. http://www.theheritageportal.co.za/article/plague-gandhi-and-parliamentary-clerks-daughter [accessed 12 June 2020]

Desai, Narayan. 2009. *My Life is my Message*, Vol 2: *Satyagraha, 1915-1930*, translated by Tridip Suhrud. Hyderabad: Orient BlackSwan.

Erikson, Erik H. 1969. *Gandhi's Truth: On the Origins of Militant Nonviolence*. New York: W. W. Norton & Company.

Evans, Charles M., Joseph R. Egan, and Ian Hall. 2018. Pneumonic Plague in Johannesburg, South Africa, 1904. *Emerging Infectious Diseases* 24, no. 1 (January): 95–102.

Gandhi, M.K. *The Collected Works of Mahatma Gandhi* [CWMG]. New Delhi: Ministry of Information & Broadcasting, Publications Division. https://www.gandhiheritageportal.org/the-collected-works-of-mahatma-gandhi

Gandhi, M.K. 1928/1950. *Satyagraha in South Africa*, translated by Valji Govindji Desai. Ahmedabad: Navajivan Publishing House.

Gandhi, M.K. 1909/1939. *Hind Swaraj or Indian Home Rule*. Ahmedabad: Navajivan Publishing House.

Gandhi, M.K. 1909/1997. *Hind Swaraj and Other Writings*, edited by Anthony J. Parel. Cambridge: Cambridge University Press.

Gandhi, M.K. 1927/1940. *An Autobiography or the Story of My Experiments with Truth*, translated by Mahadev Desai. Ahmedabad: Navajivan Publishing House.

Gandhi, M. K. 1905. Florence Nightingale. *Indian Opinion*, September 9, 1905; also in *CWMG* 5: 62-63.

Gill, Gillian. 2004. *Nightingale: The Extraordinary Upbringing and Curious Life of Miss Florence Nightingale*. New York: Random House.

Lal, Vinay. 2000. Nakedness, Nonviolence, and Brahmacharya: Gandhi's Experiments in Celibate Sexuality. *Journal of the History of Sexuality* 9, nos. 1–2 (January-April): 105–136.

Nightingale, Florence. 2006. *The Collected Works of Florence Nightingale*, edited by Gérard Vallée. Waterloo, Ontario: Wilfrid Laurier University Press.

Nightingale, Florence. 1860/1969. *Notes on Nursing: What it is, and what it is not*. New York: Dover.

Pakenham, Thomas. 1979. *The Boer War*. New York: Random House.

Scovil, E.R. 1920. The Later Activities of Florence Nightingale. *The American Journal of Nursing* 20, no. 8 (May): 609–12.

Spinney, Laura. 2017. *Pale Fire: The Spanish Flu and How It Changed the World*. New York: Public Affairs.

Tendulkar, D.G. 1961. *Mahatma: Life of Mohandas Karamchand Gandhi*, 8 vols. New Delhi: Government of India, Ministry of Information and Broadcasting, Publications Division.

Thomas, Sandra P. 1993. The View From Scutari: A Look at Contemporary Nursing. *Nursing Forum* 28, no. 2 (April–June): 19–24.

TOWARDS ALTERNATIVE HISTORIES
Gandhi and the Inter-constitutive Impact of the Colonial Encounter

Karen Gabriel

I

The impact of British rule in India was multifaceted. As M. N. Srinivas noted decades ago, 'the British brought with them new technology, institutions, knowledge, beliefs and values' (1995, 40), some of which were part of the processes of founding the modern nation-state. As such, they were to have a profound impact on what came to be consolidated as British India, and then—following the Partition of 1947—independent India. Srinivas identified quite a few of these as part of the process of the 'Westernization' of India, including the bureaucracy, the railways, the post and telegraph service, the setting up of law courts, the codification of laws, the introduction of the printing press, journalism, school and university education, political ideas such as secularism and electoral representation, the abolishing of customs like *sati*, female infanticide, human sacrifice, etc. The modernity of the Indian nation-state that emerged was thus undoubtedly defined by its European, specifically British, origin. But there were other components of this emergent entity that were not so much of European origin as products of that colonial encounter—the socio-religious reform movements of the nineteenth century, the creation of personal laws specific to each religious community, the community-based system of electoral political representation, etc. (Zavos 2000).

Apart from these facets of the impact of British rule in India though, there was also another facet, a reverse flow—i.e., the impact of British rule in India on Britain itself, and more generally, on Europe. The most obvious aspect of this reverse impact of course, is the enormous economic gains made by Britain from its imperial colonies—an aspect that has been much studied, discussed and debated from the time Dadabhai Naoroji first identified it as a 'drain of wealth' (Naoroji 1901) especially by postcolonial scholars (e.g. Chandra 1980, Mukherjee 2008, Sarkar 1989, Moxham 2016). A significant part of this debate is about whether colonialism had 'any major impact on the modernisation process of the colonizing countries of Europe (or of the US and Japan)'; the view that it 'has many adherents and has not been critiqued adequately. In fact, there has been a tendency…to underplay the role of 'colonial plunder' in primitive accumulation leading to the rise of capitalism in Europe' (Mukherjee 2010, 74). The quantum of this 'plunder', specifically in terms of the wealth transferred over the two centuries of British rule from India to Britain, has also been hotly debated; but a recent, rigorously argued estimate pegs it at about USD 45 trillion (Utsa Patnaik 2017).

Both Mukherjee and Patnaik (cited above), among others, make strong arguments for the economic impact of colonialism on the colonizing powers, not just in the direct terms of a massive financial 'drain', but in indirect economic terms as well. After abolishing slavery, for instance, the massive labour requirement that arose in the British colonies in South East Asia, Africa, and the Caribbean was met substantially by the 'export' of indentured labour from India. 'By one estimate more than two million indentured labourers were exported from India between 1831 and 1920' (Mukherjee 2010, 78). By another, 'between 1834 and 1937, thirty million Indians left India as part of the global division of labour, and just under twenty-four million returned'—so, more than six million (Mahmud 2013, 227). Their labour was crucial to the continued growth and consolidation of the British empire outside India, as well as to the maintenance of the supply of goods and services—e.g. sugar, coffee, domestic and menial work—earlier provided through slave-labour, that the British (and other European) populace had grown accustomed to enjoying. Further, 'Slaves from Africa and indentured labour from colonial India were the mainstay of global accumulation during the phase of emergence and consolidation of capitalism as a mode of production' (Mahmud 2013, 243). The actual economic volume and value of this labour, as a fraction of that European (and American) capital accumulation, remains a matter of debate (Williams 1944, Kale 1996, Morgan 2000, Solow and Engerman 2004). Even estimates such as those calculated by Patnaik for the transfer of wealth (above) are difficult to make, since this is capital accumulated through non-payment of wages for the productive labour of slaves, and minimal payment to indentured migrants. But there is little doubt that it 'can be conservatively described as large' (Williamson and Cain 2020).

Apart from these direct and indirect economic factors that shaped British society, during and after empire, there were other, very significant qualitative—and therefore perhaps difficult to quantify—gains to the British, from the colonization of India. These range from the shaping of the British education system and bureaucracy, to meet the requirements of colonial administration (Mangan 1993, Stoler 1995, Hyam 2010); to the vast numbers of cultural artifacts that were expropriated from India, and now adorn (among other places) the British Museum in London (besides bringing in income for it by way of fees); to the massive impact of Indian cuisines on British food (from mulligatawny soup to the chicken tikka masala that is now considered Britain's unofficial national dish); to the shaping of the British imagination itself, in many ways. For instance, the revolt of 1857, also often referred to as the 'mutiny' of 1857, had a big impact on both art (McAleer 2017) and literature (Chakravarty 2009). India had an impact on and shaped the British imagination in literature, more generally too: for instance, Wilkie Collins's novel, *The Moonstone*, often acknowledged to be the first crime novel in English, has a strong India-centric theme and plot. So also the work of writers like Somerset Maugham (especially drawing from his Malaysia experiences), Rudyard Kipling, E. M. Forster, and even George Orwell (among many others). Even more generally, the fascination with India's religious, spiritual, philosophical and literary traditions seeped into and moulded the writings of many 'Western' writers, from Ralph Waldo Emerson and Walt Whitman, to W. B. Yeats and T. S. Eliot, to Herman Hesse (Lal 2020). This continued into the postcolonial period, in popular bestsellers (like M.M. Kaye's *The Far Pavilions*, Paul Scott's *Raj Quartet*, J.G. Farrell's *The Siege of Krishnapur*, Ruth Prawer Jhabvala's *Heat and Dust*), that fed the British nostalgia for the glory days of 'the Raj'. This is also evident in the making of the 'Empire films,' and films like David Lean's *A Passage to India* (see also Cowans 2015). There is also a large number of Indian words that have now become an integral part of the English language—e.g., jungle, bungalow, bangle, etc—as collated in the famous *Hobson-Jobson* dictionary (Yule and Burnell 1886).

These other kinds of less easily discernible impacts, however—on social and cultural relations, education and governance; on literary, philosophical and political ideas; on language; on notions of self and identity, etc.—remain relatively much less studied than the economics of colonialism; more importantly, they remain mostly unexplored in terms of their significant implications for how the *constitution of subjectivities shape* history, politics and international relations. Some notable exceptions (apart from those cited in the previous paragraph) do engage with some of these qualitative impacts: these include Cain and Hopkins (1987), Cooper and Stoler (1997), and the fairly comprehensive entry by Laura Tabili in Stearns, et al. (2001). Tabili, in fact, argues that 'the mechanisms and practises of colonization, including aggression and exploitation, were intrinsic to European social formation and economic and political development. It follows that imperialism was inherent in domestic societies even before overseas colonization.' For Tabili, 'European identity itself was constructed through these processes' (2001, 503).[68]

But apart from these few works, there is little scholarship on how the colonial encounter shaped the colonizing subject and its social relations. Perhaps most significantly, this paucity of work registers a continuing tendency in the popular social and academic imaginary to see the relation between colonizer and colonized as mainly a 'bestowal' of 'modernity' by the former onto the latter. Further, it reinforces the concomitant and related tendency to disavow the massive economic gains to the 'West' from colonization. This disavowal—of both the quantitative and qualitative gains from colonization for the colonizers—needs to be challenged, not so much to establish claims of reparation—'it is not practisable for Britain to do so, for it is not rich enough to repay even a fraction of what it extracted from India over nearly two centuries' (Patnaik 2017, 312)—but to register, and strive to right, the underlying imbalance of power that continues to drive these tendencies. In particular, the disavowal of the manner in which the colonizing subject was constituted as an empowered one, in relation to the disempowered colonized subject, continues to dominate discourses around the colonial encounter as a kind of deep-racism.

This essay seeks to take a few preliminary steps towards addressing this lacuna, as well as the distorted perspective it reflects. It will attempt to do so through two related arguments: (a) by identifying and sketching some of the ways in which the British social order itself was affected by the colonial encounter, focusing specifically on its formulations of gender; and (b) examine the ways in which these reformulations were shaped by commensurate reformulations of gender in the colonies, specifically India. With regard to the reasons for the academic lacuna, the paper will address it in the form of a reply to Gayatri

---

[68] This can be corroborated, for instance, by the fact that the personification of British identity in the figure of 'Britannia' preceded British colonialism by at least two centuries—as she is seen in Edmund Spenser's failed epic, *The Faerie Queene* (1590).

Spivak's famous question, 'Can the subaltern speak?' It will argue that, often, an auditory space must first be created where the subaltern's speech can be heard at all. Without that space—that silence—whether or not the subaltern can speak cannot be known because, even if the subaltern speaks, s/he cannot be heard. In this instance, as noted above, the loudest conversation around the colonial encounter has been and remains about its impact on colonial societies and economies.

This paper therefore seeks to at least expose the evasiveness, if not silence, around the impact of colonization on the colonizers, and thereby create the discursive space within which another history can emerge. By doing so, it hopes to draw out the subaltern voices and forces that had (unobtrusively and unnoticed) contributed to shaping the articulation of the colonizer's subjectivity, imagination and social relations. The paper will examine the figure of Mohandas Karamchand Gandhi, in particular, and his engagements with these gender-reformulations, in this light—as setting out to rewrite the relations between gender, sexuality and power in the colony, in such a way as to destabilize their relations for the colonizer too.

II

Angela Woollacott, writing almost twenty years ago, noted that, 'It is now well established that colonialism has been an inter-constitutive process that shaped British society and culture' (Woollacott 2001, 9). She cites some well-known works in support of this observation, such as Edward W. Said's *Culture and Imperialism* (1993), Mrinalini Sinha's *Colonial Masculinity: The 'Manly Englishman' and the 'Effeminate Bengali' in the Late Nineteenth Century* (1995) and Anne McClintock's *Imperial Leather: Race, Gender and Sexuality in the Colonial Contest* (1995). These, along with the earlier cited works, seem to challenge, if not contradict, the argument above, about the scarcity of scholarly work on this 'inter-constitutive process'. However, as we noted above, although these works—and Woollacott's own work—do engage with this 'inter-constitutive process', they have had little to no impact on the dominant orientation in the study of colonialism.

Tony Ballantyne similarly argues that there are 'large bodies of work on imperial questions in British politics, the impact of slave trade and slavery on Britain, the place of the 'fruits of empire' in British cultural and commercial life, and the influence of the empire on British literary production' (Ballantyne 2010). Almost all the works that he reviews, however, explore the administrative *innovations, actions and activities* that were initiated to facilitate the imperial-colonial project, and in response to the metropolitan-colonial programmemes and policies. For instance, H. V. Bowen's *The Business of Empire: the East India Company and Imperial Britain, 1756–1833* (2006), we are told,

> ...demonstrates the ways in which the EIC's access to land revenues from India exposed it to new pressures and how, in response, the EIC created new managerial structures, decision-making systems, and relationships with investors, stockholders, and key political figures (431).

Most of the other work reviewed by Ballantyne is along similar lines. In contrast, there is little work on the ways in which the colonial encounter itself, i.e., the economic, social, cultural and political *transactions* between the colonizer and the colonized, had an impact on 'British cultural and commercial life'—specifically, on the British subject constituted as a colonizing subject.

There are some notable exceptions covered in Ballantyne's review, including Daniel Rycroft's *Representing Rebellion: Visual Aspects of Counter-insurgency in Colonial India* (2006), Douglas Hamilton's *Scotland, the Caribbean and the Atlantic world, 1750–1820* (2005) and Catherine Hall and Sonya Rose's *At Home with the Empire: Metropolitan Culture and the Imperial World* (2006). These are closer to the work that Woollacott refers to, and undertakes herself—and like them, these too, continue to have little impact on the colony-centric orientation of scholarship on colonialism. One heuristic measure of this is evident from using the search-string 'impact of colonialism' on Google Scholar: of the 86 results that were thrown up just for this year (i.e., 2020), the overwhelming majority of works cited remain focused on the erstwhile colonies, with just 3, perhaps 4, exceptions.[69] In the anthropology and historiography of Europe, the theatre in which colonialism was seen to unfold therefore continues to remain the colonies, and rarely ever Europe; its actors and agents continue to be perceived as carrying Europe to the world, and rarely ever as themselves constituted in and by that theatre, as it also played out within the European metropole. Far from being 'well established' then, the ways in which metropolitan Europe was shaped by colonialism remains a marginal and understudied area of research.

This steadfast resistance to exploring and studying the impact of colonialism on almost all of European, certainly British, society and culture is arguably a consequence of the colonial construction of the 'European subject' itself. This construction derived substantially from the understanding of colonialism as not just the cultural 'exporting' of Europe, but as a 'civilizing mission'. The construction of colonialism as a 'mission' (in the sense of a selfless vocation or calling), served thereby to justify the violence and coercion that were necessary to carry out the economic expropriations from the colonies. As importantly, it helped to distract from the cultural 'importing'—of both the appropriative and expropriative kinds—that was also happening apace—and as noted above, on quite a large scale. It is also important to note that this economic pillaging would inevitably have social and cultural consequences for its beneficiaries in Europe; just as the global spread of European technologies, and

---

[69] And even those are not all concerned with the impact of colonialism on 'British cultural and commercial life,' but have the phrase 'impact of colonialism' coming up tangentially, in relation to other issues.

the concomitant industrialization, has wrought massive social and cultural changes everywhere. However, these points are rarely acknowledged, let alone examined. It is, in fact, probably worth exploring whether this is a consequence or cause of the separation of culture from economics, that has been maintained for several decades now in the academe—with an almost casteist vehemence—and continues to be; but that must wait for another occasion. Whether as cause or consequence, though, this separation certainly strengthens the case we are making—that the impact of colonial plunder on the social and cultural aspects of European subject-formation must be examined.

Hall and Rose propose a Lefebvrian explanation for the blindness to, and refusal to acknowledge, the cultural impact of colonialism on Europe; they write:

> ...prior to decolonization, 'being imperial' was simply a part of a whole culture, to be investigated not as separate from but as integral to peoples' lives. Britain's imperial project affected the everyday in ways that shaped what was 'taken-for-granted' and thus was not *necessarily* a matter of conscious awareness or deliberation. With the exception of those in some official or quasi-official roles, for most people, empire was just there—out there. It was ordinary (original emphasis; Hall & Rose 2006, 22).

They suggest thereby, that the very 'everydayness of empire' (23) resulted in the kind of familiarity that breeds blindness, if not contempt, and a consequent inability, or at least unwillingness, to investigate it 'not as separate from but as integral to peoples' lives'. That is, the alchemy of imperialism ensures that the 'separateness' of the colonies (that warranted, and continues to warrant, the gaze of the entire postcolonial studies industry), gets integrated into the 'everyday' life of colonial Europe, and thus into the very academe that spawned the postcolonial studies industry in the first place, thereby also ensuring its invisibilization to that very industry. In the felicitous words of Namvar Singh,

'The spirit that we seek to exorcise has thus infiltrated the very *mantra* through which we seek to exorcise it' (Singh 1992, 153).

One very significant consequence of this was the representation and perception of agency. Edmund Burke III remarks:

> We tend to see colonial histories as taking place in a space that is separate from that in which European history occurs. Accordingly, colonial histories appear as derivative histories, rather than shaped by the same world historical processes as modern Europe. In this 'sleeping beauty' theory of modern history, agency resides alone with Europe, while the non-West is seen as without history, fatally blocked from change because of its alleged cultural defects (eg., Islamic obscurantism, oriental despotism, the Asian mode of production) until awakened from its millennial slumber by the kiss of the West. (Burke III 1998).

Burke is evidently critiquing the separation of European history from the histories of its colonies; the perception of the latter as derivative from the former, because of colonialism; and the consequent attribution of agency to Europe alone. Paradoxically, this is also the basis for a defence of the paucity of Europe-focused studies of colonialism. The argument is that Euro-focus is just another form of Eurocentrism which, besides drawing scholarly attention away from how the colonized apparently enjoyed agency, ignores the pre- and non-colonial histories of the latter, thereby effectively denying those histories.

The fallacies in this argument are obvious: firstly, Burke's comment on the denial of the historical agency of the colonized in 'colonial histories', seeks to reaffirm the historicity of the latter, outside and independent of European history. In the arguments alluded to above, however, the assumption seems to be that any examination of the agency of the colonizer somehow effectively implies denying the historical agency of the colonized. Secondly, the interest in the historical agency of the colonized seems primarily in exploring the ways in which the latter actively participated in their own colonization and exploitation. Under the pretext of avoiding Eurocentrism, the agenda appears to be to minimize the intents and extent of European agency in—and thus responsibility for—colonization, and maximize that of the colonized. Thirdly, the emphasis on the agency of the colonized arose out of the ostensible concern with denying the pre- and non-colonial histories of the colonized; but these histories are rarely evident in discussions of colonialism—possibly precisely because they are pre- or non-colonial histories. In other words, the emphasis on the agency of the colonized seems to be more about shifting responsibility and accountability for the colonial project from the colonizer to the colonized, than about reclaiming the agency of the latter as empowering and enabling.

Besides the 'everydayness' thesis and the 'Euro-focus = Eurocentrism' argument, noted above, there is also the 'minimal impact' theory, which (as would be clear from the name) denies that cultural inflows from the colonies had any discernible impact on European society and culture in the metropole, or any significance in shaping European sensibilities (Ballantyne 2010, 448). The denial of any significant cultural impact is now being accompanied by an increasing number of arguments denying any significant economic gain to European societies from colonialism—and indeed, that it may have actually hampered economic growth in the metropole (Cooper & Stoler 1997, 19). The 'minimal impact' understanding, however, is quite at odds with the 'everydayness of Empire' theory: if the presence and significance of Empire was so pervasive as to become quotidian, unremarkable, invisible, then its impact—whether cultural or economic—was clearly far from minimal. Contrarily, if it was in fact 'minimal', it could not possibly be so pervasive as to become 'everyday'.

Taken together with the 'Euro-focus = Eurocentrism' argument, these contestations are indications of a desire to avoid engaging with the European end of the colonial stick, on multiple, rather contradictory grounds. They couldn't, because its 'everydayness' rendered it invisible; or they needn't, because it was apparently too 'minimal' in impact to warrant much study; or they wouldn't, because of the fear of the charge of Eurocentrism. The awkwardness of these multiple protestations speak of a persistent and continuing unwillingness in the metropolitan academe to acknowledge the actual significance of this impact. I propose here that this actual significance lay, and lies, in the unexpected *intimacy* of Empire to European lives. The resistance to opening this to examination arises from the inevitability of having to acknowledge that very intimacy, and its implications for understanding the constitution of European subjectivity—of the 'European identity'. When psychologist Ashis Nandy first wrote of the 'intimate enemy' (Nandy 1983), he was writing about the making of the 'Indian' self under, and in the wake of, colonialism. What I am proposing here is the converse of the case that Nandy was making, viz., that the colonized other was as much of an 'intimate enemy' to the colonizer—only, the terms of that intimacy have yet to be acknowledged, let alone explored, in all their complexities.

Two of the earliest works, that Nandy also draws from and refers to, that offered a map to undertake such explorations, were, firstly, Algerian psychoanalyst Franz Fanon's *Black Skin, White Masks* (1967). Its searing analyses of the psychology of colonial relations were also alluded to by the second text—Edward Said's controversial *Orientalism* (1977). Fanon's work, like Nandy's, is limited in usefulness, in that they both confine themselves to examining the shaping of 'the colonized self' under and by colonialism. Said's text was severely critiqued from several quarters (e.g. Ahmed 1993, Cohn 1996) for being unoriginal, essentialist, too sweeping, and so on. However, one of the most significant outcomes of the publication of *Orientalism* was the attention it drew to ways in which imperialism and colonialism shaped the self-perceptions of the European ruling classes. It demonstrated convincingly that Europe's 'civilizing mission' was not just a justification for conquest but an ideological recasting of the European self. However, in exploring the dynamics of this recasting, Said's focus too, remains on the colonies, and not on the metropolitan impact of colonialism.

In this regard, a point of some significance is the general tendency to treat 'nationalism' as a 'third-world' reaction to colonialism, and hence as a 'third-world' phenomenon, often with associations of primordialism, and/or chauvinism, and/or religious fanaticism. However, it is arguably the case that nationalism emerged with the emergence of the nation-state as a political formation in Europe, and is closely related to the imperial project itself, as its justification (Kumar 2006). A striking example of this is in Daniel Defoe's famous fictional creation, Robinson Crusoe, who epitomized the English imperial impulse and colonial enterprise (Flynn 2000). In short, in order to fully explore the ways in which colonialism shaped the colonizer—i.e., how it impacted on European lives and moulded European subjectivities in Europe, and not just in the colonies or on the colonized—we must, deliberately and diligently, turn our gaze on the European subject of colonialism, and examine the ways in which that subjectivity was shaped, if not produced, by the colonial encounter. We must overcome the reluctance, even resistance, of that subject to being examined.

III

So, how is such an examination to be undertaken? The academic lacuna referred to earlier means that there is not much readily accessible material on the central question of this paper, viz., what was, and remains, the impact of the colonial encounter on the colonizer? How then does one study it?

Cooper and Stoler, acknowledging this issue, write that,

> Part of the problem is that the task is unwieldy and not easily carried out…[W]e can no longer confine ourselves to the units of analysis on which we have relied. We need to create…new archives of our own…We need to understand more fully how… these civilizing missions provided new sites for clarifying a bourgeois order, new definitions of social welfare, new ways in

which the discourses and practises of inclusion and exclusion were contested and worked out (Cooper & Stoler 1997, 16).[70]

Given that the material components of that bourgeois order were substantially from the colonies—marks of empire that were simultaneously pervasively present and invisible, as observed above—tracing their significance in the making of the 'European self' would certainly be a daunting task. Daunting, not just because of the sheer number and variety of such components, but because of the difficulty in recognizing them as the products and effects of imperialism and colonialism; and then possibly in coming to terms with their intimacy and integrity to the making of the 'European self'. Be that as it may, it is clear now that one way of undertaking such an examination would be through an 'anthropology of things' (Appadurai 1986) with imperial-colonial antecedents.

Another promising approach would be to explore a phenomenon we had flagged above: viz., the ways in which the establishment and consolidation of the colonial administrative machinery generated particular requirements—intellectual, physical, social—of the colonizing populace. These in turn instituted fundamental changes within European social space in terms of education, professional opportunities, occupational and vocational status, recruitment procedures, and related to these, the very important process of the gendering of functions and roles within the imperial machinery.[71] The instituting of competitive examinations to enter the Indian Civil Services and the Home Civil Services, for instance, was a response to the demands of

---

[70] A few pages after this acknowledgment, Cooper and Stoler refer in acquiescence to the theory that the economic gains of imperialism were not of any significant magnitude. This is a tellingly ironical comment on the tenacity of the resistance to being examined, noted earlier.

[71] These issues have been explored to varying degrees by several scholars (e.g. Ballhatchet 1980, Hyam 1990, McClintock 1995, Sinha 1995, and Stoler 1997), but still remain poorly represented in the literature.

Empire: Macaulay hoped it would 'fill the magistracies of our Eastern Empire with men who will do honour to their country, with men who may represent the best part of the English nation' (cited in Hyam 2010, 33). If the task of conquest-and-rule was thus rendered masculine, specifically feminine (or rather, feminized) occupations also evolved like nursing, or the role of the governess. The ideal of the housewife as mother, home-maker and charitable social activist evolved especially in the colonies (Burns 1998, Reidi 2002); but in particular, it inculcated a definitive relation of masculinity to power that was steeped in an industrial language:

> In the later half of the nineteenth century...self-control was often expressed through industrial or mechanical analogies; manliness represented disciplined control over natural forces, just as the steam engine and other industrial technology managed 'the natural energy of water and fire'...The Empire was a natural place for such masculinity to be expressed and to be textualized in stories of adventure...which would then reproduce manliness as an object of desire for young readers (Holden 1998, 2).

This approach engages directly with the constitution of the colonizing subject—i.e., with the ways in which the enterprise of colonialism impacted and shaped European subjectivity, especially through the intimate formulations of gender and sexuality. In the rest of this paper, I will attempt to follow this approach, in my exploration of the significance of Gandhi and Gandhian thought to the shaping of the European identity.

Since colonial hegemony is crucially about embodiment and power, since gendering is always processual and interrupted, and since subjects, subjectivities, and selves are formed in the intersections of culture and history, colonialism—rough and inorganic as it was—interrupted local gender dynamics (among many other dynamics) and their formative contexts. In this encounter, disparate rules of economic, social, institutional, and personal engagements came into conflict. Colonization, and then the nationalist struggle, brought structural, institutional, and legislative changes, as well as an unprecedented degree of social, spatial, and occupational mobility, all of which effected ruptures in the sex-gender system. Illustratively, the decades-long controversy over the passage of the Contagious Diseases Act in 1864, which tried to regulate the itinerant sexualities and bodies of colonial soldiers and metropolitan sex-workers, generated a massive moral and medical discourse that profoundly affected British sexual perceptions and practises (Cox 2007). The encounter itself left the colonial subject split, epistemologically destabilized, and faced with the challenges of dealing with theoretical, ideological, and practical changes in sexual, social, political, cultural, and other practises.

Moreover, the transformations in sexualization effected by the encounter impacted the perceptions of the encounter itself, as well as on the subjects engaged in it.

> In many colonial contexts, European women became the excuse for—and custodians of—racial distinctions that took the form of class-specific prescriptions for bourgeois respectability and sexual 'normalcy'...Medical discourse on the danger of physical contagion via colonized women slipped into a discourse on cultural and moral contamination and as such placed adherence to respectability and safeguards against racial degeneracy as imperatives of white rule...Colonial elites saw psychological dispositions and sentiments (toward work, consumption, children, nation, and authority) as contagious, dangerous, and identity defining as well (Cooper & Stoler 1997, 24-5).

These changes in perception of 'self' and 'other' were subsequently and, perhaps, inevitably rendered in terms of an opposition between 'tradition' and 'modernity,' with the organization of sexuality serving as the site on which this encounter was played out. Significantly, there were other gendered, even sexualized, criteria, which also drew on this same opposition between 'tradition' and 'modernity,' by which these constructions of 'self' and 'other' came to be cognized, assessed, and evaluated—e.g., the practise of meat-eating, or more specifically, of abjuring it in vegetarianism. This, in turn, was promoted as a crucial aspect of the non-violence that Mohandas Gandhi propounded as the basis of his anti-imperialism—a point we will return to shortly.

Within this nexus, the prevalent gendered binary was extended to the colonized subject disadvantageously as colonizer-colonized, masculine-feminine, civilized-barbaric, powerful-powerless, thereby modulating the organization and meanings of race, gender, and sexuality. However, what is not often acknowledged is that the colonial encounter was also one between two different, even conflicting conceptions of self, community, the relations between the two, as well as the processes by which self and community are constituted. Broadly speaking, the English understanding of the self, and of the individual in relation to the community, is as impermeable, isolated rather than processual and reciprocal; it is a product of individualism, capitalism, and then colonialism itself. Indic conceptions of self and community, in contrast, were (and are) not only as variable as the number of (definitions of) community—e.g., caste, language, religion, region, occupation—but were (and are) the products of a more complexly mixed political economy. This is not the space to elaborate on that fairly vast topic: suffice it to note here that the engagement of this mixed political economy with capitalism and colonialism did not erase the existing conceptions of self, or overwrite it with English conceptions of individualism. Rather, it became the basis of the splitting of the colonial subject that we had noted above. Under pressure to emulate the 'modernity' of the colonizer, the colonized subject sought to become both, English and Indic (Chatterjee 1986).

Recognizing this, Gandhi began to innovate notions of subjectivity and selfhood designed and tailored to salvage the 'defeated' (male) subject. This operation was located fundamentally in the dual senses in which Gandhi deployed the concept of swaraj, or self-rule: in its Gandhian formulation, this meant both control over the self, as well as freedom from British rule, with the first understanding emerging as a prerequisite for the fulfilment of the second. Before we engage in some detail with these Gandhian conceptions, it is worth noting that Gandhi 'developed his political philosophy and political tactics in the context of his direct involvement with the Indian indentured labour in South Africa' (Mahmud 2013, 239). If we recall that the 'export' of indentured labour was itself a significant way in which the colonies contributed to the making and shaping of European social and cultural life, we see that Gandhi's early political steps among these people were already signalling the impact that he would have on Britain. It led Gilbert Murray to comment that:

> Persons in power should be careful how they deal with a man who cares nothing for sensual pleasure, nothing for riches, nothing for comfort or praise or promotion, but is simply determined to do what he believes is right. He is a *dangerous* and uncomfortable enemy—because his body, which you can always conquer, gives you so little purchase upon his soul (cited in Lal 2009, 283; emphasis added by Lal).

Murray's words not only give us a clear sense of how Gandhi inverted the conventional European sense of a powerful, masculine self, to the point of making him an 'uncomfortable' person for the British. It also signals the strategy that Gandhi would employ to make arguably his biggest impact on Europe and European imperial thought—which is that it could, and would, be defeated. Gandhi's biggest impact in this sense, was his enormous contribution to the ending of empire.

There were two important aspects to the strategy that he adopted for this: the first linked self-rule to, and represented it as, ahimsa, or non-violence. The second modelled that non-violence on (what Gandhi perceived as) women's adoption and practise of it—i.e., he deliberately feminized the practise of non-violence[72] in order to represent British colonial masculinity as lacking self-control. Gandhi's own active feminization of himself is epitomized in the image of him at the spinning wheel, where both posture and activity are distinctly feminine. He also actively courted an image of motherliness through his intense, even obsessive involvement in nursing. The valorisation of women's suffering (a) deflected, by inversion, the European criticism of the treatment of women in India, seeking to represent Indian women, in particular, as imbued with, as well as being the embodiment of, the principle of shakti (energy/force/strength), the implicit argument being that (Indian) women suffered because they were strong enough to take it; (b) consequently they did not need any rescuing by the 'civilized' white man from the hands of the 'barbaric' Indian man, because the Indian man was now going to feminize himself, in order to become 'strong' like his woman; and (c) it served to present the masculinities of British imperialist patriarchy as crude, rapaciously materialist, violent, hypocritical, and profoundly lacking in self-control and discipline, in contrast to the spiritually stronger, scrupulously nonviolent, disciplined Indian patriarchy that Gandhi sought to forge.

Gandhi's espousal and even valorisation of the feminine, and his recuperation of femininity as a form of moral superiority, is an index of the inventiveness with which a paradigmatic shift was conceptualized and undertaken. These complex and innovative mechanics whereby Gandhi injected gender-sexual politics into political transformation, was arguably a major factor in the British government's inability to contain him politically. However, this does not yet give us a sense of how Gandhian

---

[72] 'I have suggested…that woman is the incarnation of *ahimsa. Ahimsa* means infinite love, which again means infinite capacity for suffering. Who but woman, the mother of man, shows this capacity in the largest measure? She shows it as she carries the infant and feeds it during nine months and derives joy in the suffering involved. What can beat the suffering caused by the pangs of labour? But she forgets them in the joy of creation' (*Hind Swaraj*, 24 February 1940: 13–14).

politics impacted on the European sense of self; in order to understand this, we need to look at one more important aspect of this Gandhian refabrication of gendered politics. This was in his inversion of the British perception of the Indian as passive and lazy: Gandhi chose to rewrite this as a spiritual superiority that rejected the pursuit of worldly gain.[73] The charge of passivity is inverted into the superior (and gendered) moral position of non-violence, and that of laziness into the quest for spiritual goals.

Not only does this wrest moral superiority out of British hands, it recasts the terms of assessment, so that it is now the conqueror and his actions that stand under scrutiny, rather than the conquered. Most importantly, perhaps, for us, this inversion not only called out the objectives of British imperialism and colonialism for what they were—exercises in conquest, rapacity, exploitation and pillaging, rather than any 'civilizing mission'—but, by doing so, it rendered the accumulated spoils of these exercises 'obscene'—i.e., that which must be hidden. It exposed the hollowness of 'Western' claims to have ruled India for the latter's benefit, as well as the silence around imperial expropriation. Gandhi's well-known aversion for 'Western', industrial and technological modernity is thus not just some form of Luddite morality: it is a reaction to what he perceived as the massively exploitative, oppressive and hypocritical basis of that 'modernity'. This is also the sense in which we must understand the apocryphal story about what Gandhi is reputed to have said, when asked what he thought of 'Western' civilization: 'I think it would be a very good idea' (cited in Lal 2009, 281).

---

[73] 'There is a charge laid against us that we are a lazy people and that Europeans are industrious and enterprising. We have accepted the charge and we therefore wish to change our condition. Hinduism, Islam, Zoroastrianism, Christianity and all other religions teach that we should remain passive about worldly pursuits and active about godly pursuits, that we should set a limit to our worldly ambition and that our religious ambition should be illimitable. Our activity should be directed into the latter channel' (1997 [1909], 42-3).

In this sense, the British (and other European) reluctance to engage with the intimacy of empire, and the consequent blindness to its everyday impact on society and culture, may be seen as a direct fallout of Gandhi's political inversion. Gandhi's refusal to acknowledge—indeed, outright rejection of—the power of material trappings, fundamentally undid the capitalist basis of colonial modernity. Further, his inversion of the gendered associations of this power was a direct and 'uncomfortable' challenge to the capitalist, colonialist impulse at the heart of the (gendered) European sense of self and identity. The almost obsessive concern with 'individuation' in the 'West', idealized in a kind of Robinson-Crusoean self-sufficiency, is a far cry from Gandhi's idea of swaraj, which links individual self-rule to national self-rule. But the fact that Gandhi's idea of self-rule could be such a major force in overthrowing 'Western' imperialism, remains one of the least acknowledged, and perhaps most potent, challenge to the West's self-perception. In this sense, the tendency to associate Gandhi with non-violence alone is to miss the far more fundamental challenge he had posed—it is to focus, in fact, on the method, rather than the substance of his thinking.

It is not surprising then, that the greatest subsequent impact that Gandhi's ideas have had in the metropole, has been in similar situations of political and/or social crises, where exploitation and oppression happen in the name of civility, freedom, rights, democracy, etc. Gandhian ideas and methods have proven themselves most effective when they engage with hypocrisies of these kinds, precisely because of the moral force that is derived from exposing that hypocrisy, and presenting the oppressor (the colonizer in this instance) with a perception of himself (rarely 'herself') that is difficult to sustain. This explains how and why figures like Nelson Mandela and Martin Luther King Jr could draw so successfully on him—but it also explains why, when the crisis does not involve such gendered dynamics of intimacy, in the representation of oppression and/or exploitation, these very methods do not prove very successful. Non-violence in itself, in other words, is not a sufficiently moral politics, in itself: it can at best be one strategy among others, to articulate a deeper moral challenge—one that must recast the sense of self of both oppressor and oppressed. This can, and often does, lead to the castigation of such dissidents as anti-national, anti-social, etc. Vinay Lal, for instance, notes that:

> Among those constituencies in the West that have championed him, vegetarians, naturopaths, anarchists, luddites, ecologists, teetotalers, walkers, and even nudists come readily to mind. Quite characteristically, Gandhi himself had cause to remark on this phenomenon: 'I have been known as a crank, faddist, mad man. Evidently the reputation is well deserved. For wherever I go, I draw to myself cranks, faddists and mad men' (2009, 282).

It is not difficult to see how, in this sense, any radical political challenge must necessarily recast the very terms on which self-hood, subjectivity and identity are cast, because any other challenge can only be, at best, a change of guard within a perpetuating system. The Gandhian contribution to the world, and not just to Europe, in this sense, is the conceptualization of the insurgent subject as one who is insurgent on his/her own sense of self, his/her own subjectivity.

The success of Gandhi's methods thus required not only a sense of moral superiority, but the possibility of rendering the opposition's sense of self itself suspect. The theatre of imperialism-colonialism provided this: but in order to understand this fully, studies of imperialism-colonialism must be able to look at the European end of this dynamic squarely, and analyze the significance of colonial dynamics to European self-fashioning, without automatically feeling complicit in the imperial project— because, by not doing so, paradoxically, they do, in fact, become complicit in it.

References

Ahmed, A. 1993. *In Theory*. Oxford University Press.

Appadurai, A. 1986. *The Social Life of Things: Commodities in Cultural Perspective*. Cambridge University Press.

Ballantyne, T. 2010. The changing shape of the modern British empire and its historiography. *Historical Journal, 53* (2), 429–452. https://doi.org/10.1017/S0018246X10000117

Ballhatchet, K. A. 1980. *Race, Sex and Class Under the Raj: Imperial Attitudes and Policies and Their Critics 1793-1905*. St Martin's Press.

Burke, III, E. 1998. Theorizing the histories of colonialism and nationalism in the Arab Maghrib (Beyond Colonialism and Nationalism in North Africa). *Arab Studies Quarterly (ASQ), 22 March*. http://www.encyclopedia.com/doc/1G1-21187376.html

Burns, C. 1998. 'A Man is a Clumsy Thing Who does not Know How to Handle a Sick Person': Aspects of the History of Masculinity and Race in the Shaping of Male Nursing in South Africa, 1900-1950. *Journal of South African Studies*, 24: 4, 695–717.

Cain, P. J. & A. G. Hopkins. 1987. Gentlemanly Capitalism and British Expansion Overseas II: New Imperialism, 1850-1945. *The Economic History Review*, Feb., 40: 1, 1-26

Chakravarty, Gautam. 2009. *The Indian Mutiny and the British Imagination*. Cambridge: CUP

Chandra, B. 1980. Colonialism, stages of colonialism and the colonial state. *Journal of Contemporary Asia*, 10: 3, 272–285. https://doi.org/10.1080/00472338085390151

Chatterjee, Partha. 1986. *Nationalist Thought and the Colonial World: A Derivative Discourse*. London: Zed Books.

Cohn, B. 1996. *Colonialism and its Forms of Knowledge: The British in India*. Princeton University Press.

Cooper, F., & Stoler, A. L., eds. 1997. *Tensions of Empire: Colonial Cultures in a Bourgeois World*. University of California Press.

Cowans, Jon. 2015. *Empire Films and the Crisis of Colonialism, 1946-1959*. Baltimore: John Hopkins University Press.

Cox, Pamela. 2007. Compulsion, Voluntarism, and Venereal Disease: Governing Sexual Health in England after the Contagious Diseases Acts. *Journal of British Studies*, 46: 1 (January), 91-115.

Fanon, F. 1967. *The Wretched of the Earth*. London: Penguin.

Flynn, Christopher. 2000. Nationalism, Commerce, and Imperial Anxiety in Defoe's Later Works. *Rocky Mountain Review of Language and Literature*, 54: 2, 11-24

Gandhi, Mohandas K. (1997 [1909]). *Hind Swaraj and Other Writings*. Ed. Anthony J Parel. Delhi: Cambridge University Press.

Hall, C., & Rose, S. O., eds. 2006. *At Home with the Empire: Metropolitan Culture and the Imperial World*. Cambridge University Press.

Holden, P. 1998. The Significance of Uselessness: Resisting Colonial Masculinity in Philip Jeyaretnam's Abraham's Promise. *Jouvert: A Journal of Postcolonial Studies* 2:1. https://legacy.chass.ncsu.edu/jouvert/v2i1/HOLDEN.HTM

Hyam, R. 1990. *Empire and Sexuality: The British Experience*. Manchester University Press.

Kale, Madhavi. 1996. 'Capital Spectacles in British Frames': Capital, Empire and Indian Indentured Migration to the British Caribbean. *International Review of Social History* 41: 4, *'Peripheral' Labour? Studies in the History of Partial Proletarianization*, 109-133.

Kumar, Krishan. 2006. Empire and English Nationalism. *Nations and Nationalism* 12: 1, 1–13.

Lal, P. 2020. Indian Influences on English, American and European Literature. URL: https://asiasociety.org/files/Indian-Influences-Literature.pdf

Lal, Vinay. 2009. Gandhi's West, the West's Gandhi. *New Literary History* 40: 2, *India and the West* (Spring), 281-313.

Mahmud, Tayyab. 2013. Cheaper than a Slave: Indentured Labor, Colonialism and Capitalism. *Whittier Law Review*, 34, 215.

Mangan, J. A., ed. 1993. *The Imperial Curriculum: Racial Images and Education in the British Colonial Experience*. London: Routledge.

McAleer, John. 2017. *Picturing India: People, Places and the World of the East India Company*. Washington, DC: University of Washington Press.

McClintock, A. 1995. *Imperial leather: Race, Gender and Sexuality in the Colonial Contest*. Routledge.

Morgan, Kenneth. 2000. *Slavery, Atlantic Trade and the British Economy, 1660-1800*. Cambridge: CUP.

Moxham, Roy. 2016. *The Theft of India: The European Conquests of India, 1498–1765*. New Delhi: Harper Collins, India.

Mukherjee, A. 2008. The Return of the Colonial in Indian Economic History: The Last Phase of Colonialism in India. *Social Scientist*, 36: 3/4, 3–44. http://www.jstor.org/stable/27644268

Mukherjee, A. 2010. How Colonial India Made Modern Britain. *Economic and Political Weekly*, December 11-17, 45: 50, 73-82.

Nandy, A. 1983. *The Intimate Enemy: Loss and Recovery of Self under Colonialism*. Oxford University Press.

Naoroji, Dadabhai. 1901. *Poverty and Un-British Rule in India*. London: Swan Sonnenschein & Co. Ltd.

Patnaik, Utsa. 2017. Revisiting the drain, or Transfers from India to Britain in the Context of Global Diffusion of Capitalism. In *Agrarian and Other Histories: Essays for Binay Bhushan Chaudhuri* eds. Shubhra Chakrabarti and Utsa Patnaik. New Delhi: Tulika Books.

Reidi, E. 2002. Women, Gender and the Promotion of Empire: The Victoria League, 1901-1914. *The Historical Journal*, 45: 3, 569–599.

Said, E. 1977. *Orientalism*. London: Penguin.

Sarkar, S. 1989. *Modern India, 1885-1947*. Palgrave Macmillan.

Singh, N. 1992. Decolonising the Indian Mind. *Indian Literature*, 35: 5, 145–156. http://www.jstor.org/stable/23337172

Sinha, M. 1995. *Colonial Masculinity: the 'Manly Englishman' and the 'Effeminate Bengali' in the Late Nineteenth Century*. Manchester University Press. https://doi.org/10.2307/4051878

Solow, Barbara L, & Stanley L. Engerman (2004 [1987]). *British Capitalism and Caribbean Slavery: The Legacy of Eric Williams*. Cambridge: CUP.

Srinivas, M. N. (1995 [1966]). *Social Change in Modern India*. New Delhi: Orient Longman.

Stoler, A. 1997. Carnal Knowledge and Imperial Power. In *The Gender/ Sexuality Reader: Culture, History, Political Economy* eds. M. di Leonardo & R. Lancaster. Routledge.

Tabili, Laura. 2001. Imperialism and Domestic Society. In *Encyclopedia of European Social History*, ed. Peter N Stearns et al, Vol I, Section 4. Detroit: Charles Scribner's Sons.

Williams, Eric. 1944. *Capitalism and Slavery*. Chapel Hill: University of North Carolina Press.

Williamson, Samuel H. & Louis P. Cain. 2020. Measuring Slavery in 2016 Dollars. *MeasuringWorth*. URL: www.measuringworth.com/slavery.php

Woollacott, A. 2001. *To Try Her Fortune in London: Australian Women, Colonialism, and Modernity*. Oxford University Press.

Yule, Henry & A. C. Burnell. 1886. *Hobson-Jobson: The Anglo-Indian Dictionary*. Hertfordshire: Wordsworth Editions.

Zavos, J. 2000. *The Emergence of Hindu Nationalism in India*. Oxford University Press.

Part Two

ACTIVISMS

REVISITING GANDHI'S *INDIA OF MY DREAMS*

Globalization and Village Republics in the 21st Century

Saurabh Chaturvedi and Niharika Ravi

Technological advancements, the computer, and the internet of things: products of globalization and western civilization have facilitated the publication of millions of research documents on an eclectic range of pedagogical concentrations spanning every significant discovery made by humankind. However, it seems with research in general, and contemporary academia in the social sciences in particular, there exists an insufficiency of viable and practically implementable solutions to the research problems. In stark contrast, *India of my Dreams* manifests as a futuristic handbook for Indian governance, or rather, a practical manual of the Father of the Nation's vision for the motherland. It is most appropriate, then, to examine this striking piece of literature in the context of the given theme: then and now.

India of My Dreams is timeless in conception and reception. A compilation of Gandhi's thoughts and writings amassed from pre-existent literature delivered by him over a span of many years, arguably, the most compelling part of this compendium of ideas is the preface note addressed 'to the reader' which acknowledges any discrepancies that may be found in Gandhi's writing, advising the reader to consider the later published idea on the same subject. Gandhi insists that he, too, is human: an organic being, capable of growth and change (Gandhi 1947, 1). However, the underlying theme of almost all 75 chapters of the book is coloured by the author's aspiration for India to evade the so-called 'ill-effects' of globalization, European culture, and

Western Civilization. This is, debatably, a fierce stand against change itself.

The dichotomy of the Mahatma's ideas about a globalized world and his advocacy of village republics is an intriguing feature of the book, especially when the time period in which it was written is considered. Historian R.G. Collingwood declares contemporary history a myth, and considers a historian's task as a 're-enactment of past thoughts' (Smith 2012). Doing justice to Gandhi's thoughts 'then and now' can only mean that one must study his beliefs in the setting of his time and ours. It is evident that his ideas cannot be assessed in a vacuum, but they are relevant now, more than ever, in the face of a global pandemic and the de-urbanization it has caused in the country.

The representation of Gandhi's views on globalization and villages is a vast ocean of knowledge in the given book. Applying interpretations of these views to contemporary India would prove to be an arduous task that may bear little fruit. It is hence, that this paper deals with Gandhi's writings on these subjects in modern socio-political praxis relevant majorly to this crude juncture in human history brought forth by the present pandemic. Decentralization, migration, and de-urbanization during the COVID-19 pandemic, education and women's safety are examined under a village-globalization lens in this paper.

Globalization and Village Republics: Then and Now

While Ambedkar and Nehru treated the Indian village as a site of oppression and backwardness respectively, to Gandhi, the village was a symbol of authenticity. The former, much like the colonial administrators of their time, neglected the pulse of the Indian village as the soul of the nation and regarded it as an object to be liberated from social evils and transformed into urban suburbs, akin to those found in the West (Jhodka 2002, 3343–3344). We inspect globalization in relation to Indian villages here forth, rather than examining them as separate entities.

The 'village republic' fashioned by Gandhi in his writings is not one he created in idealistic or romantic imagination, but one that had existed as an 'autonomous republic' for eons under various rajahs in the erstwhile kingdoms of what is today called India. It is hence that traditional Indian life is still conceptualized as one that resides in the village, which is regarded as the basic unit of Indian civilization and social structure. However, the hegemony of the Zamindars, Ryotwars and Mahalwars over the village economy only added fuel to the fire that was the plethora of social evils that haunted rural Indian society during colonial and post-colonial times (Jhodka 2002, 3350). Nonetheless, Gandhi, unlike his contemporaries, insisted that India was found, not in her cities but in her (then) 7,00,000 villages. He states that not only was the town dweller ignorant of the plight of his village brethren, he was also their greatest exploiter (Prasad 2001).

The idea of exploitation in the milieu of globalization and village societies is an interesting one to analyze. Towns, in Gandhi's time, were said to be secluded havens of progress and industrialization. Migration, and subsequently urbanization, was a mandate if one aspired to partake in the so-called wonders of the 19th-century industrial revolution that was imposed upon the naïve Indian population by its colonial overlords. While towns thrived and, moreover, cities began to develop as urbane hubs of prosperity, Mother India bore a new child. The newfound Indian middle class emerged as a significant player in the Indian Independence Movement. However, the middle class's substantial influence on the Indian economy made it central to the tussle between upcoming Indian industrialists and the Colonial Raj (Oonk 2015 43–47). The discernible chain of exploitation in 20th-century industrialized India comes off as a nightmare of Marxian proportions as the industrial workers here, akin to their brethren in Russia, were plagued by social alienation—not only from the product and the process, but also from their people and government. However, it is questionable if the license raj born out of the subsequently adopted Soviet-inspired five year development plan model did much good to these industrialists either.

While the industrialists and other 'town-dwellers' exploited the village people, they, in turn, were exploited by the colonizers who 'supported' them, while simultaneously imposing trade restrictions, barriers and unreasonable taxation. This is reflected in Dadabhai Naoroji's 'Drain of Wealth' theory as well, that blamed the tax burden levied on the average Indian and the lack of immigration into India that grossly affected industrialization as some of the many reasons for the failing Indian economy in the moderate era (Naoroji 1901, 628).

This exploitation is characteristic of erstwhile insular colonialists across the globe, and was probably indoctrinated in the Indian mind-set as well, especially in the cities and towns. Gandhi wrote of villages that were deserted for many months every year as villagers went to Bombay to work under 'unhealthy and...immoral conditions' (Jhodka 2002, 3345). Upon return, they would bring with them corruption, drunkenness and disease to the villages. So impressionable was the mind of the lay Indian that exposure to the urban would cause him to absorb habits and behaviour that, perhaps, were ill-suited for him. It is astonishing that this aspect of Indian thought and behaviour stands true even today, and is further explored in this paper under the lens of women's safety.

Surinder Jhodka presents Gandhi's changing points of focus regarding Indian villages in three distinct phases. While, at the outset, the Mahatma concentrated on equating Indian villages to the West, his later writings sought to pit village life against urban life, offering the former as an alternative to modernity, and by extension, globalization. The latter phase encompasses Gandhi's focus on reforming the existing villages in India (Jhodka 2002, 3346). This is a predominant theme in the part of *India of My Dreams* that deals with villages wherein Gandhi describes the idyllic village, outlining acceptable standards of health, sanitation, food and work. The creation of such utopian village republics is greatly dependent on globalization, or lack thereof, especially in the current state of things. This idea is explored further in application to the migrant crisis during the COVID-19 pandemic.

Gandhi's resentment of globalization is established by his challenges to industrialization, which he refers to as a 'curse'. He declares that 'this mania for mass-production is responsible for the world crisis' (Gandhi 1947, 36). However, what Gandhi neglects to express is that the values of liberty and fraternity that he preaches, his learnings from Thoreau and Tolstoy and the idea of democracy itself are all Western inheritances and, for India, products of 18th- and 19th-century globalization. Notably, world-wide anti-globalization movements portray Gandhi as someone who shared their ideology, in spite of the fact that Gandhi, himself, was a 'product of globalization' having been educated in London and having started his political activities in South Africa (Mukherjee). Yet, it would be arrogant to assume that the Mahatma did not realize this. This aspect of the compilation of Gandhi's philosophies is evidence of the multi-layered and multi-faceted nature of his writings and the deliberate omission of specific ideas that may have been a hindrance to the realization of his dreams for India.

Dr. Tabassum Sheikh speaks of 'Gandhi and globalization' in relation to economic development, which she deems unimportant if it fails to uplift the impoverished and those from the lowest rungs of society. Her contention is that each man who contributes to or participates in economic development has the right to reap the benefits of the same and fully realize their fundamental and human rights. Therefore, 'development' that favours the elite's narrow interests in society then, or the already developed global north now, at the cost of denying rights to the underprivileged or the global south respectively, is not development at all (Sheikh). In fact, the application of the Marxian theory of alienation may be fitting to this form of economic un-development, wherein the working class is alienated from the product of its hard work and denied the right to participate in making decisions about the process of production. To this end, Gandhi says that when production and consumption are both localized, one would see the temptation to speed up production at any price disappear (Gandhi 1947, 35). While he insists that such localization would bring an end to all the perils of the modern economic system, this equilibrium of production and consumption is a feature of perfect competition that economists have been vying to establish practically for decades. This is a pertinent example of the aforementioned gap between theory and practise in social science research that *India of My Dreams* has inevitably fallen prey to as well.

Gandhi's characterization of Western industrial society vis-à-vis the Indian village society and economy as 'one man's food is another man's poison' is aptly representative herein as well (Gandhi 1947, 35). Indeed, the marvels of industrialization, globalization and development have been incredibly gainful for Western civilization in the colonial and post-colonial periods, at the cost of nurturing Indian village economies. Many a study about the decline of economies in colonies around the globe has indicated that 'the white man's burden' was a façade that masked the undertaking of mass plundering by European colonizers and overlords. Of these, the most eminent in recent times is Dr. Shashi Tharoor's speech titled 'Britain Does Owe Reparations' delivered at the Oxford Union. Herein, Dr. Tharoor illustrates how India was governed for the benefit of Britain and that the latter's rise was financed by the depredation of India. Gandhi's charkha and khadi, which Nehru called 'the livery of India's freedom,' are symbols of protest against British industrialization which led to the complete fall of the traditional Indian handloom. The entire premise of toxic colonialism in contemporary times can be equated to this aspect of 19th- and 20th-century industrialization—and while the colonialist, under his garb of nobly endeavouring to civilize the native people of the colony, fooled the masses into serving his every wish and command, the burden of silently accepting and painstakingly managing his off-cuts fell on the poor colony. Needless to say, this is a widely prevalent phenomenon that can be observed in most erstwhile colonies and present-day third world nations alike, including Vietnam, which was a French Colony and The Philippine Islands: Rudyard Kipling's inspiration for his poem titled 'The White Man's Burden'.

The British colony of India was an agrarian economy. Over 75% of the Indian population was made of agriculturists who lived in villages in the 1900s. Inadvertently, these village dwellers faced the brunt of Britain's aforementioned conscious de-industrialization of India. In this light, Gandhi's emphasis on village industries and mill industries and discouragement of the passive or active exploitation of villagers was highly relevant to his time. Mechanization, according to Gandhi, is good when the hands are few but evil when there are more hands than are required for the work, like in India (Gandhi 1947, 101).

Herein, one can recognize the visionary that Gandhi was as India, in the present-day, is plagued by the ills of disguised unemployment, which is most rampant in the primary sector in India today. To Gandhi, decentralization and focus on the village republic could solve many of the problems that we still face today. Hence, it is only fitting to analyze Gandhi's ideas of decentralization from the 20th century and ascertain if the same could be viable in 21st-century India.

Decentralization and Public Policy in Globalized India

Economic development, in Gandhi's eyes, would only be possible if the state achieved complete decentralization. To him, 'independence must begin at the bottom' and so, decentralization was essential to the establishment and the sustenance of the village republic system. In 'Non-violent Economy', Gandhi insists that the establishment of said non-violent economy is impossible if the gap between the rich and the impoverished persists and advocates dignity of labour. He states that India must adopt a policy of decentralization to evolve along non-violent lines, and in doing so proposes a system of socialism that he advertises as a 'Ram Rajya', commonly perceived as the ideal form of society in Hindu philosophy (Gandhi 1947, 72–74).

Gandhi's evident fear of economic divide between the top 1% and bottom 20% or so of society, and his distress regarding the lack of dignity of labour destroying society and economy are more than justified in the 20th-century setting (Gandhi 1947, 75–79). The discussed trend of migration to cities and the growing perils of a capitalized, industrialized economy led to the creation of an Indian bourgeoisie. While this new Indian industrialist class flourished in the city lights, the failed crops in the drought-stricken villages pushed farming families over the edge. A grand divide was born. The then-town dweller was ostentatiously wealthy, whilst the average farmer was impoverished and hungry (Madhumati 2011, 63–64).

The famines of 1896–1897 and 1899–1900, both caused by drought, struck particularly hard on the Indian village economy, but hardly affected the towns. However, in context of creating a 'Non-violent Economy' in Gandhi's Ram Rajya (Gandhi 1947, 72–75), one must note the controversies surrounding the officially recorded mortality rates of the Bihar famine of 1966 and the Maharashtra famine of 1972–73. Here, it is pertinent to question the socialistic ideals that were adopted by Nehru, and further promulgated by Indira Gandhi, since the bureaucratic and institutional apathy exhibited by the government during these famines is arguably nothing short of violence in the economy. Moreover, the present politico-economic standing of a post-industrialized and largely centralized India is characteristic of what the Mahatma feared for India's future. The lack of decentralization and the limitations and shortcomings of the comparatively recently introduced system of local self-governance, along with the legacies of the licence raj have marred the Indian economy with rampant corruption, gross economic inequality and most recently, the risk of foreign invasion in urbanized India that Gandhi seemed to dread the most (Sharma, Singh and Singh 2008, 729–731).

A reconstruction of the entire social order is recommended in the writings as the way to equal distribution (Gandhi 1947, 75–78). While this system does not deny each man what he wants, it provides him only with how much he needs. This was the case for the Indian middle and lower classes who sustained themselves on the ration administered by the government for many decades post-independence. However, present-day India, with its system of 'federal governance with a central bias' is a confused, yet overly centralized economy when looked at through a Gandhian lens (Chakroborty and Pandey 2009, 10). This is evident in the Indian State's handling of the COVID-19 pandemic, for while the centre issued a certain set of guidelines, each state issued other guidelines that rarely ratified the former. Interestingly, the centre, in its guidelines for September 2020, censured this behaviour by mandating that no state shall issue separate orders contrary to the ones released by it. On the other hand, such a system is essential in a land as vast and varied as India, not just in this scenario but in all situations. Then again, one cannot ignore the inherent contradiction with regard to centralization and, indeed, de-centralization herein.

The recent uproar regarding the Central Board for Secondary Education's next edition of textbooks for its higher secondary social science students was majorly concerned with the elimination of concepts like federalism and decentralization from the texts. For many, this move was seen as an aggressive shift towards a more centralized system of governance in the future, departing from the legacy of the Gandhian values discussed here.

Wilfred Wellock takes an interesting stand on the internationalism of decentralization in 'Is there a Nonviolent Road to a Peaceful World?' wherein he submits that a world peace order could be established by following a two-sided revolution leading to personal resistance of all war and nuclear armaments, along with a social and industrial decentralization that fulfils each individual's right to responsibility, expression and cooperative participation in an industry (Wellock, 261–264). One may identify the roots of this interpretation, once again, in Gandhi's counsel on running a village industry. The 'Khadi mentality' speaks of decentralization of production and distribution of the necessities of life and the simultaneous nationalization of heavy industry, striking a balance while also providing 'choice before labour' and fundamental worker's rights to the village workforce (Gandhi 1947, 106).[74]

The COVID-19 Migrant Crisis and the Village Republic System

The focus on the village workforce and its rights manifests in Gandhi's discourse on unemployment and migration as well, both in *India of My Dreams* and in *My Experiments with Truth*. It is thought-provoking to assess the continuing dominance of the migrant population in the urban economy and the psycho-social relevance of migration in colonial India and in the 21st-century modern nation.

In keeping with Dadabhai Naoroji's assessment of the economy in 1867 (Naoroji 1901), migration into India was sparse at this time. On the other hand, emigration was widespread. In *My Experiments with Truth*, the Smuts-Gandhi agreement and Gandhi's general displeasure with the system of indentured emigration are brought to light along with his activism for the immediate abolition of indentured labour (Gandhi 1927, 447–450). UNESCO observes that the first Indian indentured immigration was recorded in the 1830s. Nearly 12 lakh Indians were relocated to 19 countries over a span of 100 years since

---

[74] In *India of My Dreams*, Gandhi speaks of tanning industries and other industries as separate from the khadi industry. He illustrates the practical implementation of his ideas under the heading 'how to begin'.

then (UNESCO). Gandhi made his first petition against this 'semi-slavery' in 1894. His actions, at Madan Mohan Malviya's behest, warranted a blanket ban on the indentured labour system that was levied by the English in 1917 (Gandhi 1927, 447–450).

On the other hand, his disapproval of migration from villages to towns and cities is also evident in his many writings. His model of village republics promulgated in 'The Gospel of Swadeshi' promotes the inculcation of an attitude for every Indian to prefer an indigenous good to a foreign-made one, and moreover, a good produced by a village industry to one made in the mills. However, he does not wish for the extinction of landlords and capitalists, who facilitate most migration (Gandhi 1947, chapter 31). In 'Class War', Gandhi writes that he wishes for a transformation in the existing relationship between the capitalists or landlords and the masses into something purer and healthier as the idea of a class war does not appeal to him (Gandhi 1947, chapter 8). However, from his writings, one can infer that Gandhi wants labour, and indeed good labour, to be brought to the labourer who must continue living in his sovereign, independent village republic. Astonishingly, the idea of bringing the labour to the labourer has taken tangible form as the Work from Home policy that global society has been forced to adopt in the present pandemic. Unfortunately, however, such policies in 21st-century India are financially viable only for the upper and upper middle class and deprive the lower class that migrant labourers belong to of financial, social and psychological support.

The Hindu BusinessLine, in June 2020, looked back at Gandhi's 'gram swaraj' in light of the migrant crisis that emerged due to the spread of COVID-19. It called for an independent village with self-governance that was built on the principles of sustainability. Indeed, the exodus of the migrants and their plight pushed the nation to realize that these workers are the backbone of the modern Indian economy. Many thousands of these labourers, stranded in cities without money or transport, began making long inter-state journeys home on foot during the global pandemic (Chandurkar 2020). The World Economic Forum reported that India had 139 million internal migrants in 2017. In the same report, the forum urged that these internal migrants 'must not be forgotten' (Krishnavatar 2017). COVID-19 has reminded India of the role that migrant labourers play in our society, despite their low income sustenance. Adopting Gandhian socialism and de-centralized village republic governance would certainly have benefitted this section of the population greatly in the past 73 years. However, sustaining a village republic economy in a globalized world would have proved to be a challenge in the long run.

Feminism and Village Globalization: Bane of the Glocalized Indian Village

Once again, Gandhi admired the Indian village as a symbol of authenticity. The village republic was, once, the innocent playground of traditional Indian life and the cradle of culture, values, customs, languages, clothing and administrative systems, often unique to each specific village. Pre-colonial villages were independent units, governed with minimum intervention from the monarchical seats of power. The village heads held legislative and judicial functions and while there was rampant caste and gender-based bias in society, these were the realities of those times and must not be judged in the light of present socio-cultural progress. However, the tenacity of the village culture in compromising with certain 'traditions' mandates criticism in the era of 'glocalization', which takes into consideration both global and local practises.

The advent of globalization was fatal to the independent realm of village culture. The emergence of the global village diminished the sovereignty of the local one. The penetration of Western sociological thought, the values of liberty, equality, fraternity and democracy were borrowed hand-me-downs acquired by modern India, worn out, and lent in the form of shreds to glocalized village systems. It is no wonder, in this scenario, that the village society became prone to the sociological theory of culture lag. Acquired knowledge of modern, Western ideas that were pitted against age-old traditional values imparted by misinterpreted religious texts in addition to the arrival of modern technology proved lethal to one particular section of society: women.

A glaring piece of evidence of this phenomenon is the Indian saga of prenatal ultrasounds, popularly known as the sex determination test. While Indian customs entailed traditions like dowry and child marriage that led to a preference for the birth of a male child who could 'carry the family name forward' and simultaneously earn for the family, technological advancements facilitated the opportunity to completely eliminate the 'burden' of the female child by murdering her before birth itself. Female foeticide became so rampant by 1994 that a legislative ban on prenatal ultrasounds was imposed in the country. Amrita Tripathi has traced the history of the male-female ratio in the nation alongside the introduction of affordable ultrasound technology in India. She notes that while in 1982, the female to male ratio was 962:1000, it dropped to 945 females in 1991, 927 in 2001 and 918 in the 2011 census (Tripathi 2016). The preference for male children resulting in this skewed ratio of male to female population in the country is notably documented in 'No Country for Young Girls' funded by the United Nations Population Fund that portrays the struggle of a young woman who must choose between staying with a man who does not wish to have a girl child or leaving him to live a life of difficulties in abject poverty. Indeed, the ever-dipping male female ratio only substantiates the claim that India is no country for young girls.[75]

---

[75] 'Son Rise' and 'The Unwanted' are more documentaries that have been made on the subject of gender ratio in India. However, despite widespread media coverage, the sex ratio has only depreciated over the years and globalization has not aided women.

Here, one must note that the gruesome 2020 Hyderabad vet gang rape case was compared to the 2012 Nirbhaya gang rape case that made world headlines at the time because of the socio-economic and geographical backgrounds of the rapists. The fact that the alleged and convicted rapists respectively were migrants from villages was highlighted by the media. The underlying message herein is another proof of the pervasiveness of culture lag in glocalized Indian society. Free access to pornography and child pornography, in addition to sexualization of children and the sensationalized and grossly misogynistic depiction of the 'woman of the city' in Indian films seem to have birthed misconceptions about 'modern' city life in the mind of the impressionable village dweller. These are products of globalization that have penetrated the narrow-minded outlook of traditional village society, constructing an unsafe environment for women and children.

This complicated web of socio-cultural realities conform to Gandhian ideas to some extent. However, the internet would have permeated the hypothetical 21st-century village republic just as easily as it has the 21st-century globalized republic. In fact, what little gender equality that India can boast of would have been negligible without globalization.[76]

The looming truth of the 21st century, as reflected in the 2011 census, is that female foeticide and, by extension, dowry and child marriage are still extremely prevalent in Indian

---

[76] At this time, the divide between the so-called city and village mentalities is so great that for the 'modern' city-dweller, exposed to the full brunt of globalization, the very notion that sex on the pretext of marriage can be awarded with legal punishment seems outlandish. On the other hand, in more conservative societies, sex before marriage is a punishable offense and, moreover, a sin. The difference in opinion on such an essential question of law runs so deep in the globalized urban and the conservative rural, that one speculates that each village republic, having a separate ideology, would require not just a separate civil code but also a separate criminal code, making the Indian Constitution itself, along with the Indian Penal Code and the Civil Procedure Code, etc., null and void.

society. Moreover, *The Hindu* noted that the coronavirus-induced lockdown led to a significant rise in the cases of child marriage with more than a 100 cases between mid-March and July occurring in the Mysore district alone (Khan 2020). One can only imagine the hidden realities of rape within families as the country celebrated a drop in reported rape cases during the lockdown. Reports suggest that cases of domestic violence, which is often a consequence of unmet dowry demands, are also at an all-time high at this time. This is evidence to the fact that a glocalized system of education is the need of the hour in order to combat these social evils in 21st-century physical India that mentally resides in the 18th century.

Assessing the National Education Policy (2020): A Glocalized Lens

Globalization is always relevant to education. Education is always relevant to the village lifestyle. Gandhi believes that education should be capable of connecting children of both cities and villages to all that is 'best and lasting in India.' He opines that physical, intellectual and moral development should be the objects of basic education. Moreover, he states that all education must be imparted in the provincial language and that college education should be revolutionized to fit national necessities. He recommends practical learning and apprenticeship alongside theoretical studies, especially at the side of certified luminaries in the concerned fields. Additionally, despite his belief that knowledge of religious books is no equivalent of that of religion, he makes a powerful case for the involvement of religious studies, if not in the school curriculum, then as a co-curricular or extra-curricular undertaking. Lastly, he strongly wishes to oust any influence of the West from the Indian Education System (Gandhi 1947, 178–188).

Fascinatingly, these are some of the major aspects of the revolution of education that seems to be set in motion with the advent of the National Education Policy (Government of India 2020). In fact, the National Education Policy is a champion of Gandhi's views on education. However, the imposition of the provincial language as a medium of instruction, the incorporation of religious studies in the curriculum and the introduction of apprenticeship at the primary school level have all been questioned by the critics of this new education policy as well. It is evident to the city-dwelling, English-speaking privileged student that being educated in a provincial language shall be depredatory to one's opportunities to work in a world that is dominated by English speakers. The measure of success in the 21st-century globalized world is to be gainfully employed by multinational corporations or international organizations after being educated outside one's third world nation, and this is true of both city and village dwellers. These modern aspirations shall be gruesomely hit if the average school-goer is deprived of his English education, even if he finds that being educated in the provincial language is more convenient at that time. Even so, one must not assume that learning in the provincial language shall necessarily be easier, more so when one considers the high numbers of internal migrants in the country.

Next, the incorporation of religious studies in the curriculum as a mode of moral education (that has also been encouraged by Gandhi), while excellent on paper, raises questions about the capability of those who impart such knowledge and their commitment, not to secularism but to pluralism, for Gandhi would also agree with the fact that pluralism is the most fundamental feature of a truly glocal society.

Lastly, in a third world nation like India wherein the standard of both education and skills of teachers are questioned, and where a negligible portion of the national budget is pledged towards education, the layman has been found asking himself if the National Education Policy, especially in terms of its ultramodern ideas like primary school apprenticeship, could stand the tests of lack of funds and incompetency of educational authorities.

Concluding Notes: Endeavouring to Provide Solutions

'To the preliterate man of integral vision a fable is what we call a major scientific truth...our own self-amputations can today provide the beginnings of a new science of man and technology.'

—McLuhan, *War and Peace in the Global Village*

Gandhi's writings indicate that he understood the consequence of a Western form of industrialization as destructive of Indian society. Such destruction, in his views, would purge decentralized rural industries and effectively obliterate the village lifestyle. The emphasis he lays on reviving, improving, encouraging and conserving various facets of the village republics effectively rejects centralization, globalization, industrialization and, by extension, technology and progress. Of course, Gandhi probably never imagined the impact of technology on the village republics. Foreseeably, technology, if nothing else, would have coaxed these village republics out of their sovereign, independent cocoons, only a few decades later than globalization primarily did.

A systemic revolution, akin to the National Education Policy, must be initiated in order to pander to the socio-economic and political issues born out of globalization and industrialization. Moreover, the environmental impacts of the same must be tackled in a mindful manner, keeping all the concerned stakeholders in mind while making any decision and consulting them while framing laws. This can only be done by mastering the necessary skills of management and governance. Hence, the root to all solutions can be traced back to reforming the system and standard of education being imparted in the country.

The National Education Policy is not a liability, but an opportunity to impart these values to future lawmakers and citizens. In keeping with Gandhi's belief that college education should be designed with national interests in mind, this new policy has already shown the inclination to impart humanitarian and sociological lessons to all students. Moreover, the policy's intention to focus on the positive use of technology can be a turning point in guiding the youth of the nation to make meaningful use of technology and the internet of things, lest technology itself be the ruin of the 21st century. More importantly, a focus on making young Indians educated and not just literate must be adopted in order to truly host progress on the various fronts discussed in this paper.

While it may be too late to completely reform the structure of Indian society to accommodate Gandhi's village republics, there is still the opportunity of investing time, money and concentration on the villages themselves. The social evils discussed herein are still widespread in rural India and have proved to be immune to the educational aspects of globalization. Hence, the most feasible solution to the impacts of industrialization and globalization in the Indian village is a reformed, all-inclusive, modern, comprehensive, practical and pluralistic educational system.

References

Chakroborty, Bidyut and Rajendra Pandey. 2009. *Indian Government and Politics*. New Delhi: SAGE Publications.

Chandurkar, Dharmendra. 2020. Migrant crisis calls for revival of Gandhi's Gram Swaraj. *Hindu BusinessLine*, June 1.

Gandhi, M.K. 1947. *India of My Dreams*. Delhi: Rajpal and Sons.

Gandhi, M.K. 1927. Abolition of Indentured Emigration. In *My Experiments with Truth*, edited by Shriman Narayan. Ahmedabad. https://www.mkgandhi.org/autobio/chap135.htm.

Government of India, Ministry of Human Resource Development. 2020. National Education Policy. https://www.education.gov.in/sites/upload_files/mhrd/files/NEP_Final_English_0.pdf

Jhodka, Surinder S. 2002. Nation and Village: Images of Rural India in Gandhi, Nehru and Ambedkar. *Economic and Political Weekly* 37 (32): 3343–3353. https://www.jstor.org/stable/4412466.

Khan, Liaqh A. 2020. Sharp rise in child marriages during lockdown. *The Hindu*. August 18.

Madhumati, M. 2011. The Gandhian Approach to Rural Development. *IJCRT* 1, no. 2. http://www.ijcrt.org/papers/IJCRT1133061.pdf.

Mukherjee, Aruni. Gandhi and Globalisation. *Articles: About Mahatma Gandhi.* Sevagram Ashram. https://www.gandhiashramsevagram.org/gandhi-articles/gandhi-and-globalisation.php. (Accessed September 15, 2020).

Naoroji, Dadabhai. 1901. *Poverty and Un-British Rule in India.* Ministry of Information and Broadcasting.

Oonk, Gijsbert. 2015. The Emergence of Indigenous Industrialists in Calcutta, Bombay and Ahmedabad 1850-1947. *Business History Review* 88 (1): 43–72. http://doi.org/10.1017/S0007680513001414.

Prasad, Rajendra. 2001. Gandhi, Globalization and Quality of Life: A Study in the Ethics of Development. *Gandhi Marg* 22, No. 2. https://www.mkgandhi.org/articles/gandhi_globalization.htm.

'Records of Indian Indentured Labourers.' Memory of the World. *United Nations Educational, Scientific and Cultural Organisation.* http://www.unesco.org/new/en/communication-and-information/memory-of-the-world/register/full-list-of-registered-heritage/registered-heritage-page-7/records-of-the-indian-indentured-labourers/. (Accessed September 14, 2020).

Sharma, Krishnavatar. 2017. India has 139 million internal migrants. They must not be forgotten. *World Economic Forum*, October 1, 2017. https://www.weforum.org/agenda/2017/10/india-has-139-million-internal-migrants-we-must-not-forget-them/. (Accessed September 14, 2020).

Sharma, Sanjeev K., Sarbjeet Singh and Sarabjeet Singh. 2008. Gandhian Strategies for Democratic Decentralisation and Development: Dimensions on Rural Development, Gram Swaraj and Sarvodaya. *The Indian Journal of Political Science* 69 (4): 727–744. http://www.jstor.com/stable/41856465.

Sheikh, Tabassum. Gandhi and Globalisation. In *Gandhi in the New Millennium-Issues and Challenges* https://www.mkgandhi.org/articles/gandhi-and-globalisation.html.

Smith, R.B. 2012. R.G. Collingwood's Definition of Historical Knowledge. *History of European Ideas* 33 (3): 350–371. https://doi.org/10.1016/j.histeuroideas.2006.11.010

Tripathi, Amrita. 2016. Sex determination in India: Doctors tell their side of the story. *Scroll.in.* April 13. https://scroll.in/article/805064/sex-determination-in-india-doctors-tell-their-side-of-the-story.

Wellock, Wilfred. Is there a Nonviolent Road to a Peaceful World? In *Gandhi—His Relevance for our Times*, edited by G. Ramachandran and T.K. Mahadevan, 260–267. New Delhi: Gandhi Peace Foundation.

SPACE, PLACE AND *PEACE*

Engaging with Mahatma Gandhi in the Discursive Alternative

Aparna Phadke

Introduction: Referencing the Context

The contemporary time(s) are marked with increasing complexities in socio-cultural and politico-economic structures. There has been aggravation of several issues threatening the very existence of human societies. The developmental discourses that have been extant so far work on the principles of *capital*ism. Here when I say *capital*ism, I mean to refer to the 'invisible hand' present in all political regimes. At least, the contemporary time(s) do not exhibit any substantial difference in attending the current socio-cultural and politico-economic problems. Why I choose to talk simultaneously about development and geopolitics is because the contemporary discourses on development and geopolitics are intrinsically connected with each other and revolve around the workings of capital. So it is the developmental geopolitics that needs to be scrutinized in the light of the current situation of economic crisis and associated consequences. There had been critical discourses in analyzing the 'development geopolitics' in the late 1950s which remained prominent till almost the last decade of the 20th century. Raul Prebisch in the late 1950s, Andre Gunder Frank (1971), Paul Baran (1957), and Paul Sweezy (1966) all contributed to the concept of 'underdevelopment' and theories of dependency while exploring the link between political agendas and developmental discourses. The classical and neoclassical economic theories on development remained mainstream, leading to marginalization of every other analysis of developmental geopolitics.

The 1980s witnessed a forceful shift in the perspectives on development. Several national governments especially from the Global South were forced to realize that international capital flows were a must for economic development. Interestingly, it wasn't the World Bank or International Monetary Fund that was involved in pushing these agendas but the United Nations that abruptly hijacked 'development' as their prime objective. The abrupt shift was justified by interlinking 'Peace and Security' as the prime objective with achievement of better levels of economic and social development. Following the same, the Millennium Development Goals or MDGs were designed, keeping socio-economic development at their core. Ironically, a supranational body that was meant for maintaining peace and security got converted into a puppet regime and started serving the interests of international capital. The resolution passed in 1997 by the UN reiterated the need to take measures that have larger implications on economic development with international capital as a primary driver (United Nations 1997). In the year 2015, the UN declared that the goal of poverty eradication had been met by most of the countries as it claimed that more than one billion people had been lifted from extreme poverty worldwide (UN website, accessed in 2020). Following the same, in the next step, the Sustainable Development Goals (SDGs) were introduced where there is no mention of poverty eradication and associated key issues. With this backdrop, now the UN is pushing the agendas of sustainable development, thus falsifying the very objectives of economic and social development. It is interesting to note that such a shift in the policy of the UN is responsible for intensifying the contradictions in the national policies on development and environment as they are set in the times of neoliberal governance and shaped under finance capitalism.

With the economic aftershocks of neoliberal reforms and intensification of global economic integration, anti-globalization trends are already creating space for themselves in developed economies, for example, Brexit. With extremist regimes in the US, Great Britain, China and other European countries, there have been efforts to reframe the regulations on visas and citizenship status. All kinds of restrictions on trade and commerce interactions are in the pipeline. The importance of 'local' is gaining much more attention than ever. With the recent COVID-19 pandemic, the world could observe a complete set back to the economy. There has been a re-realization of geography and self-reliance. To revive this economic situation, we need various resources, a strong local network of inter-spatial linkages and political vision.

What especially, does India have in its account currently? Our resources are already depleted and we are on the verge of complete exhaustion of some of the very important energy resources. Our environmental protection policies and 'development' policies contradict each other and stand compromised on the quality of the environment. There is a complete stagnancy at the level of the economy with all-time low GDP i.e. -23.9 in quarter 1 (*The Economic Times* 2020). An estimated 122 million people lost their jobs in the Coronavirus pandemic (*The Hindu* 2020). At the social and societal level we continue to experience complete anarchy with the rise of post-modern and neoliberal regimes setting the narrow agendas of identity politics over real concerns of socio-economic and ecological development. Nonetheless, the policies on economic development also emanate from capitalist market ideology and continue to exclude everything else that does not fit into the capitalist logic. This includes the poorest of the poor, the children, women, farmers, workers and countless numbers of people who are not consumers or taxpayers. The COVID-19 pandemic has made the situation far worse and has witnessed a complete wiping out of the 'progress' so far. Ironically, to deal with this situation, almost all governments are falling back on options of localization. Recently, there has been a policy envisioned by the Central Government, titled 'Aatmanirbhar Bharat' launched on 12th May 2020, whose five pillars are 'economy, infrastructure, system, vibrant demography and demand' (Ministry of Finance, 12th July 2020). It is an effort towards self-reliance and localization, as per what has been described by the Ministry.

So we are back to square one—1947 and Gandhi's vision of self-reliant villages. It is Gandhian economic principles that would be the most appropriate for making India self-reliant in terms of economy.

Development and Geopolitics

What is development is the key question today. Capital-centric economic and societal development is equivalent to materialistic growth and product consumption. How much one consumes decides his worth in the market economy. Noam Chomsky in his book *Manufacturing Consent* (1988) suggests that the market has the deepest influence on our everyday life. The circuits of consumption, production and distribution imply more or less the economics of profit maximization over satisfying the basic needs and demands of people, especially the masses. It is obvious to see that the economy is subservient to the capitalist interest and occupies a peripheral position in serving the interests of the masses. Capital continues to be the soul of economic organization whether it is founded on capitalist, communist or socialist ideologies. None of the political ideologies has ever created an alternative to capital. These three economic and political systems may differ in their approaches vis-a-vis distribution of profit to different sections of society. But ultimately, reaching the poorest of the poorer has remained equally difficult for all the systems. The geopolitics—structures that are set to work again in the interest of international capital—basically capitalizes on development that has 'creative destruction' (Schumpeter 1950) at its core. The global geopolitical structures and international relations have been reconstituted frequently, following the vested interests of the developed economies in resources, territories and people. China as a major power now, too, emerges as equally expansionist, authoritarian and exploitative. The world system theory proposed by Wallerstein (1974) fits perfectly here. It suggests that the world is a single entity having several hierarchical levels denoting specific power parity and with exploitation as its integral component. All the countries are positioned in core, semi-peripheral and peripheral positions depending on their politico-economic status. They may change their positions as per the altering developmental and geopolitical scenarios. Both upward and downward mobility are possible. It is interesting to see how in the past three decades, the frequency of altering the political equations between several countries has been accelerating under the regime of international finance capital. The formation of BRICS, for example, is the best example of such altering geopolitical equations. The recent changes in the geopolitical relations of India with its neighbouring countries and their closeness to China is another example of such temporary geopolitical structures that are largely guided by vested interests. Though it is claimed that there has been no war since World War II, the period since then has been witnessing several 'peace efforts' in the form of 'war on terror'; 'saving people from the authoritarian regime'; 'peace army' and so on. These 'peace efforts', ironically, take the form of military interventions, stirring political instability against unwanted governments, supporting the anti-government groups and organizations and so on. The dominant nations from every continent have probably applied all these methods to regain regional control and domination. India, too, has not shied away from them. The killing race for territorial domination in the name of financial aid and help, economic growth and so on has already killed and uprooted billions of people from their everyday lives. 'No direct war between superpowers' cannot be equated to peace (Gregory 2010).

In this backdrop, what is the status of India is another key question. India spent almost 71.1 billion dollars in 2019, making it world's third biggest military spender (Shukla 2020). India spends only 3 percent of its budget on education. Is it affordable for a developing country like India to spend so much on defence? Can peacekeeping efforts be made in an innovatively creative manner that would balance out all odds? These would be policies that keep peace as their essential core. Could India emerge as a leader that can create space for peaceful international deliberations? Here the conceptualization of peace by Gandhi becomes most significant as he believed international relations could also be governed by the principles of nonviolence. He further proposed that 'there is no path to peace, peace is the path'. I would extend this by saying 'peace is space' (Shukla 2020).

Geography, Gandhi and Space

In critical geographical praxis, 'space' is one of the most widely used constructs to understand the interrelationship between people, nature, resources, economies, cultures and social structures as spaces are the productive reflections of their amalgamations. That further suggests that spaces are mirrors of socio-cultural, economic and political amalgamations at a particular time and get represented explicitly in a particular place. The major determinants of any socio-cultural space, thus, would be people, communities and structures. What a particular space would contain will be decided by the process of production of space. Lefebvre (1996) explains the production of space as though 'being' and 'becoming'. He also suggests a triad to decode the production of space—perceived, conceived and lived spaces. The spatial approach reinstates space as a dynamic element. Most of the conventional geographers look at 'time' as a decider. The debate goes on around how to place space and time vis-à-vis each other. For many, time is active, dynamic, decisive, hence masculine, whereas spaces are passive, static, dependent, hence feminine. The narrative of 'everything changes with time' dominates the understanding of any change, whether social change or political change. Interestingly, in the process, one conveniently ignores the conditions of 'spatial fixity' where in the absence of any stimulus, irrespective of 'passing time', the spaces remain unchanged. But spaces are not passive and do not wait for 'time' to transform them. There are volatile forces, processes and influential people that shape any space and punctuate imprints of those changes in time. How the space has evolved over the period of time will decide what fundamental ethics have been put to work, produce and 'run' that space. So what constitutes the socio-political space and which political ideologies are shaping the political spatial mending and so on, becomes vital. For instance, the entire history of world politics is dominated by the discourses of expansionism, domination and control. From a geographical perspective, 'peace' has always been equated with a 'no war' situation, putting peace as a secondary element of political space. The very secondary position of peace in geopolitical studies engulfs the discourse on peace and shifts it to the conflict resolution mode and weakens the independent thinking on centralising peace in the alternate discourse. In fact, peace research as a discipline has been polarized as much as peace as a concept (Swisspeace 2014).

It could be interesting to see how Gandhi dealt with space in his several proposals when it comes to development and geopolitics. The analysis of his models of development as well as international relations suggest that he firmly believed in the continuous production and reproduction of space at various levels of individual and collective life.

It is the coherence and interconnectedness of all principles he proposed in his lifetime that allows us to have Gandhian principles at the core of an alternate discourse on development and geopolitics. For example, he has given tremendous emphasis on mental space that includes ethical and moral training not just to an individual but also its application in different situations and varying scales. As suggested by Rathi (accessed in 2020), Gandhi continues to emphasize a creation of mental space that would encourage the moral regeneration of an individual and

FIGURE 1: Conceptualizing Production of Space through Gandhian Principles

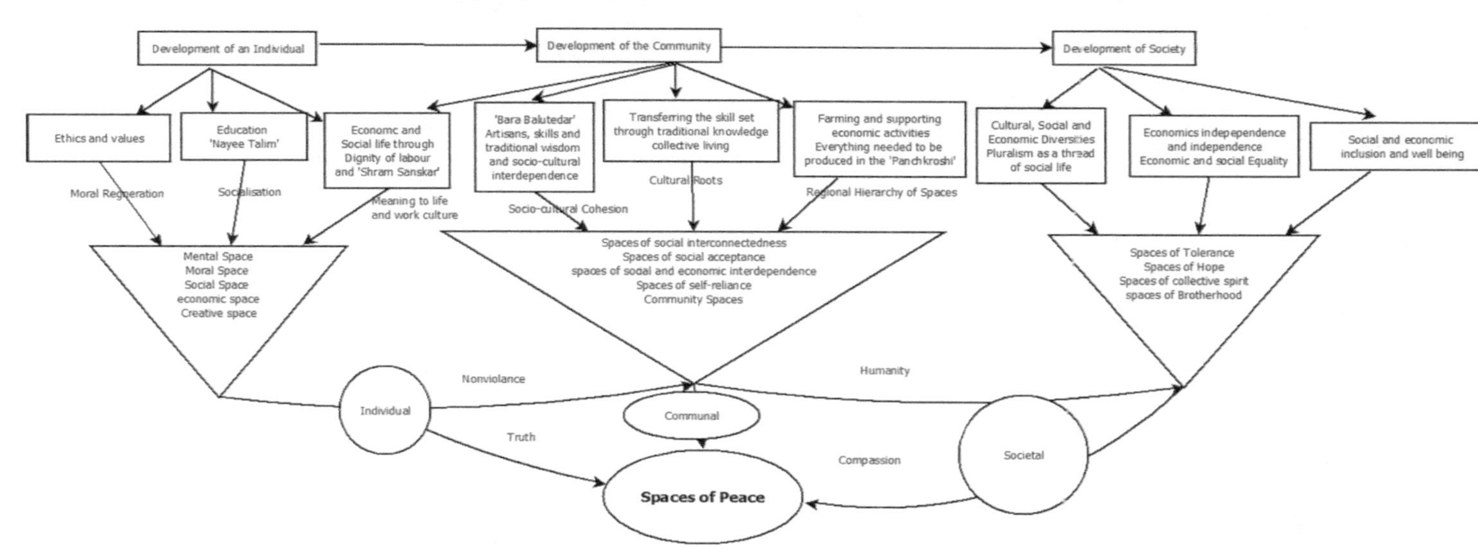

imbibe non-violent values. The creation of 'ethical moral space' thus not only remains the core of individual moral regeneration but also implied in the larger socio-political spaces at the level of community and society. His emphasis on dignity of labour and 'Shram Sanskaras' to be imbibed in formal education suggests his keen interest in rebuilding a society that respects all kinds of work and there is no caste identity attached to it. His emphasis on education through 'Shram Sanskar' and insistence on developing skill sets pertaining to 'Bara Balutedar' (12 types of artisans interdependent on each other in rural settings) in students got reflected through the experiment of 'Nayi Talim' in school education. The moral education through *My Experiments with Truth* and philosophy of nonviolence and 'simple living, higher thinking', were the key elements in reaching the level of self-actualization and spiritual intimacy. Finally, his directives on the natural environment, 'The earth, the air, the land and the water are not an inheritance from our forefathers but on loan from our children. So we have to hand it over to them at least as it was handed over to us' (Koushik 2021). The same would instill the values of social equality in children. There can be simultaneous economic space generated through the internal interdependence of various artisans, farmers and other elements of villages to create a self-sustaining and self-reliant local economic space. He expected the same would promote social and economic interdependence that would keep the village society together and encourage collective life. The creative space would allow people to engage in the development of appropriate technologies and sharpen the traditional skill sets to solve the problems that are locally created. Such social and economic cohesion of different communities will lead to the development of a healthy society. The core principles of these societies would be socio-cultural pluralism, respect for diversity, tolerance, acceptance and nonviolence to achieve a creative, truthful and peaceful individual and societal life at the end. His firm belief in 'simple living and high thinking' can also guide society to reorientation on how to 'consume'.

Reconstruction of 'peace' and 'space' must be simultaneous; in fact, both should be intrinsically linked, as Gandhi suggests. With the advent of globalization, there has been, on a massive scale, abrupt, hurried and leap-frog patterns of social transformation. Probably at every scale there is a rush to grab the maximum. We continue to equate joy, happiness and peace with materialistic consumption—more or less—which is a passive mode of consumption. There is a complete lack of creativity and originality in what we do as we have been trained to believe that consumption is creativity. Peace needs to be constructed in spaces by integrating and interweaving the mental peace at individual level with socio-economic peace at community level and political peace at societal level—as per one of Gandhi's sayings, 'there is a sufficiency in the world for man's need but not for man's greed'.

The model of holistic development had already been offered by Mahatma Gandhi. His ardent follower Vinoba Bhave successfully moderated the Bhoodan Movement. Experiments rooted in Gandhian vision are success stories, like Popatrao Pawar and the experiment of Hivarebajar, Mendha Lekha, rights to forests and empowerment of scheduled tribes, Vanrai by Mohan Dharia, etc. Gandhian principles become extremely important here in societal regeneration because of his emphasis on the individual's moral and ethical development.

Interestingly, the principles with which he suggests a reconstruction of society at local levels, are the same principles he has suggested to attain world peace. The geopolitical world structure is so complex that one may be confused by how such simple principles can solve the complex conflicts and war-like situations. Rathi suggests that Gandhi envisioned a World Federation or International League founded on the principles of non-violence and international cooperation. He also expected the proposed world federation to maintain a nonviolence policy where the soldiers of this force would bear no arms (Rathi, accessed in 2020).

Secondly, Gandhi believed in the attainment of peace through establishing economic equality as the 'master-key' to a nonviolent world order. Peace must have its roots in fraternity rather than in fear. He believed that global peace could not be possible unless the exploitative world economic and social hierarchy is replaced by a new world that is committed to nonviolence and an exploitation-free social order (Rathi, accessed in 2020).

Nazareth, in his speech delivered at the National Defence College, Delhi, in 2008, expresses the views of Antony Copley who stated that Gandhian-style resistance to apartheid was part of the wider struggle against colonialism and neo-colonialism. He also sheds light on the influence of Gandhi on Nehru, who was behind the Non-Aligned Movement. On international relations, when Gandhi was asked about India's relations with Great Britain, he had answered that India could be completely cut off from the Empire but not from the British nation. 'I would prefer an equal relationship with Britain' (Fischer 1954).

There have been many struggles and freedom movements that got inspiration from Gandhian principles of nonviolence. Nelson Mandela, Martin Luther King and many others have engaged themselves in promoting peace as the core of geopolitical relations. Many environmental movements also have their roots in Gandhian philosophy. Right from the Chipko movement to the recent Aarey movement, the young generation too have followed satyagraha as a way of exhibiting opposition to the decision of state governments to cut down trees. Internationally the German Green party has acknowledged Mahatma Gandhi for inspiring them to rethink lifestyles and methods of production which rely on an endless supply and a lavish use of raw materials (Nazareth 2008). Megaron (2011) offers an interesting concept of 'Everyday Peace' which can be connected here, as its basic premise is communal and societal harmony. Gandhian principles have always been relevant in reconstructing the socio-cultural fabric of society in the most pluralistic way they are now.

Places with Spaces of Peace

The experiments of reconstructing spaces of peace through Gandhian philosophy thus emanated from the effort of reconstructing communities, or rather, reconstructing people into communities. There is a tremendous scope for geographers to emerge with innovative concepts inspired by Gandhian economics and philosophy in reconstructing 'peaceful spaces'. In fact, internal and external peace are intrinsically linked with each other. Bhutan, a tiny country, ranked 15 in the Global Peace Index in 2019 whereas India ranked141, with deterioration of 4 points in the last 5 years. The choice is ours.

What can really bring us peace, homogeneity or diversity? It is definitely diversity—environmental, social, cultural and so on. In fact, the whole world economy thrives on diversity. Geographical diversities can be translated into spatial uniqueness. The planning should be such that most of the people have the right to not only resources (physical, financial and infrastructural) but also the right to plan their resources and livelihood in a sustainable manner for the long term and larger communal welfare (Phadke 2019). The larger sustainability can be brought through inclusion, equity and responsibility, and peace rests there.

References

Dudziak, Mary L. 2014. War and Peace in Time and Space. *Seattle Journal for Social Justice* 13 (2).

Fischer, L. 1954. *Gandhi: His Life and Message for the World*. New York : New American Library; London: New English Library.

Foucault, M.1976/1980. *Power/Knowledge*. Brighton: Harvester.

Freud, S. 1909. *The origin and development of psycho-analysis [Five lectures on Psychoanalysis]*. In *Standard edition of the Complete Psychological Works of Sigmund Freud* edited by J. Strachey, vol. 11, 7–55. London: Hogarth.

Gregory, D. 2010. War and Peace. *Transactions of the Institute of British Geographers* 35(2).

Herman, Edward S., and Noam Chomsky. 1988. *Manufacturing Consent: The Political Economy of the Mass Media*. New York: Pantheon Books.

Kumar, Satish. 2011. Gandhi's Way to Peace. *The Sun* May 2011. https://www.thesunmagazine.org/issues/90/gandhis-way-to-peace

Lefebvre, H. 1991. *The Production of Space* trans. D. Nicholson-Smith. London: Blackwell.

Megoran, N. 2011. War and peace? An agenda for peace research and practise in geography. *Political Geography* 30, 178–189.

Nazareth, A. 2008. A Gandhian Approach to International Security. Speech delivered at National Defense College. Accessed in 2020 from https://www.mkgandhi.org

Phadke, A. 2019. Geography and Planning : An Alternate Development Discourse. In *Global Policy Regional Planning for Sustainable Land Use in India*, ed. by Rumi Aijaz and Felix Knopf. ORF and Global Policy Journal, New Delhi: Willey Blackwell.

Rathi, S. 2020. International Peace and Gandhian Thoughts. Accessed in 2020 from https://www.mkgandhi.org

Shukla, A. 2020. REVEALED: How much India really spends on defense. *Rediff News* May 8, 2020.

Swisspeace. 2014. Challenges of Peace Research: Assessing Quality in Peace Research.

The Economic Times. 2020. GDP growth at -23.9% in Q1; first contraction in more than 40 years. September 2, 2020.

The Hindu. 2020. An estimated 12.2 crore Indians lost their jobs during the coronavirus lockdown in April: CMIE. May 2, 2020.

Yadav, S. 2005. International Peace and Gandhian World Order. *The Indian Journal of Political Science,* 66 (3): 443–462

SAARAAKASSH–AN ATTEMPT TOWARDS VILLAGE REPUBLIC

Following the Footsteps of M.K. Gandhi

Shital Ravi and Ravi Narayanan

Vision Statement of Saaraakassh Trust: To bring a smile to every wanting soul.

सारा आकाश

झोप त्याग, श्वास भरू, जयाची ललकार रे
चाल चाल चाल चला ध्येय करू साध्य रे
चाल चाल चाल चला ध्येय करू साध्य रे
हो जी हो जी हो जी जी

कठीण आहे खेळ, त्यात्यून नाही मेळ
करू नका हे भेद, तुमच्यात आहे देव,
जाळू मनाचे जाळ, घेऊ चला ही झेप,
सैतान तुमच्या पाठी, द्यावी तयास मात
स्फोटरे...विस्फोटा रे...स्फोट करू युक्ती अन—पेटवूया रान रे
चाल चाल चाल चला ध्येय करू साध्य रे
चाल चाल चाल चला ध्येय करू साध्य रे

हो जी हो जी हो जी जी

होऊ नको उदास, अग्रीचा भारी श्वास
आकाशी घेई झेप, मन पाखरा जणूच,
मन घे तू ही भरारी, काही नाही कठीण
कुचळू रे सारी भीती, दे बजरंगी हुकार

पेटवू...अरे पेटवू...पेटवूया आज...मनाची ही मशाल रे
चाल चाल चाल चला ध्येय करू साध्य रे
चाल चाल चाल चला ध्येय करू साध्य रे
हो जी हो जी हो जी जी

Saaraakassh Anthem
(English Adaptation)

Sacrificing sleep, taking a deep breath, giving the clarion call
Let's march, march, march ahead to accomplish our goal
Let's march, march, march ahead to accomplish our goal.
Ho ji, Ho ji, Ho ji, ji.

The game is difficult; there is no option to that
Do not discriminate, in you resides God
Burn the mind's cobwebs, let's take this leap
The Devil is behind you, Defeat him!

Explode. Blast. Let's explode with ideas and burn the jungle.

Let's march, march, march ahead to accomplish our goal
Let's march, march, march ahead to accomplish our goal.
Ho ji, Ho ji, Ho ji, ji.

Do not be sad, there is fire in your breath
Take a giant leap towards the sky, as if the mind is a butterfly
Oh my mind, take this flight, nothing is difficult
Crush all fear, Shout Bajrangi's name.

Burn, burn, let us burn today, the torch in our mind.

Let's march, march, march ahead to accomplish our goal
Let's march, march, march ahead to accomplish our goal.
Ho ji, Ho ji, Ho ji, ji
Ho ji, Ho ji, Ho ji, ji
Ho ji, Ho ji, Ho ji, ji.

This is how we dreamt a dream! At first it was a small dream, of helping others in our own small capacity, thus trying to bridge the gap between the haves and the have-nots. For the last 5 years, the Trust, in the Dombivili area, has been distributing food packets to around 40–50 poor people on a daily basis. What started as an Annadaanam initiative later spread its wings in many directions.

Saaraakassh Trust, a Sarvadaanam initiative, started work on 2 October 2015, by doing its first Annadaanam distribution on this day. Though not planned, it was by a happy coincidence that Gandhiji's birthday became the Foundation Day of the Saaraakassh Trust, too. Saaraakassh believes in the principle of Sarvadaanam which encompasses daanam in any capacity, which includes not only Annadaanam but also Aushadadaanam, Vidyadaanam, Vastradaanam and Vastudaanam; based on the needs of the downtrodden, underprivileged, and poor people of our society.

However, if this large and widespread goal was to be implemented and executed well then it needed to be streamlined. Meetings and discussions with likeminded people such as Dalal bhai of the Motilal Dalal Trust led us to the interiors of Maharashtra to the adivasi villages of Murbad district. The trustees were able to understand the new scope of rural development which became a major impetus to take the Trust's work forward. This led to the Saaraakassh Trust starting its work

Saaraakassh Trustee Ravi Narayanan in discussion
with villagers of Musrundi Village.

with tribal villages in Murbad district in the year 2017. Over the days, the model was to adopt a village and try and render all possible help that they required by holding discussions with the villagers about their requirements. Thus, a partnership and an inclusive model was put in place where the villagers too were actively involved.

To quote Gandhiji, 'Take the village people and slum-dwellers in your hands and give them the benefit of your knowledge, skill, insight, constructive work and patriotic spirit. Give the people this true education through the example of your own lives. Let all your activities be directed to the welfare of the people.' This became the roadmap for Saaraakassh, too.

Thus the long-term vision is to keep adopting villages one by one and reach out to the maximum numder of people. Till date, Saaraakassh has worked extensively in three villages, namely, Musrundi, Pezwadi and Karpatwadi. Here we showcase the journey of Saaraakassh through each village in its attempt to make it a model village to the best of its capacity.

Village Musrundi

Situated just 18 kilometres away from Kalyan, which is a hustling and bustling city with all the latest amenities, is a village called Musrundi. The Saaraakassh Trust team visited the adivasi village of Musrundi on 14 January 2017 to distribute Tilgul and clothes on the festive day of Makara Sakranti.

It was unbelievable that a village which is only a couple of hours away from Mumbai had only one well of potable water for a population of 400. That too, this well starts drying up by February until the rain gods are benevolent and fill it up by July! And hence the thought germinated that something had to be done to get potable drinking water for this village through the year. We realized this was easier said than done as the nearest river body, the Murbadi river, was 4 kilometres away from the village and the path in between is through hilly terrain.

However, where there is a will, there is way. And after a couple of meetings with the villagers, work started on 26 January 2017. It was decided that the villagers would contribute by doing the physical labour. Thus, the villagers were going to be involved partners in this project and not just passive beneficiaries. The cost was nothing less than 7 lacs for this whole project. Being a novice in such grassroot-level work, Saaraakassh did not know that many documents are required to be in place before such work can be undertaken. Getting the forest department's permission was mandatory, which the Saaraakassh team realized only after the electric poles had been delivered to the village! However, once the required documents were in order, the permission from the forest department too was forthcoming.

Jain Irrigation came into the picture and at a very reasonable price gave the underground water pipes. Their engineers themselves came to survey and later supervise the laying down of the pipes. Many of the villagers had by then lost steam and on the day of the laying down of pipes there were hardly any menfolk in the village. The Saaraakassh team went from house to house to gather the womenfolk to come and help in the physical labour as promised. With the Saaraakassh team leading from the front, and the womenfolk and children of the village, the laying down of the water pipes over a stretch of 4 kilometres was achieved in a single day. Thus, the Herculean task of bringing water to the village from the Murbadi river through the mountainous terrain by laying a pipeline was achieved by 17 June 2017. However, this water was not potable. And hence to make the water potable, a filtration plant too was installed. A year went into achieving this project. But there is much gratitude towards all those people who made this dream project turn into a reality.

Though the Saaraakassh team has moved on to do *shramadaan* in the further villages, the connection with Musrundi village is still deep, and the team visits for the Zilla Parishad school functions, festivals and even weddings. Distribution of school items, stationery, toys, clothes and so forth is also done regularly at the village.

Village Pezwadi

On the first visit to the adivasi village of Pezwadi on 14 January 2017 on the festive day of Makar Sankranti, the Saaraakassh Team observed that all the children appeared to be undernourished. A preliminary health checkup was organized on the same day, and our team realized that most kids do not have a healthy diet, which negatively impacted their growth and development, thus hampering their overall health and wellbeing.

This led to the creation of the Pilot Milk Project with Ashwagandha Powder for the children of the Pezwadi ZP School.

Various research studies have reported that together, milk and ashwagandha make a remarkable difference in the overall growth of children. An associate organization of Saaraakassh Trust, the Vaishnavi Trust, had been successfully running this project for some time in Chennai and the surrounding region, and it was from there that we got the inspiration to do the same.

Before beginning this pilot project, firstly we took the permission of the Upamukhya Karyakari Adhikari, Mahila va Balvikas Vibhag, Zilla Parishad, Thane Zilla and requested their assistance in monitoring and assessing the health of the children before and after the implementation of this project.

After acquiring the necessary permission, this project was rolled out in a full-fledged manner. Dr. Niraj Dandekar and Dr. Yadnya Dandekar, who are Ayurvedic practitioners running Arogyakiran in Panvel, headed a proper medical camp. Ayurvedic medicines and supplementary food such as gul-chana chikki and kharik was distributed along with the milk and ashwagandha powder to arrest the issue of malnutrition. We, as well as the doctors, organized and conducted talks with villagers to help them understand the importance of good dietary habits and maintaining daily hygiene. A slight modification in their mid-day meal along with all of the above mentioned measures helped us combat malnutrition to a large extent. When the doctors visited the village 6 months later the weight of almost 52 children out of the 55 children had increased. Imagine our joy when the doctor declared that 52 children had crossed over and were no longer malnourished!

Dr. Niraj and Dr. Yadnya of Arogyakiran, Panvel, conducting the Ayurvedic Medical Camp in Pezwadi.

'Village sanitation, domestic cleanliness, personal hygiene and health care have the first place and also full scope, the underlying idea being that this done there can be no disease' (Gandhi in a letter to D.D. Joshi, 1-8-1946). Borrowing from Gandhiji's idea on village sanitation we realized that we needed to go beyond.

Thus we decided to make Pezwadi a model village and not just stop at one goal of eradicating malnutrition. The first initiative was to provide the village with a regular drinking water supply through a water tank. 'Sauch Khaddaas' were also constructed to help drain the dirty sewage water. To make the village an area free of open defecation, we took up the project of building 38 toilets at the cost of Rs.11,000 per toilet. It was not an easy task! However, knowing that open defecation in a closely settled place leads to numerous health issues along with contaminating the nearby water body, we took up this daunting endeavour. After a lot of fundraising events, publicity of the project through word of mouth, and such sustained efforts, by October 2018, we had built toilets for all the families in the village.

Pezwadi has been our 'Karma-Bhoomi' in terms of learning. We realized that just having the desire to help is not enough and that arbitrary decisions cannot be made about the plans of action. Certain processes needed to be in place.

Thus, our vision was streamlined into certain processes that have been practised henceforth. Hereafter, our three major aims would be the Three E's:

1. Eradicating Malnutrition
2. Encouraging Sanitation
3. Enabling Education

Saaraakassh Trustee Shital Ravi exhibiting and selling adivasi village products in the exhibition, Samanvay, arranged by the Rotary Group of Dombivli on 2 October every year.

Thus, school bags, uniforms, school stationery, and toys and games for education and learning are distributed on a regular basis. Before the arrival of the monsoon, Saaraakassh also ensures the upkeep of the school building by way of plastic sheets, etc., to keep the school dry and free from leakages.

Also, to give impetus for employment, mahua oil, honey and bamboo products are bought from the Pezwadi villagers, and then showcased in exhibitions and sold through word of mouth.

It was in Pezwadi that we first organized the Urban-Rural Student Programme, through which urban children visited the village and helped teach the rural children through various activities such as drawing competitions, science experiments, skits, dance competitions and so forth. The takeaway from this experience for the urban children was no less. To actually see adivasi places with minimum facilities like Pezwadi makes anyone who experiences it realize the immense opportunities and conveniences that one has in cities, allowing things to fall into perspective immediately. Guardian School of Dombivli

Dombivli's Guardian School students with Pezwadi Zilla Parishad school children in the Urban-Rural Student Programme.

was the first school to partner with Saaraakassh on this student programme. For the entire academic year 2018-2019, children of various classes visited Pezwadi with teachers and other school staff every month. Words fall short for expressing the hard work put in by all the teachers and students to make this programme a success.

Continuing on the path of the third E, Enabling Education, Saaraakassh finally launched its dream project on 20 October 2019: the P4 series—Pudchi Pidhi, Pudcha Paul, with the children of Pezwadi, undertaking the first Lifeskills workshop of the P4 series.

Saaraakassh Trustee Shital Ravi holds a postgraduate degree in Counselling Psychology from Mumbai University and is also the founder of Disha Counselling Center. Saaraakassh trustee Ravi Narayanan too holds a postgraduate degree in Social psychology from Mumbai University. Having conducted many Lifeskills workshops previously, the P4 series had been a dream project in the pipeline for a long time which finally got rolled out. Under the initiative of Vidyadaanam, the vision is to

The first Pudchi Pidhi Pudcha Paul Lifeskills
workshop in action.

conduct a series of life skills workshops with the underprivileged adivasi children to help them develop better leadership skills, self confidence and an ability to face the world that lies beyond their remote and secluded environment, thus hoping to help them become part of the mainstream society seamlessly.

In many ways, Pezwadi has been our testing ground where we conducted many of our firsts, be it the life-skills programme, urban-rural student programme, building of Sauch Khaddaas and toilets, putting up big water tanks to store drinking water for the village, cleaning of wells before the monsoon, among many others. Even though we have moved on to our third village now, Pezwadi holds a dear place in our hearts and work goes on.

Village Karpatwadi

Karpatwadi is an adivasi village which we used to pass by while going to Pezwadi. By and by, it became familiar to us as the Sarpanch used to come to visit Pezwadi, and children from Karpatwadi used to join some of the Saaraakassh distribution programmes done in Pezwadi school. With the growing connection with people from Karpatwadi, we realized that here was a village with a difference! Education and overall awareness of the Sarpanch (Nathu Pardhi) and Upa-Sarpanch (Chandar Rama Pardhi) made a sea of difference in facilitating the Saaraakassh work that we wanted to start there.

It was indeed a pleasure to know that there was a Karpatwadi Gaon Sudhar Samiti which had been established with a few villagers on board and a bank account too had been opened. This samiti, with the inputs of all the villagers, came up with ideas to make their village a model village. Also, with the passage of time and growing experience, we too had learnt our lessons. We had gotten more focused, and kept ourselves within the fold of our vision. Within the Saaraakassh framework we first began with the repairing of school toilets, building a common kitchen shed for the Zilla Parishad school and Aanganwadi with all facilities and distribution of stationery and sports equipment to the ZP school.

While we were working on all this, we came across the problem of alcoholism in the village. Thus, it was decided to arrange a programme in the village to address this. On the decided day, the rain gods decided to send a huge shower of untimely rain. However, though the whole place was damp and the stage too had become wet, it did not dampen the indomitable spirits of the villagers and the Saaraakassh team. On 19 October 2019 a full-fledged programme was conducted with cultural events by the villagers, children and our team as well, and a motivational speech by Shri Ranjan Rao against alcoholism. We also had a demonstration and talk on the benefits of doing daily Agnihotra to help purify the environment. The programme ended with Sankirtan by none other than the budding team from Pezwadi (to whom we had donated musical instruments such as the harmonium, tabla, dholak, flute and mike systems). This was followed by a dinner for the entire village where we all sat and talked together under the moonlit sky and could sense a spirit of positivity already seeping in. With sustained efforts the alcoholism rate has come down to a small extent, though much more work needs to be done on this front.

Next was the Ayurvedic medical camp for the villagers. Though malnutrition was not a problem here, the villagers, especially the women, were anemic and had health issues. A medical camp with two senior Ayurvedic doctors and two juniors was conducted on 14 December 2019 for the villagers of Karpatwadi. Medicines were also distributed on the same day by the doctors.

The next big project undertaken was the eye camp. We were fortunate to team up with the Essilor Vision Foundation for this event. The team from Optifocus, Pune, did the work of getting all the required machinery for the check up. We had a training session for the Saaraakassh team and a few enterprising villagers who would carry out the initial screening process. This was done over a two-week period and on 26 January 2020, we had the mega eye camp. We covered a total of 8 villages in the camp and 250 people got their eyes tested after the initial screening of 1500 people in these 8 villages. It was a Herculean task to manage the crowd and 9 hours of hard work by the team of 3 doctors and 2 technicians. Spectacles were distributed free of cost on the same day and for a few they were sent after 10 days.

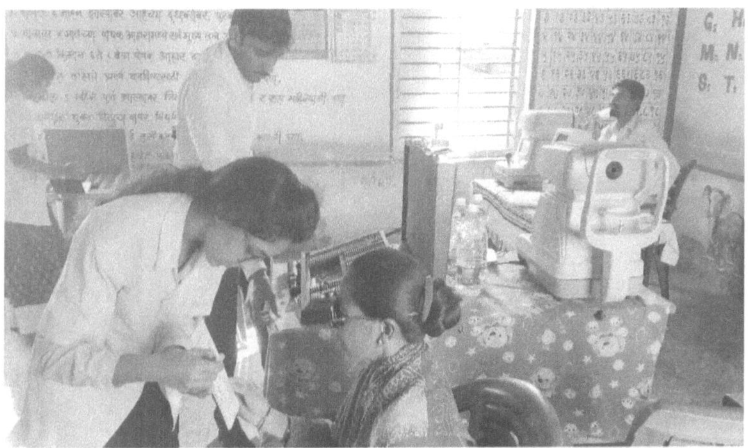

Eye Camp in progress.

At the request of the villagers, Saaraakassh has now taken up the task of building a Samaj hall and a Vithal Rakumai temple in the village. The work for this has begun already. The purpose of a Samaj hall is to have a place where meetings, bhajans, and the life skills camps for the children could be conducted. Any place of prayer helps the community to congregate and have an exchange of positive ideas. Since there was no temple in the village, we felt that this would be a right step to sustain the atmosphere of positivity and brotherhood amongst the villagers.

While our work went on, the whole world was gripped by the Covid-19 pandemic. As soon as the lockdown was announced, we realized that Karpatwadi and the surrounding villages were completely isolated and would be without any means of food as most of these villagers work as daily wage labourers. Thus in this lockdown period, they would be in urgent need of ration supplies. Saaraakassh appealed to its well-wishers and donors to help in these challenging times. With the help of many such good Samaritans, Saaraakassh supplied groceries worth Rs.1200 per family, for immediate relief to help them tide through these tough times.

Sarpanch Shri Chandar distribing food in one of the villages on behalf of Saaraakassh.

In the first week of April 2020, Saaraakassh reached out to many adivasi families across five villages and in the coming days was able to reach out to many more such villages. In May 2020, Saaraakassh covered 11 such villages. This would not have been possible without the tireless hard work done by Shri Nathu and Shri Chandar of Karpatwadi who spearheaded the ration supply distribution across the 11 villages. The grocery distribution was done over 4 months to sustain the villagers over these troubled times.

Here is a village which has shown us how much can be achieved by simple unity and team work. Beautiful learnings that we are learning from our fellow adivasi brothers and sisters. Thus the work in our third village goes on.

We hope to now achieve what Gandhiji had envisioned for an ideal village or village Swaraj, that it is a complete republic, independent of its neighbours for its own wants and yet interdependent for many others where dependence is necessary.

'That village may be regarded as reformed, where everybody wears khadi, which produces all the khadi it needs, which uses only oil produced in indigenous oil-presses, which consumes only jaggery manufactured in the village itself or in its neighbourhood and only hand-milled flour and hand-pounded rice; the village, in other words, where the largest possible number of village industries are flourishing, in which nobody is illiterate, where the roads are clean, there is a fixed place for evacuation, the wells are clean, there is harmony among the different communities, and untouchability is completely absent, in which everybody gets cow's milk, ghee, etc., in moderate quantities, in which nobody is without work, and which is free from quarrels and thefts, and in which the people abide by the sevak's advice in all matters. This is possible in the existing conditions. I cannot of course say about the time required' (Gandhi's letter to Munnalal Shah, 4-4-1941).

Yes, Saaraakassh too does not know the time that may be required but it has definitely started taking steps in this direction, hoping to achieve this dream someday soon.

References

Gandhi, M. K. 2002. *Gandhiji on Villages*. Selected and compiled by Diyva Joshi. Bombay: Mani Bhavan, Gandhi Sangrahalaya.

Gandhi, M.K. 1946. Letter to D.D. Joshi, 1-8-1946; 85:105.

Gandhi, M.K. 1941. Letter to Munnalal Shah, 4-4-1941; 73:421.

Radhakrishnan, Sarvepalli. 1957. *Mahatma Gandhi—Essays & Reflections*. Jaico Publishing House.

YOUTH, COMMUNITIES AND SWARAJ
A Gandhian Lens

Anita Patil-Deshmukh

We are currently living through unprecedented times—an era filled with collective human experiences of trauma, loss, anxieties, fear and hopes. The pandemic has upended the world, triggered partly by the insatiable greed of humankind for more comfort and wealth and a conquering attitude towards Earth. Competition, rather than collaboration, became the coin of the realm. There has been a cavalier encroachment of the spaces of other living creatures. This condescension brought on this pandemic and with it, floundering economies, helpless governments, collapsing institutions, mounting mortality and global gloom and doom. It has created massive migrations, deepening the marginalization and destitution of many vulnerable communities around the globe.

In such a moment of complete rupture, we seek inspiring leaders to pull us out of this apocalypse. To help us bring about the much-needed change in the way we conduct our lives, who else to turn to but Mahatma Gandhi and his principles of *Hind Swaraj*? This timeless document, written by Gandhi in 1909, still stands as one of the finest blueprints for different civilizational practises.

Hind Swaraj is a commentary that is both a scholarly argument as well as an opinion anchored in a few eternal truths that Gandhi believed in and lived. Some of the principles he talked about in that document are the fundamental principles of the working of Partners for Urban Knowledge Action and Research (PUKAR), as well as the foundation of nearly all PUKAR's programmes and projects.

Hence, I take the liberty of quoting some of his thoughts, his ideas, his principles to show how deeply PUKAR's work is influenced by them and how PUKAR has tried to implement those ideas in practise.

One thing this pandemic has taught us is that we cannot go on living the way we have been for the past 200 years. The modern industrialized world's practises, our arrogant exploitation of Earth's precious resources for our 'Greed and not our Needs,' the onslaught of globalization and the deep inequalities created by its systems, the failure of economic and political systems to provide the basic necessities of life to every human being, as Gandhi had cautioned about in Hind *Swaraj*, the destitution of the marginalized and the exclusion of the rural poor—all these factors have brought us into this mess in the first place. The time has come to think, alter and gain 'Swaraj' from our greed and our exploitative and lazy attitudes and to learn to build a mutually respectful relationship with Earth and all her creatures.

For Gandhi, 'It is Swaraj when we learn to rule ourselves!'

And for Gandhi, the basic aim of education should be to 'Bring our senses under our control and to help imbibe ethical behaviour in our life.'

At PUKAR, we believe that we can learn to rule ourselves only when we learn to understand ourselves as individuals. That is the principle we have used very successfully over the past 14 years in PUKAR's flagship programme called Youth Fellowship. This eleven-month long fellowship creates a cadre of Community-Based Youth Leadership from five districts around Mumbai covering over 26 million people. It empowers youth with participatory research skills to conduct research on problems in their own communities and come up with community-based solutions, thus becoming changemakers in their own communities. Youth who are mostly from subaltern communities are accepted as participants but only as a group.

The Youth Fellowship learning process has followed an alternative pedagogy of Community Based Participatory Action Research (CBPAR), the mantra being 'Karake Sikho'. Sustainable communities form a big part of SDGs and hence occupy central space in discourses in every field. This has only strengthened our resolve to foster and scale up the Community Based Participatory Action Research.

Professor Arjun Appadurai, the Founder of PUKAR, in his seminal essay 'Right to Research', argues that Community Based Participatory Action Research 'democratizes research, gives credence to community based indigenous knowledge and enables the community members to have a voice in envisioning of their own future, thus making the communities sustainable.' This also devolves power and places it into the hands of local communities, urban or rural, which Gandhi strongly advocates in *Hind Swaraj*.

Decentralization of power and inclusivity form a critical part of his argument in *Hind Swaraj* when he talks about villages. Gandhi also strongly advocates a self-reflective, inward-looking attitude towards one's own identity in *Hind Swaraj*. In PUKAR, this aspect forms the first step that all the participants must take as soon as they join PUKAR's Youth Fellowship.

Writing an autobiography and looking at one's own life as a bystander is a difficult, yet essential, first activity that each youth is encouraged to undertake. Resolving struggles of layered identities through self-reflection and writing one's own biography to know oneself better is usually an eye-opener for many. Engaging with prevalent social issues such as caste, religion, gender, language, region and cultural practises, reflecting upon one's own space and location in their communities as youth, leaders, consumers and aspirants, and learning to negotiate all these positions under the prevalent social construct, are both frightening and liberating experiences for the Barefoot Researchers.

The realization that in many areas some of them are

privileged, but that even victims of some social structures can be perpetrators within other social categories, especially in areas of gender and environment is a sobering thought for many. With the help of the expert Resource Persons, the ever-smiling Facilitators and Alu-mentors, the Barefoot Researchers walk through and reflect upon a maze of complexities. In addition, they are enabled with some of the most critical skills that are necessary to live a successful life in the 21st century. These include problem location and problem solving, teamwork and cooperation, collective decision making and consensus building, critical thinking and empathy, many of the qualities Gandhi talks about in *Hind Swaraj*. He gives particular importance to local small technologies. In YFP that is exactly what is fostered. Local problems, local small solutions, based upon evidence collected locally by the local youth and implemented locally.

Let me share with you a few stories of resolute-minded youth who were empowered through the Youth Fellowship and how they changed the lives of the people from their communities through their small but significant actions.

The Sexual Harassment Faced in Local Trains

A group of young women who travelled by Mumbai's local train network to their colleges decided to explore the sexual harassment they all faced. In addition to interviewing many of their colleagues who attended colleges in the same vicinities as theirs, they also mapped and photo-documented the areas where they faced the most harassment.

Some stations and neighbourhoods around these stations stood out. Many of those areas shared one thing in common: the lack of adequate lighting. The women shared this research and these maps with the railway authorities, requesting them to increase the lighting in these areas. Small improvements led to large dividends.

Improving Connectivity of a Village for Decreasing Deaths and Morbidity

A youth group from Amboli conducted research on health and mortality in their village. They found that a large number of deaths and non-institutional deliveries took place on the roads. People had to wait at the railway crossing gate since there was no overhead bridge. With local trains passing by frequently, people's lives were at risk. They shared this evidence with the local corporator who in turn shared the information with the respective authorities, who finally sanctioned a budget for an overhead bridge, thus bringing relief to their community.

To Continue Education

We had a spirited group of Adivasi youth from Kalomboli village. To reach this village, one has to first reach Khopoli by train, then take a bus for half an hour that drops one off at the bottom of a hilly region. From there, it is an hour-long uphill walk to reach the village.

The village has a primary school up to the 4th grade. The entire village becomes vacant during summer since there is no drinking water. The villagers come down to the bottom of the hill to the brick kilns for work. Children who wish to continue their higher education have to walk to the school located in another village, which is a walk over difficult terrain.

The PUKAR youth researched and documented the villagers' plight through photography that was taught to them at Youth Fellowship workshops. They used cameras, rather than smartphones, to take pictures. After the research and documentation was completed, they took the data to the bus service company and pleaded that the bus should come all the way to the bottom of the hill and take them to the other village so that at least a few of them could continue their education. The bus service staff agreed, which was a huge achievement for these youth.

We have many such stories to share of the 5,000-odd youth we have trained in 14 years and more than 400 communities we have reached. Each of these stories echoes the same principle that Gandhi reiterated many times:

> Whenever you are in doubt, or when the self becomes too much with you, apply the following test. Recall the face of the poorest and the weakest man whom you may have seen, and ask yourself if the step you contemplate is going to be of any use to him. Will he gain anything by it? Will it restore him to a control over his own life and destiny? In other words, will it lead to Swaraj for the hungry and spiritually starving millions?

Gandhi always emphasized the importance of self-reliance and had deep-seated respect for manual labour. In one of his speeches during his tour in 1934 he vowed, 'We have to become speechless manual labourers living in the villages.' He believed that unless one does manual labour oneself, one may never understand the efforts and pain behind it, and one may never learn to respect it and value it. Keeping this cardinal principle in mind, in PUKAR the entire team decided that we would undertake the cleaning of our office by ourselves. No outsider should clean the space that we use every day. So, once a month on a designated morning, all of us gather at the office, with brooms and cleaning material and water buckets. Over the next four-six hours, every nook and cranny of the office is cleaned, including the toilets. Listening to music and eating snacks in between, we make it a joyous team activity and not only enjoy it but also value it. Gandhi's influence does not ever seem to leave our horizons.

Another area where we have followed Gandhi is in our ability to build collaborations. In *Hind Swaraj*, Gandhi talked specifically about 'curbing unnecessary competitiveness'. At PUKAR, this principle has been observed minutely. In everything we do, propose and implement, a spirit of collaboration and cooperation and equal treatment for all are encouraged. We have always believed strongly that synergy is the fuel that allows ordinary people to achieve extraordinary accomplishments. This word occupies a significant space in PUKAR's organizational principles, from the daily functioning of the teams to research conducted by our Barefoot Researchers in teams of 10-12 youth.

Group work remains an important part of PUKAR projects. We believe that by working in teams, we learn to respect diversity of opinions and differences, resolve conflicts, learn to build consensus, and gather the skills necessary to foster inclusivity and democracy. We pool our strengths, capabilities, talents and creativity so that as a collective, we can achieve exponentially rather than individually. Our efforts are not just additive but multiplied. In each of our projects, this notion is fostered and executed with ease. Believing strongly that ground-breaking, inclusive partnerships will lead to synergies in every sphere of development will give measurable outcomes for the communities we work with.

So, where did we build our partnerships? All over. From the Municipal Corporation of Greater Mumbai, (MCGM) to the BMN College and Khalsa College of Mumbai, which cater mostly to lower middle-class students belonging mostly to minority groups. From the prestigious Tata Institution of Social Sciences (TISS) of Mumbai to globally renowned academic institutions like Harvard University, University of Chicago and Max Planck Institute of Germany. The main focus of these collaborations has always remained the empowerment of youth through knowledge, skills and attitudinal changes.

Municipal schools draw some of the most deprived students from mostly migrant and marginalized communities. They lack information, knowledge and exposure on varied fronts, leading to a deep inferiority complex within many of them. PUKAR decided to address this issue by partnering with MCGM. The main focus of this partnership was to empower adolescent girl students of 7th and 8th grades with knowledge of puberty, menstrual health and hygiene, gender identity and gender violence. This triangulation between MCGM school students, communities and

PUKAR lead to exhilarating outcomes not just for the girls and their mothers but also for our team members, who felt equally empowered with the spirit of disseminating knowledge.

Our collaboration with Harvard University led to exploring the social determinants of health in an informal settlement. This in turn led to increasing the immunization rates of children from 32% to 89.6% over 18 months with door-to-door education of mothers and collaboration with MCGM to bring health camps to this settlement. This research helped us to publish seven important papers published in peer reviewed international journals that are cited more often than we had ever imagined. (These are available on www.pukar.org.in).

Finally, one of the most difficult yet most rewarding partnerships emerged between PUKAR's E-Governance team and rural tribal youth of over 40 villages in the tribal district of Palghar. This partnership has been difficult to execute mainly due to its massive scale, the hilly and inapproachable terrain and poor connectivity between the villages scattered across 150 kilometres. The PUKAR team members overcame all these hurdles with their resolute minds and determination. They inhabited the area for months, kept an ear to the ground through their Adivasi E-Sevaks, and were agile on their feet as the situations demanded.

The synergy of this partnership has brought about a revolutionary turnaround in the capacities of the rural population. The knowledge of the 73rd Amendment delivered to each and every household, the importance of the participation of tribals in the working of Gram panchayats, their demand for good governance from the Gram panchayat by raising their voices in Gramsabhas; all of this has been a new and exhilarating experience for the tribal villagers.

The schemes specifically created for tribals by the Government of India are being delivered to their doorsteps by our trained local E-Sevaks. The villagers get their Aadhar cards, voter registration cards, land ownership records and marriage certificates in their own villages without having to make multiple trips to the local district office. This not only saves them money and time but also spares them the humiliation they face at the hands of the officers, bankers and office staff. This gift of dignity is beyond any measurable value to these tribal communities—which they have conveyed to their local E-Sevaks over and over again. And in this process, the villagers have also been empowered towards the Self-Rule that Gandhi so deftly advocated.

He wrote in *Hind Swaraj*:

> It is swaraj when we learn to rule ourselves! There is a symbiotic relationship between swaraj as 'self-rule' of individual Indians and swaraj as the home-rule or self-government for the Indian people.

Through such partnerships, we have been collaborators, not competitors. We have been inclusive, not exclusive. We have created synergies that are much larger than the sum total of our partners and us. The real beneficiaries of these energies and synergies are not just all of us but the marginalized and disenfranchised, repressed and oppressed, the ostracized and excluded, voiceless and invisible citizens of our country—the millions of people Gandhi cared for the most! He advocated, 'If we (individuals) became free, India would be free.'

To Gandhi, the recognition of the responsibility of duty was the very essence of freedom.

He wrote:

> Our freedom does not lie in expanding our choices at the expense of others. That is power. Our freedom lies in expanding the choices of those beyond ourselves, those of the human community sans any exclusion.

That is what we have been trying to inculcate in the community-based youth. To look beyond themselves to their communities, cities, countries and nature. As social beings, we must learn to respect the importance of communities as social units and their space in shaping our lives. Social media cannot replace social communities. Technology that creates band-aid solutions but fails to ask questions as to why the situation has been created in the first place cannot become a panacea for our problems. It can complement our efforts but not replace it.

In today's interdependent world that has been capsized by a tiny micro-organism, connected by the internet and yet divided by increasing inequality, endangered by cyclones, tsunamis, floods, drought, forest fires, hunger and malnutrition, and steeped in the mirage of technology as the ultimate solution, we need Gandhi's ideas of Swaraj and Freedom.

References

Gandhi, M.K. 1909. *Hind Swaraj or India Home Rule*. Ahmedabad: Navajivan Publishing House.

Gandhi, M.K. 1988. *An Autobiography or The Story of My Experiments with Truth*. Ahmedabad: Navajivan Publishing House.

Pradhan, R.C. Gandhi's Hind Swaraj: A Summary and Centennial View. Bombay Survodaya Mandal and Gandhi Research Foundation.

Lelyveld J. 2011. *Great Soul*. New Delhi: Harper Collins.

Patil-Deshmukh A. 2008. *Mumbai's Barefoot Researchers*. PUKAR Publication.

PUKAR Youth Fellowship Research Archives 2018-2019 https://www.goodreads.com/quotes/695582-whenever-you-are-in-doubt-or-when-the-self-becomes Accessed Sept 2020

THE COVID-19 PANDEMIC

An Opportunity to Revisit the Gandhian Perspective

Suchita Krishnaprasad

Introduction

Covid-19 pushed the world into a pervasive crisis encompassing every aspect of human life. It altered our consumption patterns, shocked our smart production systems, changed the modes of education and entertainment and made us take a serious relook at the 'social animal' definition of ourselves as a race that has increasingly learnt to dominate this planet. Paradoxically, the most civilized species that has pushed so many other species to the brink of extinction suddenly appears precarious and vulnerable mainly due to having chosen perilous ways of living. We live on the brink of an energy crisis, climate change and hunger, made worse by inequitable access to resources and opportunities. The pandemic has been a rude shock to our comfortable but unsustainable ways of living, and hence it is an opportunity to revisit the Gandhian perspective of human society. Mainstream economics directs us to maximize resource utilization for the highest level of gratification. Gandhian economics, grounded in the premises of non-violence, truth, and non-covetousness, is instantly antithetical to mainstream economics, as it begins with the need to contain one's wants. Dignity of labour, self-sufficient and strong village economy and the principle of trusteeship emerge as logical corollaries of this system of thought with an inbuilt thread of morality running through it, thus offering an integrated view of managing the economy, polity and society harmoniously. Gandhian thought can provide some critical insights during this exercise in introspection. This paper is an attempt in this direction.

Section I: An Overview of the Covid Crisis

The year 2019 ended with a few cases of infection of Covid-19, first in China, which soon gripped all the nations across the world in an unprecedented manner, disrupting every possible human activity. Within months it took the form of the worst pandemic in recent human history with the only known way to restrict its spread being lockdown and social distancing along with scrupulous standards of cleanliness and hygiene. This in turn wiped away millions of jobs across the world, severely affecting global supply chains, and totally freezing certain sectors such as aviation and hospitality. Forced unemployment meant loss of income for many, and hence a severely constrained demand. With the two market forces losing steam, there were predictions of a dip in global production, which have been revised downwards within a few months. Globally, a loss of nearly 400 million full-time jobs has been estimated in the year's second quarter (April-June 2020) according to the ILO. An IMF estimate projected a loss of 9 trillion dollars to the global economy and a dip of 3% in the global economic growth rate in the year 2020.

In India unemployment reached a record level of 27.1% by the end of April 2020. According to a CMIE report, about 122 million workers lost their jobs by April end, of which nearly 70% were small traders and wage labourers. And though resumption of agricultural operations with the onset of monsoon helped in reducing unemployment in the following months, reports suggested a likely resurgence in unemployment once this peak activity in agriculture was over. This was borne out by the fact that just in the month of June, 62 million people demanded work under the Mahatma Gandhi National Rural Employment Guarantee Act (MGNREGA) programmeme at minimum wages. Macro-economic indicators reveal the bruises suffered by the economy. To take a snap shot, during the April-June quarter, India's GDP contracted by 23.9%. It is estimated that there could be a permanent loss of 13% of real GDP over the medium term and to catch up with the pre-pandemic trend value of real GDP would require average real GDP growth to surge to 13% annually for the next three fiscals.

A sector-wise growth in GVA (Gross Value Added) presented in the monetary policy report of RBI (October 2020) provides a brief view of the economy.

TABLE 1: Sector-wise Growth in GVA

Sector	2018-19 (FRE)	2019-20 (PE)	2020-21 Q1
Agriculture, forestry and fishing	2.4	4.0	3.4
Industry	4.5	0.8	-33.8
Mining and quarrying	-5.8	3.1	-23.3
Manufacturing	5.7	0.0	-39.3
Electricity, gas, water supply and other utilities	8.2	4.1	-7.0
Services	7.5	5.0	-24.3
Construction	6.1	1.3	-50.3
Trade, hotels, transport, communication	7.7	3.6	-47.0
Financial, real estate and professional services	6.8	4.6	-5.3
Public administration, defence and other services	9.4	10.0	-10.3
GVA at Basic Prices	6.0	3.9	-22.8

FRE: First Revised Estimates; PE: Provisional Estimates.
Source: NSO.

Barring agriculture, forestry and fishing, every other sector has had a negative growth in GVA. Unsurprisingly, as noted in the RBI report, both customer confidence and the business sentiments have also been on the decline.[77] When the two components of private expenditure slide down, the gloom spreads from the real sector to the monetary sector and banks have to struggle with NPAs (Non-Performing Assets) on the one hand and poor demand for borrowings on the other, thus arresting the future economic growth.

What is further worrisome is the fact that the states which have a major share in India's GDP (~36%), Maharashtra, Tamil Nadu, Karnataka and Andhra Pradesh, together accounted for ~54% of India's total confirmed cases as on September 7, 2020.

While all these numbers are enough to indicate the overall gloom that looms over the economy, one of the worst fallouts of the pandemic was the flood of 'reverse migration' of workers back to their home states, by every possible mode of transportation including walking painfully for long distances across the subcontinent. Some have even compared it to the turmoil around partition time. Even if this is seen as an exaggeration, it cannot be denied that it has been a human tragedy of colossal proportions, and that it does represent an indecent side of India's growth story.

Section II: India's Growth Story

It is well known that the growth rate of the Indian economy crawled up to 3.5% in the first three decades of planning which have been boldly described as the decades of state control. A few notable achievements during this period were: the setting up of major irrigation projects, setting up of IITs, the Green Revolution and near self-sufficiency in food production, the White Revolution (production of milk) and bank nationalization, expansion of banks and rise in the saving rate. The 1980s began with some window of opening up and India adopted liberalization, privatization and globalization (LPG) through

---

[77] https://www.rbi.org.in/Scripts/PublicationsView.aspx?id=19439

her New Economic Policy, which ushered in a new era of a phenomenal expansion of opportunities along with of rising aspirations of her people.

TABLE 2: India's Decadal GDP Growth and Investment Rates

	Annual GDP growth rate	*Investment rate*	*Savings rate*
1951–61	3.91	11.82	-
1961–71	3.68	14.71	9.03
1971–81	3.09	17.86	12.96
1981–91	5.38	21.04	17.32
1991–2001	5.71	24.14	24.27
2001–11	7.68	32.44	31.42
2011–18	6.61	35.78	31.17

Source: Basu, Kaushik 2018

The table speaks well of the impressive economic growth achieved by India with both savings and investment rising hand in hand, especially after opening up of the economy, which also did well to attract foreign direct investment (FDI) and to accumulate the foreign exchange reserves, as is visible in Table 3.

There was also a significant reduction in extreme poverty, and the fact that India could maintain her annual growth rate between 8 to 9% even during the years of global financial crisis, gave rise to the hope that India was about to emerge as an economic power in the world, especially with the so-called demographic dividend in her favour.

However, this glorious growth story is not without its shadow. And there are several indicators of this. Malnutrition and high mortality among children,[78] high rates of dropouts

---

[78] https://www.thehindu.com/news/national/68-of-under-5-deaths-in-india-due-to-child-maternal-malnutrition/article31570050.ece

TABLE 3: Growth in FDI and Foreign Exchange Reserves

India's foreign exchange reserves		Total reserves
Year	₹billion	US$ million
1954–55	9	1,873
1959–60	4	762
1964–65	3	524
1969–70	8	1,094
1974–75	10	1,379
1979–80	59	7,361
1984–85	72	5,952
1989–90	63	3,962
1994–95	798	25,186
1999–00	1,659	38,036
2004–05	6,191	141,514
2009–10	12,597	279,057
2014–15	21,376	341,638
2017–18	27,930	405,810

Source: Basu, Kaushik 2018

from school[79] despite high enrolment,[80] and a growing gap in the rate of growth of profit vis-a-vis wages over the years, are only some of them. The graph below shows how India's growth has increasingly failed to create jobs.

---

[79] https://news.careers360.com/dropout-rates-increasing-in-classes-9-and-10-in-some-states-mhrd

[80] https://www.mhrd.gov.in/sites/upload_files/mhrd/files/statistics-new/ESAG-2018.pdf

GRAPH: India's Jobless Growth

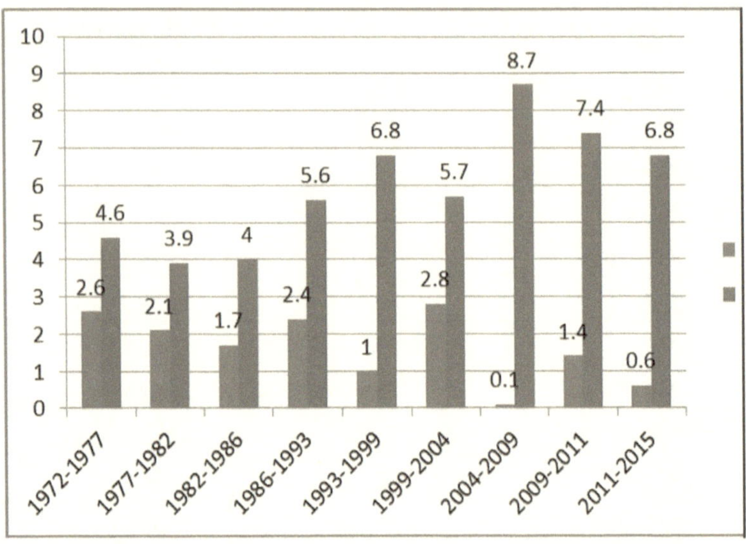

Source: Reports from Ministry of Labour and Employment, and Economic Surveys

Sluggish job creation means greater dependence on agriculture. More than 50% of India's population is dependent on agriculture, but the share of agriculture in the GDP has been falling consistently. This means that nearly half of the people are trapped in low productivity and poor growth while the other half lives the story of prosperity and growth. This may be a broad representative of the urban-rural divide, but the divide within the rural sector itself becomes clear when we account for the iniquitous ownership of agricultural land. Less than 5% of farmers control 32% of India's farmland and a 'large' farmer has 45 times more land than the 'marginal' farmer. Finally, 101.4 million people, or 56.4% of rural households own no agricultural land.

Poverty and poor productivity in agriculture and the seasonality of employment explains migration, which is roughly estimated to be 10% of the population. According to the report of the Working Group on Migration (2017) only 17 districts from UP and Bihar together account for 25% of the total male migrants in the country. Whether one understands it as a push or a pull factor, migration of this scale most certainly underlines the regional disparities and hence the pockets of abject poverty. Further, the growth that has increasingly added fewer and fewer jobs hints at the urban poverty and the fate of the migrants, who might still choose urban poverty in hope of more opportunities of earning a livelihood than the rural counterpart. Living in highly congested slums and surviving on poor wages with little safety at the workplace, largely under informally agreed terms of employment, or running a small commercial unit employing family labour, the migrant workers have been the hidden army providing support services to every sector and across the classes.

So when the nation-wide lockdown was iteratively extended in April and May 2020 to ensure that people Stay Home and Stay Safe, people living in these Dickensian conditions decided to flee because firstly, their savings had dried up, and their congested dwellings with common toilets were hardly 'Safe Homes'! And this was a saga of massive hardship for millions who only knew they had to leave where they had survived so far but did not know how to reach where they wanted to, and whether they would live to see that destination.

If the symbolic image of the consequence of the first wave of the pandemic in India was the unending swarm of migrant workers walking along the highways or railway tracks in the hot summer, that for the second wave was of people being given oxygen from cylinders in cars or even on the streets, since there were no beds. The worst image is of course that of the corpses left floating in the water bodies. Undoubtedly it was far more swift in its speed and lethal in its impact. Since it largely reached the rural and semi-rural areas, it laid bare the glaring inadequacies of our health services in these areas. Before the second wave India was already exporting masks, and though there were regions where masks were rarely used, there was an overall awareness among people about the need for social distancing, using masks, and importance of basic hygiene.

The third wave was fortunately more benign, and by this time the vaccine had been administered systematically across the population, though there were shortages once in a while. The digitisation of records made it easier to assess the work completed and what remained to be accomplished.

Section III: Why Gandhian Thought? And Why Now?

Profit drives a market economy. But profits rise when the market size expands and the market size depends on income distribution and employment generation. Economists across ideologies have pointed out time and again that a rise in unemployment would stunt the market size and hence the profit. Labour may be a factor of production, but as a consumer, the labourer should also be the 'King' of the market system; and here lies the crux of the dialectics of the growth process in a market economy. In other words, it may be possible to gather more profit by squeezing wages, but only in the short run. In the long run the same strategy will in fact usher in stagnation. Similarly regional disparities, iniquitous distribution of income and assets threaten sustainability. Again, when only 7% of the workforce is engaged in the organized sector and 93% of workers largely remain outside the ambit of social security and decent work, growth, delinked from development, may prove unsustainable. To sustain the fruits of high growth achieved through market-friendly economic policies we may need to ensure that more hands earn income, and a decent income at that, to keep the demand burning.

This brings us to the Gandhian system of thought, which begins at a position that is totally antithetical to mainstream economics. The textbook economics, aka positive economics, starts with the premise that wants in general are insatiable, and that resources are limited. The Gandhian system, steeped in normative thinking,[81] starts with the idea of containment of wants, because after all there is enough on this earth for everybody's needs but not enough for one man's greed. Greed breeds violence and gives rise to the need to exploit others, which is against the first primal principle of the Gandhian system: non-violence. Squeezing wages and exploiting workers is also equivalent to violence. Unequal land holding is manifestation of greed, which was sought to be corrected through the Bhoodaan movement by Gandhiji's illustrious disciple, Vinoba Bhave. Creating circumstances that force people to migrate because of poverty might amount to violence at a societal level. Gandhiji wanted to reverse this by making village communities stronger and self-sufficient. Empowering villages though a benevolent *Jajmani* system was his idea of nurturing the roots of community living in India that lived mostly in villages. The well-being of rural India was of utmost importance to him and people who migrated once that had been achieved would be only exercising their choice.

Gandhiji's ideas about choice of technology have been much debated, but his key idea of optimally using the local resources and skills are the basic tenets of any textbook trade theory. Machines are useful. But they should not impact the dignity of labour. Gandhiji's concept of dignity of labour has several dimensions.[82] Firstly, it means that no labour is menial. In fact he strongly recommended a few hours of manual labour every day for everyone. That would ensure physical and mental fitness besides appropriately sensitising the employers of manual workers. Dignity of labour also means more importance to the man behind the machine. It means the need to treat that

---

[81] https://www.mkgandhi.org/momgandhi/chap41.htm. Accessed on 22/11/2020.

[82] http://gandhiashramsevagram.org/voice-of-truth/gandhiji-on-dignity-of-labour-bread-labour.php. Accessed on 20/11/2020.

man with decency. Decency would include healthy and clean working conditions and reasonable wages. His intervention in the Ahmedabad textile workers' strike can be seen as an attempt to ensure decent work. He was not against industries. Industries would be necessary for progress, and they would have to make profit in order to survive, but again the profits belong to the society, that provided every possible resource to an industrialist, who is therefore a mere trustee of this wealth. It, therefore, becomes his obligation to look after the needs of the society. Using profit towards the larger social good, which is the crux of corporate social responsibility, can thus be traced back to Gandhiji's idea of trusteeship.

Although his ideas never fail to appeal to our higher consciousness, it is customary to applaud them as lofty ideals that can only be admired from a distance.[83] It is also an easier way to escape the responsibility of implementing them or even experimenting with them.

However, the current pandemic has paved the way to possibility of such experimentation, and there are several grounds to justify this position.

Changing Consumption Pattern: The pattern of consumption has changed significantly, especially during the lockdown periods. Studies have noted a substantial reduction in 'discretionary' (read as conspicuous) consumption. Consumers are less blinded by the brand-value and are increasingly alert about distinguishing between essential and non-essential consumption, even while choosing a brand.[84] This is a form of 'containment of wants', though forced by circumstances. Nudging households to choose healthy lifestyles to bolster immunity in the face of Covid is

---

[83] https://indianexpress.com/article/world/uks-labour-party-group-mahatma-gandhi-future-leaders-plan-6556198/ Accessed on 22/11/2020.

[84] For a detailed survey of changing consumption pattern, see: How the coronavirus is changing consumption patterns (livemint.com) Accessed on 22/11/2020.

another blessing in disguise. Preferences are shifting to natural and herbal remedies and learning about their goodness and lasting effects. Ceremonies have become Spartan since huge gatherings are dangerous and also illegal. However, more time at home is like a 'Razor's Edge' . On the one hand there are studies of higher incidence of substance abuse, alcoholism, anxiety and depression[85] and on the other innovative and creative ways are being devised to make home-stay more bearable. These include online learning programmes, from those aiming at honing untapped skills to the ones on self-healing, and discovering inner peace. It is true that the death and morbidity associated with the pandemic along with the financial stress and being largely homebound have led to more cases of depression and anxiety, but it is also true that more and more people in our society are willing to acknowledge these conditions as normal, and reach out to provide assistance, at least through social media.

Indeed the Subjective Well Being (SWB) can swing in either direction, as brought out by an exhaustive study based on a cross sectional survey of over 1,000 participants in China,[86] and how we tweak the support systems towards choosing a healthier lifestyle now can have a critical impact for the times to come.

---

[85] The next pandemic: COVID-19 mental health pandemic Evelyn Parrish: The next pandemic: COVID-19 mental health pandemic—PubMed (nih.gov), The assessment of lifestyle changes during the COVID-19 pandemic using a multidimensional scale (nih.gov), Effects of COVID-19 Home Confinement on Eating Behaviour and Physical Activity: Results of the ECLB-COVID19 International Online Survey—PubMed (nih.gov) Accessed on 22/11/2020.

[86] Impact of the COVID-19 Epidemic on Lifestyle Behaviors and Their Association With Subjective Well-Being Among the General Population in Mainland China: Cross-Sectional Study Zhao Hu1, MD ; Xuhui Lin1, MD; Atipatsa Chiwanda Kaminga2,3, MD ; Huilan Xu1, PhD See: JMIR—Impact of the COVID-19 Epidemic on Lifestyle Behaviors and Their Association With Subjective Well-Being Among the General Population in Mainland China: Cross-Sectional Study | Hu | Journal of Medical Internet Research. Accessed on 20/11/2020.

Changing Patterns of Production: As the world grapples with the problem of fragmentation of the supply chain, and the necessity to restart in whatever manner possible, producers may be forced to relocate their sources of supply. An UNCTAD economist, P. Fortunato, in his study on *How COVID-19 is Changing Global Value Chains* (September 2, 2020), observes a trend towards relocation of the GVC (Global Value Chain) in favour of a greater use of local skills and materials. Compelled by the pressures of circumstance we might redevelop production systems of the kind that Gandhiji advocated strongly to promote self-sufficiency.

Further, experts highlight compulsions to turn to green technology.[87] The Confederation of British Industry, for instance, has urged the government to invest in green technology and jobs.[88] In a significant move to ensure sustainability in the post-Covid scenario, the UK government has even announced a Green Recovery Challenge Fund.[89] Interestingly, investment in green technology can unleash a significant multiplier effect with a high employment potential as noted by ILO.[90]

Empathy Towards the Deprived: The migrants reaching their home states by foot, by legitimate or illegal means[91] has been a heart-wrenching story.[92] But it has also led to individuals and

---

[87] Clean, green and better: Policy priorities in a post-COVID-19 world | Climate Investment Funds. Accessed on 22/11/2020.

[88] 'Create green post-Covid recovery' urges UK industry body—Positive News—Positive News. Accessed on 22/11/2020.

[89] Building back a green and resilient recovery—GOV.UK (www.gov.uk) Accessed on 21/11/2020

[90] Microsoft Word—Methodologies for assessing green jobs March 2013 (ilo. org). accessed on 22/11/2020 Also see: Looking-for-green-jobs_the-impact-of-green-growth-on-employment.pdf (lse.ac.uk) Accessed on 20/11/2020.

[91] https://www.thestatesman.com/coronavirus/18-migrant-workers-trying-to-reach-home-hiding-in-cement-mixer-held-in-madhya-pradesh-1502883244.html. Accessed on 22/7/2020.

[92] https://www.reuters.com/article/us-health-coronavirus-india-migrants-spe/special-report-indias-migrant-workers-fall-through-cracks-in-coronavirus-lockdown-idUSKBN2230M3. Accessed on 22/7/2020.

NGOs rising to the occasion to support these unfortunate fellow beings through supply of food packets and other materials to ease their agony. The state and union governments did arrange Shramik trains to ensure safe return, but the role of individuals,[93] NGOs[94] and religious institutions[95] that extended a helping hand so spontaneously cannot be overemphasized. If the reverse migrant movement is akin to partition, so is the extent of support and help from various quarters of society. Gandhiji would have not only appreciated this spirit of empathy but would have perhaps succeeded in processing it into institution-building for longer sustanance.

When the existing patterns of socio-economic systems are shaken, they create the space for a shift. It is also an opportune time to correct the previous malfunctions of the system. For example:

Reducing Rural-Urban Imbalance: Greater dependence of our population on agriculture indicates non availability of non-agricultural jobs. Providing more jobs in the non-agricultural sector, and more so in manufacturing is the need of the hour.[96] Promoting agro-based and related commercial activities such as fisheries and food processing can go a long way in providing more opportunities of gainful employment in the rural sector, which would be a step in the Gandhian direction: reducing

---

[93] https://www.hindustantimes.com/sex-and-relationships/this-is-how-good-samaritans-are-helping-delhi-survive-in-lockdown/story-MPp9xnxZ34zCCBg1ELZACL.html. Accessed on 21/8/2020.

[94] https://timesofindia.indiatimes.com/city/dehradun/good-samaritans-social-organisations-come-forward-to-help-those-hit-by-lockdown/articleshow/74901311.cms. Accessed on 21/8/2020.

[95] https://timesofindia.indiatimes.com/city/agra/gurdwara-along-nh2-has-fed-over-a-million-people-during-lockdown/articleshow/76163085.cms, and https://www.tribuneindia.com/news/punjab/dsgmc-launches-langar-on-wheels-for-migrants-86473. Accessed on 21/8/2020.

[96] See *Reviving Jobs: An Agenda for Growth* edited by Santosh Mehrotra (2020).

circumstances that force people to choose migration as a last option to survive.

Domestic Violence and the Gender Issue: It is a well-recorded fact that there is an increase in violent, abusive, impulsive, compulsive, and controlling behaviour and aggression directed towards women during the periods of economic hardship.[97] Studies suggest an astonishing rise in the harassment of women behind closed doors. While everyone in the household may be living under a potential threat to life, financial stress, lack of opportunities to socialise, frequent violent outbursts among men desperate for alcohol or tobacco seem to be considered socially acceptable. Being trapped in a space with violent or manipulative individuals could lead to increased rates and intensity of threats, physical, sexual and psychological abuse, humiliation, intimidation, and controlling behaviour, which is heightened by the lockdown. And this is true of developed countries as well.[98] In the first five weeks of lockdown, Pune police reported an increase in the cases of domestic violence by 12 times.[99] These numbers have justified the term 'parallel

---

[97] 'Intimate Partner Violence in the Great Recession' Daniel Schneider, Kristen Harknett, and Sara McLanahan, *Demography*. April 2016, 53(2): 471–505. Intimate Partner Violence in the Great Recession—PMC (nih. gov) accessed on 8/6/2022

[98] A UN Women report confirms a global increase in emergency calls to address violence against women with 30% increase in France and Cyprus, 35% increase in Singapore and 25% in Argentina. China's Jianli county recorded 162 case of domestic violence as against 47 cases in the pre-pandemic scenario. Argentina, Australia, Canada, U.K., France, Germany South Africa, and US have reported significant increases in domestic violence reports. 'The Covid-19 Pandemic Has Escalated Domestic Violence Worldwide' (forbes. com) Accessed on 8/6/2022.

[99] According to the Crime in India Report 2018, published by the National Crime Research Bureau (NCRB), a crime is recorded against women in India every 1.7 minutes and a woman is subjected to domestic violence every 4.4 minutes. This might have only worsened during the pandemic. Crime

pandemic' to describe domestic violence, underlining the dark gender impact of the pandemic, but they have also brought out the issue of gender disparity and the disenfranchisement of women in a manner that can no longer be overlooked. That the family, which is ideally the basic nurturing cell in the society should exhibit its stark opposite during such hard times especially to the very agents that provide the nourishment, is a strong and shrill alarm which needs to be heard.

The data in India shows an inequitable access to health care systems based on gender which only became worse during the pandemic.[100] Growing number of child marriages,[101] and a high rate of school drop outs especially among girls is likely to further widen the gender disparity in the times to come. Also it is reported that as health services focussed increasingly on Covid-related issues during the pandemic, there was a rise in unplanned pregnancies owing to lack of access to family planning measures.[102] This could become an important obstacle in women joining the labour force in the post-pandemic scenario.

---

in India—2018 | National Crime Records Bureau (ncrb.gov.in) accessed on 22/11/2020 Also see: Crimes against women drop in 2020 but rule violations spike in Covid-hit year: NCRB India News (indiatoday.in) Accessed on 8/6/2022, which reports that Cruelty by Husbands recorded the highest number of crimes against women in India in 2020.

[100] See: Change (forbes.com), How India's Healthcare System Treated Women During Pandemic | NewsClick, Indian Women, Inordinately Burdened By HouseWork, Pay The Motherhood Penalty | (indiaspend.com), Glaring realities of healthcare spending in Asia: Privatization, Health inequality, and Covid-19 in the region | ADN21 | ASIA DEMOCRACY NETWORK (adnasia.org). Accessed on 6/12/2020

[101] Child marriages in Maharashtra surge by 78.3% amid lockdown as families reel under poverty—Mumbai news—*Hindustan Times*. Accessed on 6/12/2020

[102] Population Foundation of India (PFI) estimates 20 million babies born from January 2021 which is nine months after the announcement of the lockdown from this March, because 25 million couples in India did not have access to contraception. Another 1.85 million women have been denied access to abortion post the lockdown. UNICEF highlights that for every three months the lockdown continues, there will be an additional

Reverse Migrants: States like UP and Bihar faced a heavy pressure of accommodating reverse migrants. It was in fact an opportunity to deploy their expertise at home. Some of them have reportedly undertaken skill-mapping, which had never been thought of before. There is little evidence though, of how this information has been put to use. The Budget of 2022-23 lays emphasis on improving infrastructure through PM Gati Shakti, which is expected to push up the economic growth through the multiplier effect but this has come after the migrants have already returned to their work-destinations.

Albeit painful, reverse migration was a unique opportunity for the 'labour surplus' states to use this experienced labour force to work on building industrial estates for setting up new MSMEs, etc., to attract more business.

As for migrants with experience of running tiny or home-based businesses, it is possible to bring them together into clusters to form co-operatives. Having faced a similar fate of deprivation, the reverse migrants are more likely to team up with each other through trust. And trust is an intangible component of any business because it reduces the transaction costs. And this is even more true for co-operatives.[103] There are successful examples of migrant workers' co-operatives that emerged as a response to the crisis in many countries. States can benefit by collaborating with the ILO which has a rich experience of

---

two million women who will not have access to modern contraceptives. See: How India's Healthcare System Treated Women During Pandemic | NewsClick. Accessed on 6/12/2020. The countries with the highest numbers of forecast births are expected to be India (20.1 million), China (13.5 million), Nigeria (6.4 million), Pakistan (5 million) and Indonesia (4 million). Also See> Millions more cases of violence, child marriage, female genital mutilation, unintended pregnancy expected due to the COVID-19 pandemic (unfpa.org) Accessed on 8/6/2022.

[103] See: https://mfasia.org/migrant-workers-cooperatives-as-a-crisis-response/ for Indonesian experience of migrant workers co-opertives. Accessed on 22/11/2020

hand-holding many such projects across the globe.[104] Finally, co-operatives are important because they facilitate decentralization of the process of growth, which is Gandhian in spirit.

Urban Development: Covid-19 emphasized the need for cleanliness and hygiene like never before. It compelled the urban local bodies to improve and expand their health services. It has also a wake-up call to transform slums and the living conditions therein. It has made us aware that ignoring hygiene or treating it as welfare or a charitable act is not going to help because these are necessary for everyone's survival now. In a way, ensuring decent living conditions, which is implicit in the dignity of labour, is thrust upon us as a need for survival. One thing the pandemic has taught us is that an infection anywhere is a threat to health everywhere.

Decent Work, Occupational Safety and the Covid Allowance: Though only for a brief period the labour deficit States from where the migrant workers have moved out have had to raise wages due to severe shortage of labour. There are instances where workers have been given air tickets to return to work![105] These may be anecdotal instances, but they do echo the need to treat workers with dignity though under duress. One only hopes that at least some such benefits last long enough to emerge as new practises. This reminds us of Gandhiji's intervention in the Ahmedabad textile strike to negotiate the issue of plague allowance.[106] In my opinion there are several reasons that

---

[104] https://www.ilo.org/wcmsp5/groups/public/—-ed_emp/—-emp_ent/—-coop/documents/publication/wcms_221743.pdf

[105] https://timesofindia.indiatimes.com/india/3-times-more-pay-air-travel-how-migrants-are-being-wooed-back/articleshow/76210270.cms. And https://www.indiatvnews.com/news/india/construction-firms-migrant-workers-air-tickets-sops-623400

[106] https://nvdatabase.swarthmore.edu/content/ahmedabad-textile-laborers-win-strike-economic-justice-1918, https://dialogueden.com/2020/blog/from-the-1918-influenza-pandemic-time-and-gandhis-role-as-an-arbitrator/

necessitate thinking of a Covid allowance and determining some standards to calculate it, and these are:

1. The virus is very likely to stay longer than was initially feared. That makes it systemic and not temporary, and hence the need to institutionalize the support through designing a Covid allowance.

2. The lockdown inspired by the pandemic has led to what is being called the New Normal of working from home. This mode saves the variable costs of establishment such as power charges, use of computers, maintaining canteen facility, and overall housekeeping for the employer, while the employees bear a higher cost in real and money terms. This is because: i. Employees might now work for longer hours, being available 24x7, ii. They have to face the stress of managing the work-space and home-space together, and iii. They might have to make an additional investment to upgrade infrastructure. It is important to compensate the employees for this.

3. Employees who travel to their workplaces during these times run a high risk of contracting the infection themselves if they resort to public transport. Opting for safer and more personalized travel to the workplace, on the other hand, is sure to hike their travel expenses.

4. It is now becoming clear, that those recovered from Covid are indeed not far from danger, as there are cases showing serious damages affecting vital organs of the patients even after recovery. The expenditure on testing and medicines is likely to rise unpredictably for those who contracted the infection even once.

5. Lastly, of course, the ability to pay of the employer would have to be taken into account, because harmony in the employer-employee relationship is crucial to the Gandhian view of industrial relations.

It has been argued by K. R. Shyam Sunder (2021) that given its tendency to mutate and spread rapidly, Covid should be covered under the labour code meant for Occupational Safety and Health (OSH).

Environmental Concerns: Lockdown reportedly reduced the air and water pollution substantially.[107] It would be up to us to maintain it with as much caution as possible. For instance there might be greater possibilities of shifting to more eco-friendly urban transport system and manufacturing systems to enable reduction in the carbon emissions along with creation of more employment opportunities.

Reclaiming Demographic Advantage: UNICEF has reported a rise in child labour due to the pandemic[108]. A combination of factors such as: closure of schools due to lockdown, rise in the incidence of poverty due to unemployment among parents and/or rise in health expenditure of the family due to Covid have pushed more children into work,[109] and this can seriously affect India's ability to monetise its proverbial demographic dividend. The digital divide became more obvious than ever when education became an online activity.[110] Even those who had the access to digital education could not benefit much as the quality of teaching and learning remains arguably far less effective.[111]

---

[107] https://www.sciencedaily.com/releases/2020/07/200716101621.htm, https://www.sciencedirect.com/science/article/abs/pii/S0048969720323378, https://www.timesnownews.com/mirror-now/in-focus/article/covid-19-lockdown-leading-to-significant-drop-in-ganga-river-water-pollution/574016. Accessed on 25/11/2019.

[108] Child labour rises to 160 million—first increase in two decades (unicef. org) Accessed on 8/6/2022

[109] Child labour increased during COVID-19: survey—The Hindu accessed on 8/6/2022.

[110] Digital divide still a challenge in remote teaching, learning, say experts—Times of India (indiatimes.com), Covid-19 pandemic risks a lost generation in India as digital divide widens | Mint (livemint.com), Exploring India's Digital Divide | ORF (orfonline.org) Accessed on 8/6/2022.

[111] Learning outcomes for online versus in-class education | Australian Academy of Science. Accessed on 8/6/2022.

Learning a craft or a skill that needs hands on experience may be particularly difficult to accomplish through this mode. And yet it is an effective platform that can readily provide insights from experts through podcasts, webinars, and videos, at learner's convenience. Education is beyond literacy. Gandhiji advocated education that ingrained ethical values and also taught some essential skill to the learner to work with hands. Education should nurture self-esteem and team work. Though these are difficult to achieve in a state of a prolonged social isolation, a lot would depend on how effectively we manage to meet these challenges if we wish to reclaim the lost ground.

The Journey of Zomato: A Journey of Two Engineers towards a Responsible Business

Founded by two IIT graduates Deependra Goyal and Pankaj Chaddah as a Foodiebay in 2008, Zomato got its name in 2010. This aggregator that operated through food delivery app, soon spread to major metros of India from Delhi to Ahmedabad, Bengaluru etc. Pandemic turned out to be a boon for this firm as people could not visit restaurants. The sales increased by 225% in the first half of FY 2020. Soon the restaurant partners increased by 177% and Zomato became a multinational aggregator.

Zomato went for an IPO launch on July 14, 2021 in which only institutional investors were to enter. On July 23 2021 as the stock opened at Rs 116 on the NSE, a 52.63 percent premium to its final offer price of Rs 76. The listing price on the Bombay Stock Exchange was at Rs 115, up 51.32 percent. The stock closed at Rs 125.85 on BSE, up 65.59 percent with respect to the issue price, while on NSE, the stock closed at Rs 125.30, up 64.87 percent against the stock's issue price of Rs 76. By February 2022 there was a dip in the stock price.

In May 2022 Zomato announced Employee Stock Ownership Plan for the delivery partners who have been with the company for 5 to 10 years. (see Zomato CEO gifts his Rs 700-crore ESOP proceeds to delivery partners—*The Hindu BusinessLine*). As per this announcement, the ESOPs proceeds worth Rs 700 crores (net of taxes) have been committed to Zomato Future Foundation (ZFF). This will include donations toward the education of up to two children of all Zomato Delivery Partners, special programmemes for girl children and higher education scholarships, among other benefits.

The company has also announced cash benefit of Rs. 50.000/- per annum per child for a delivery partner who has worked for five years and Rs. 1, 00, 000/- per child for a partner who has worked for 10 years or more. The condition of duration of service is relaxed in case of women. Welfare schemes are also announced for girl children who complete education up to standard 12 and graduation level.

At a time when a global giant delivery aggregator like Amazon seems to neglect hygiene and safety of workers at work place and ignore their fatigue experienced due to long and hectic working hours, (See: 'I'm not a robot': Amazon workers condemn unsafe, grueling conditions at warehouse | Amazon | *The Guardian*) Zomato does stand out because of its fraternal policies towards people who contribute to its revenue on the ground.

The Economic Survey of India 2021-22 puts the number of start-ups as 14,000, with 44 unicorns (a start-up company with a value of over one billion dollars) And certainly a few of them particularly in the education sector have prospered significantly during the pandemic.

It would be interesting to find out how many of them follow the path of a responsible business, something that is in tune with Gandhiji's idea of trusteeship.

Conclusion

Any attempt to engage in greater sustainability is Gandhian in spirit, because it can be achieved only by rising above the baser instincts of greed, violence and petty self-importance. The Sustainable Development Goals can be seen as stemming essentially out of an integrated vision grounded in Gandhian thought. Interdependence and independence are no longer antithetical in the Gandhian view, which perceives the need for harmonious coexistence of human beings with each other, with nature, and other beings supported by the planet. The crisis of the pandemic has opened up opportunities to tweak our ways of living on this planet in a wiser and more compassionate way. The choices we make now can have long-term effects on our well-being.

References

Basu, Kaushik. 2018. A Short History of India's Economy: A Chapter in the Asian Drama.

United Nations University UNU WIDER Working Paper /124. October.

Bondurant, Joan V. 1958. *Conquest of Violence: The Gandhian Philosophy of Conflict*. Princeton: Princeton University Press.

Chakrabarty, Bidyut. 2006. *Social and Political Thought of Mahatma Gandhi*. London/New York: Routledge.

Chandra, Sudhir. 2020. Thinking of Gandhi Today. *Economic and Political Weekly* 55: 38.

Chatterji Rakhahari. 1976. *The Indian Journal of Political Science* 37:4, pp. 42-57.

Dasgupta, A.K. 1975. *The Economics of Austerity*. Oxford University Press.

Desai, Mahadev.1918. *A Righteous Struggle: A Chronicle of the Ahmedabad Textile Labourer's Fight for Justice*. Ahmedabad: Jivanji Dahyabhai Desai.

Erikson, Erik H. 1969. *Gandhi's Truth: On the Origins of Militant Nonviolence*. New York: W. W. Norton & Company.

Patel, Sujata. 1984. Class Conflict and Workers' Movement in Ahmedabad Textile Industry, 1918-23. *Economic and Political Weekly* 19: 20/21 (May 19-26), pp. 853-855; 857-864. http://www.jstor.org/stable/4373280

Mehrotra, Santosh, ed. 2020. *Reviving Jobs: An Agenda for Growth*. New Delhi: Penguin.

Nayak, Pulin B. 2017. A. K. Dasgupta on Gandhi and the Economics of Austerity. Economic and Political Weekly 52: 50, 16 Dec.

Spodek, Howard. 1965. The 'Manchesterisation' of Ahmedabad. *The Economic Weekly* March 13, 483-490.

Spodek, Howard. 2011. *Ahmedabad: Shock City of Twentieth-Century India*. Bloomington, IN: Indiana University Press.

Shyam, Sunder K. R. 2021. *Impact of Covid- 19, Reforms and Poor Governance on Labour Rights in India*. New Delhi: Synergy Books India.

Vyas, M. 2020. The jobs bloodbath of April 2020. CMIE, Mumbai.

Weber, Thomas. 2020 Gandhi and the Pandemic. *EPW* 55: 25, 20 June.

TRANSFORMING ADVERSITY INTO PROSPERITY

Application of Gandhian Thought to Higher Education

Sybil Thomas

Introduction

Worldwide, leaders as well as common men and women are trying to make sense of ways in which the world is trying to rebuild itself from the grassroots after the unprecedented changes that COVID 19 brought in society. In the midst of this pandemic, all agree that there is a need for the reconstruction of society based on reflection. A new society that is built on values of freedom, equality, justice and brotherhood is struggling to be born. These times are similar in many ways to the times of reconstruction of society post-independence. As a new democratic society was established, our founding fathers looked to education as an instrument of social transformation and an instrument to make democratic values a reality for every individual. Education today owes much to the thoughts and philosophy of great thinkers like Mahatma Gandhi, Tagore, Vivekananda, Aurobindo, Dr. Babasaheb Ambedkar, Tilak and many more.

The question that we often ask ourselves is whether the thoughts and philosophies of these great thinkers are relevant today in a neoliberal, post-colonial era after 73 years of independence and when the world is ravaged by a pandemic which has affected all facets of society.

For this discourse, we will look at the thoughts and philosophy of Mahatma Gandhi, the Father of the Nation, and see how this is relevant for us in higher Education. The reason for situating the discourse in the space of higher education is that universities have been conceived of as the 'sanctuaries of the inner life of the nation' through their role and functions.

Dr. Radhakrishnan, philosopher-scholar, produced the first Report on Higher Education in free India in 1948 (Radhakrishnan, 2017). Excerpts from the report, in the sections on the university, say that:

> The academic problem has assumed new shapes. We have now a wider conception of the duties and responsibilities of universities. They have to provide leadership in politics and administration, the professions, industry and commerce. They have to meet the increasing demand for every type of higher education, literary and scientific, technical and professional.

> If India is to confront the confusion of our time, she must turn for guidance, not to those who are lost in the mere exigencies of the passing hour, but to her men of letters, and men of science, to her poets and artists, to her discoverers and inventors. These intellectual pioneers of civilization are to be found and trained in the universities, which are the sanctuaries of the inner life of the nation.

Mahatma Gandhiji's vision on education was for the individual and the betterment of society, country and the world. His experience in South Africa not only changed his world view but also challenged him to commit his life to transform India and the world at large. Situating higher education in this context, it is all of us, the privileged, who are a part of the 26.3% of the gross enrolment ratio (GER) in higher education (Bhattacharjee 2020) who have the greater responsibility to ensure that this education we have received is self-transformative and in turn transforms societies that we are a part of.

After looking at the mission that we are involved with in the sector of higher education, we can now attempt to address the question of relevance in the areas of:

- Conceptions of Knowledge
- Concept of Curriculum
- Teacher and Learner in Higher Education

Conceptions of Knowledge

The ultimate objective of education as envisioned by Gandhiji is not only for a balanced and harmonious individual but also a balanced and harmonious society—a just society where nothing divides the haves and have-nots and everybody is assured of getting their basic needs satisfied, and all have the right to freedom. This provides the basis for understanding the concept of knowledge, according to Gandhiji. Knowledge evolved from the activity of the child in society. That was the basis of the Nai Talim and the Wardha scheme of education. Children learn by doing, and in doing, their educational and economic needs are fulfilled. When children learn based on craft and societal engagement, education does not alienate the individual, but gives worth and value to every child, the village child and the urban child alike.

For Gandhiji, education meant an all-round drawing out of the best in child and man—body, mind and spirit. To fulfil this aim, literacy was a means and not the end of education. He went on to say that literacy in itself is no education at all. He recommended that a child's education should begin with the teaching of handicrafts (Gandhi 1937).

Knowledge, for Gandhiji, was not limited to declarative knowledge, which is factual information but the knowledge that is valuable, the knowledge that can be connected to the students' experience in order to be remembered and used. He recommended procedural knowledge; that is, information about how to perform a task related to day-to-day life and, most importantly, conditional knowledge of 'when,' 'why,' and 'under what conditions' declarative and procedural knowledge should be used. A knowledge that is anchored in this type of thinking will contribute to an individual being more reliant, relevant to society and being able to deal with any situation with confidence. It is this kind of knowledge that prepares the individual to face ambiguity and uncertainty with confidence. This was reflected

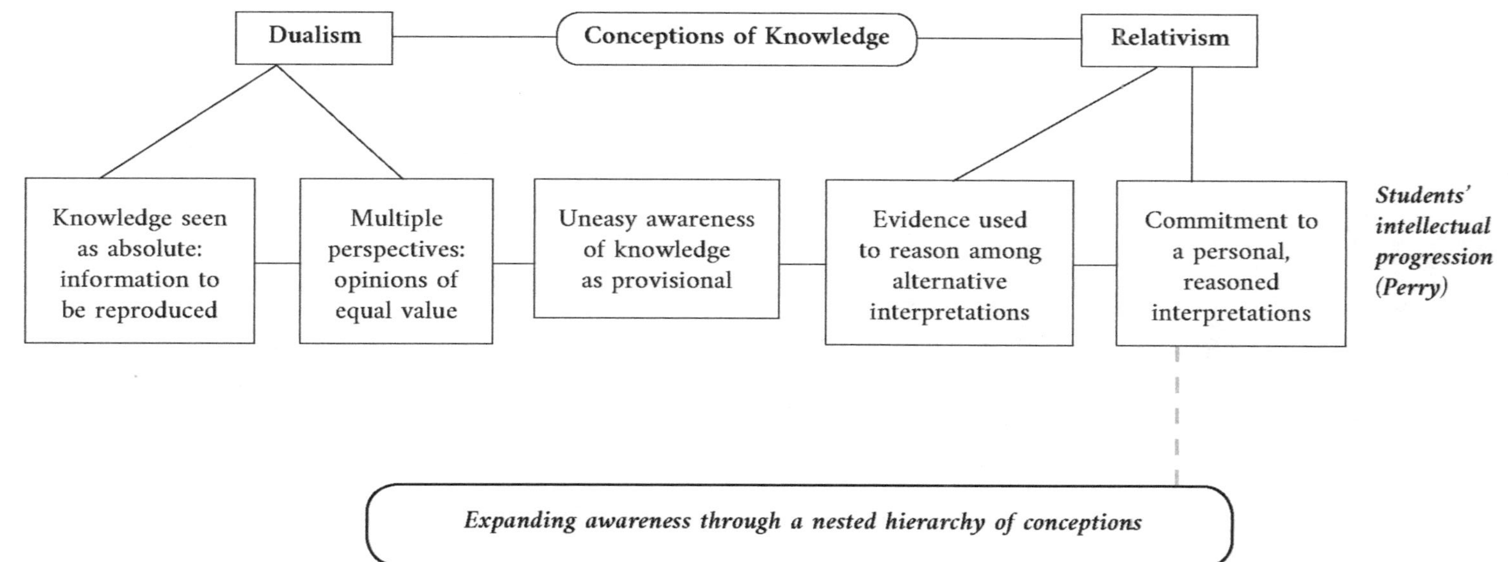

FIGURE 1: Conception of Knowledge

in his ideas of basic education. Today we see that this kind of knowledge is endorsed by contemporary thinkers. The model of students' intellectual progression, as advocated by Entwistle, as shown in the diagram below, is a reflection of an understanding of how university students progress towards a sophisticated concept of knowledge (Entwistle 2007). It also brings out the need for inculcating a commitment to relativist conceptions of knowledge, which was what Gandhiji visualized.

This is an example of the potential of the philosophy of education and more specifically, the philosophy of education of Mahatma Gandhi. It has influenced the thoughts and attempts of educationists trying to find answers to questions about:

- What is worth teaching and learning?
- What is knowable, and
- What should an individual do with education?

Attempting to answer these questions has been the concern of educationists who have tried to find ways to reach the ideals of philosophers. Our National Curriculum Framework 2005 too, envisioned education using procedural and conditional knowledge as propagated by Gandhiji.

The National Curriculum Framework 2005 of the Government of India posits that it is the child's community and local environment that are significant spaces where learning takes place. It is in this space that the child interacts with the environment and derives meaning for his/her existence which is nothing but knowledge generation (NCF 2005). Therefore, the policy urges education to blur these boundaries between the space of education and schools. It goes on to build on the notion that strengthening and capitalizing on students' knowledge which they pick up by relating to the world is what will give them meaningful learning experiences. This kind of knowledge, that is gained through activities, builds the procedural and conditional knowledge that is lasting and pragmatic. Education must strive to focus on and celebrate this kind of knowledge.

The pandemic forced us to rethink and revisit our ways of living and thinking. Mere declarative knowledge is no longer enough; to adapt and thrive in the 'new normal', higher education needs to emphasize procedural and conditional knowledge to equip learners to create a new social order.

Concept of Curriculum

Generally speaking, the term 'curriculum' refers to a variety of things. A simplistic summarization of the term curriculum is: a vision of the capabilities and values that every individual must have; and a socio-political and cultural vision for society. In curriculum studies, the moral, political and ideological aims behind the various conceptualizations of curricula have been studied for decades. A curriculum relates to the knowledge, skills and understanding that are to be mastered (rather than to rules of conduct within the school, for example) and the sequence in which they are to be taught. In addition, it is related to the whole phase of education rather than to individual lessons or even groups of lessons. The curriculum could then be defined as the prescribed content of knowledge, understanding and skill that fulfils the aims of education (Winch 1996).

Therefore, the curriculum is the vision of society for its young. It is formed through process of negotiation. In this section, the focus will be on approaches to curriculum studies and how the philosophy of Mahatma Gandhi informs and challenges us to look at the curriculum more holistically. The researches in the area of curriculum studies reflect this notion of different approaches to understanding the curriculum. It is against this model that we can see how Gandhiji positioned his conceptualization of the curriculum.

For Gandhiji, the curriculum was not restricted to content alone. Curriculum as equal to syllabus and content was a narrow understanding of what schooling should provide. This approach of, looking at curriculum as content as in McCormick's

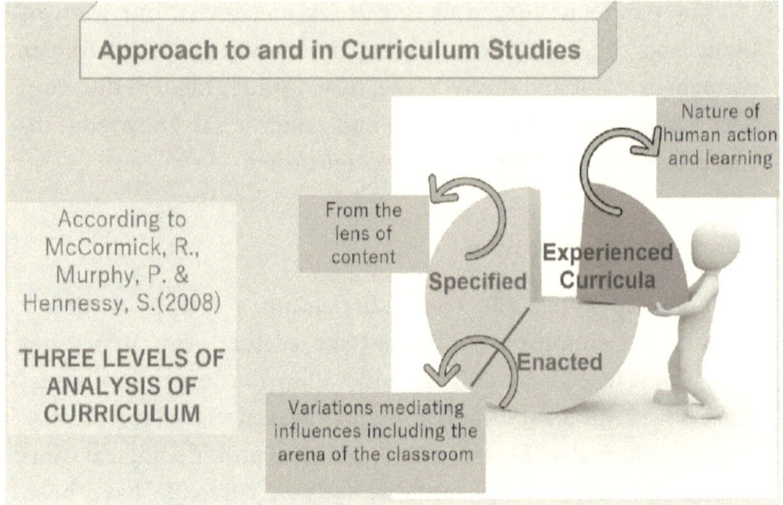

FIGURE 2: Approach to and in Curriculum Studies

approach (2000) to understanding the curriculum is termed the specified curriculum. At the specified curriculum level, Gandhiji's philosophy gives much thought to the principles guiding the choice of basic craft, art and health. On the other hand, the enacted curriculum relates to the way in which the prescribed curriculum is actualized in classroom practises. Gandhiji then moved on to recommend that experiences should be provided that are rich in educational possibilities and have scope for cooperative activity. That is the domain of content transactions in classroom spaces. He also emphasized that a proper place must be given to the planning and evaluation of every undertaking; there must be room for initiative and children must learn to take personal responsibility for their progress. These aspects of his thought are related to the experienced curriculum domain. It is here that the curriculum should not only be concerned with what and how content is transacted but also with the experiences of students and teachers. These experiences should be captured and evaluated.

As time went on, there was a growing consensus that crafts

which best met these requirements were those most closely concerned with the basic needs of human life, the production and preparation of food and clothing, the use of clay and wood to provide both shelter and the tools and utensils of daily living. So even today, we see that if this concept of craft is accepted, there is a growing demand not only in academic circles but also from the stakeholders that the curriculum should be closely related to the needs of society and the ownership of the curriculum should rest with the teachers and students. It calls for autonomy and distinctness in approach to curriculum construction. It is only when students of higher education are equipped with critical skills of thinking that arise from the procedural and conditional knowledge or relative conceptions of knowledge that they will be empowered enough to take ownership and be involved in their

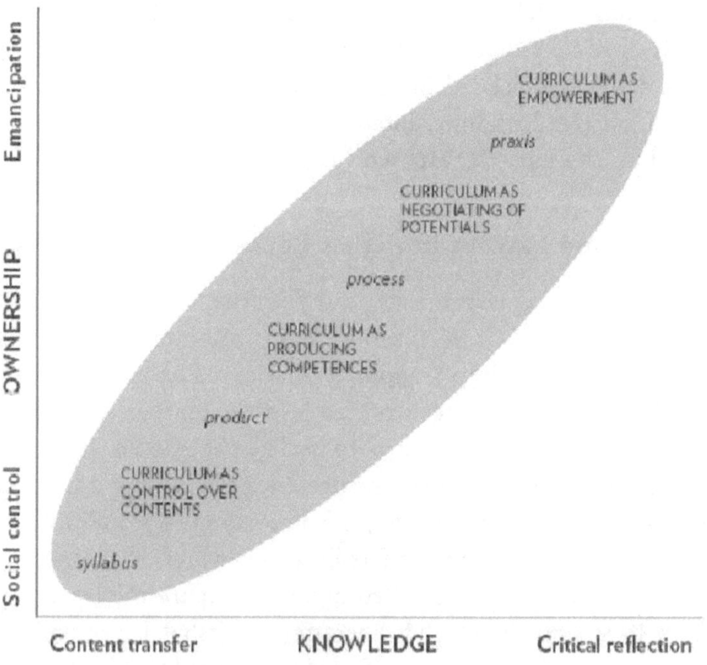

FIGURE 3: Framework for Conceptualizing Curriculum Approaches

own curricula. This is a challenge in a society that is striving to bring in homogeneity on one hand and an over-emphasis on individualism, on the other hand.

This relationship between the notions of conceptions of knowledge and ownership within the space of the curriculum and has been put diagrammatically in figure 3.

Relating Gandhiji's thoughts to conceptualizing the frameworks of curriculum approaches (Annala, Lindén & Mäkinen 2016), we see that his thoughts on the curriculum are spread into the domains of the enacted and the experienced curriculum as well. He encouraged a lot of evaluation, initiation and experiences that would build the praxis aspect of the teaching-learning process. Gandhiji's philosophy even today implores us as educationists in higher education to reflectively look at ways in which the prescribed, enacted and experienced curriculum could be made emancipating, liberating and transforming. A curriculum which is experienced and dynamically rooted in the needs of society would be flexible enough to accommodate the radical changes needed in the present times to help our youth overcome the economic, intellectual and emotional challenges posed by the post-COVID world.

Teacher and Learner in Higher Education

Every individual is precious, every learner is precious, every teacher is precious is the message that is communicated to those who delve deeper into Gandhiji's writings. For him, education should help, prepare, nurture and lead the learner towards the only purpose of life, which is to realize the Atman. It is when the person is able to realize the presence of God not only in the self but in everything around, this according to Gandhiji is the spiritual realization, the self-realization, which is the primary aim of life. Education is called upon to prepare the learner for this self-realization which is liberation (moksha). He emphasized the ancient Indian wisdom—'*Sa vidya ya vimuktaya*' (that which liberates knowledge) which should be the aim of education.

For this self-realization to be achieved, which leads to liberation, Mahatma Gandhi laid down some rules for students. Morality and righteousness always have to be considered as an essential and non differentiable part of education. He said that on one hand, students should gain education under the strict regimen of high morals, self-control and right thinking. On the other, they would also be expected to provide service to society in general.

According to Gandhiji, the purpose of education was not to teach a particular profession or occupation to the children, but to develop the 'full man or woman' through teaching an occupation. This includes respect towards parents, teachers and elders and admiration of the young. It also includes following social traditions and constant cognizance of duties and responsibilities. Moral action, values and spiritualism were some of the critical features of Gandhiji's vision for the individual and society. This, for Gandhiji, comes through engagement with craft and working together in the community and for the community. It is through work that the learner learns self-discipline and values required for community living. This has been underlined in the vision of the UGC and other statutory bodies that emphasize community engagements and internships. Like never before, there is a growing consensus around the need for these programmes in university education not only in India but around the globe.

However, the challenge lies in enriching and equipping teachers and students to commit themselves to the philosophy and in the enacted and experienced curriculum space. One sees how Gandhian philosophy is seen in the understanding of learning through the lens of the constructivist and situated cognition view to learning. Rogoff identifies three interrelated perspectives on learning associated with three planes of analysis. The three planes are 'community,' 'interpersonal' and 'personal'; the view of the learning process associated with each of these is apprenticeship (where an individual participates in activities with others), guided participation (participation with others through observation and hands-on involvement) and participatory appropriation (how individuals change through their involvement in the activity) (Rogoff 1995). It is about becoming rather than acquisition. This, too, is a testimony to how philosophical thoughts have guided different understandings and praxis.

For Gandhiji, education was an instrument to bring equality in society, and he wanted every individual to be a part of this process. Rich or poor, every child deserved to be a part of this liberating process. As we go through the various writings of Gandhiji, we see that he constantly underscores the importance of education for the upliftment of the oppressed in society, for the growth and development of the community as a whole, and thereby the building of the nation. This vision of 'Education for All' finally culminated in the Right to Education Act of 2009.

How can this be attained? It can be attained only when a person of strong moral character who has experienced true education himself leads the students through the liberating experience called education. It will be attained through awareness of the teaching methodologies that support the emancipatory approaches to learning and teaching in higher education, as summarized in the diagram below. Therefore, the teacher should also be aware of different ways of leading the student through a liberating process and using student-centred approaches. Given below is the diagram of Entwistle, who shows how the different approaches to teaching in higher education can lead a student to make movements in learning (Entwistle 2007).

During the present times of great uncertainty, conception of education as a process where a teacher is herself emancipated and leads her learners to liberation through education would help both teachers and learners find a direction to work towards. It would also help them to use education as a powerful enabler to tide over the times of crisis.

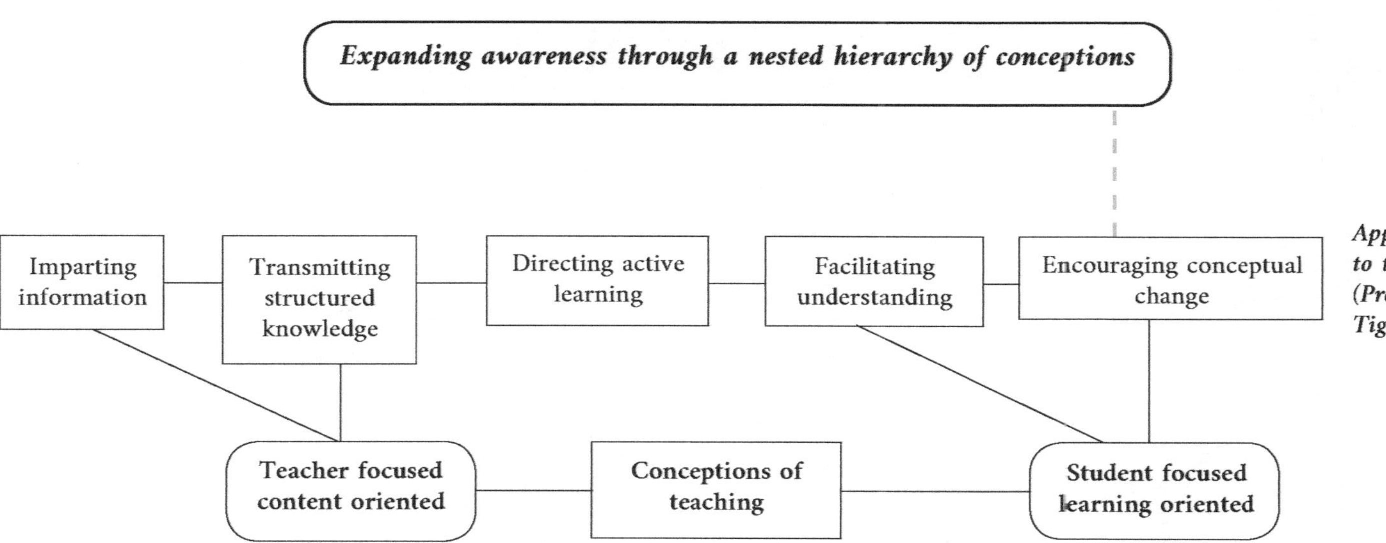

FIGURE 4: Approaches to Teaching

Conclusion

COVID 19 has brought unprecedented change to society, and Gandhiji's vision of New Education based on values of freedom, equality, justice and brotherhood is relevant and necessary to tackle the future. There is a loud cry for universities to create knowledge and train minds who would bring together material and human resources. The National Education Policy 2020 also reiterates the evolution of pedagogy towards education centred around experience, meaningful engagement and leading to gainful employment.

> While learning by rote can be beneficial in specific contexts, pedagogy must evolve to make education more experiential, holistic, integrated, discovery-oriented, learner-centred, discussion-based, flexible, and, of course, enjoyable (NEP 2020).

The policy reiterates that the curriculum must include basic arts, crafts, humanities, games, sports and fitness, languages, literature, culture and values. These subjects are in addition to science and mathematics, to ensure the all-round development of the learners as well as to ensure that the process of education is fulfilling to the learner.

Finally, the watchwords are: education for character building; education for developing ethical, rational individuals; education for compassion and care, while addressing the need for knowledge and skills for employment. These are what we are called upon to strive towards for ourselves and the ones that we are entrusted with.

Reiterating the words of The UN General Secretary, António Guterres, we need solidarity more than ever. We belong to each other. We stand together, or we fall apart. These times are similar in many ways to the times of reconstruction of society post-independence. Great leaders like Mahatma Gandhi, who were inspired by education, were willing to give their all to help the nation realize that freedom, equality, justice and brotherhood are possible ideals through education.

Through this exercise of going back and forth in time, we see how education has built on the vision of great thinkers like Mahatma Gandhi and we need to be assured of the fact that these ideals are there, and can be used as a beacon as we reconstruct society based on togetherness in the post-COVID world.

References

Annala, J., Lindén, J. & Mäkinen, M. 2016. Curriculum in Higher Education Research. In *Researching Higher Education: International Perspectives on Theory, Policy and Practise* ed. J. Case & J. Huisman. SHRE Society for Research into Higher Education & Routledge. https://doi:10.4324/9781315675404

Bhattacharjee, Sanchayan. 2020. Increasing enrolment in higher education: A quantitative and qualitative challenge | ORF. Retrieved September 4, 2020, from https://www.orfonline.org/expert-speak/increasing-enrolment-in-higher-education-a-quantitative-and-qualitative-challenge-55883/

Entwistle, Noel. 2007. Research into Student Learning and University Teaching. *BJEP Monograph Series II*, Number 4, *Student Learning and University Teaching* 1-18.

Gandhi, M.K.1937. *Basic Education*. Ahmedabad: Navajivan Publishing House.

McCormick, Robert and Patricia Murphy. 2000. Curriculum: The case for a focus on learning. In *The Routledge International Companion to Education* ed. M. Ben-Peretz, S. Brown and B. Moon. London: Routledge. https://doi.org/10.4324/9780203639061

Ministry of Human Resource Development, Government of India. 2020. National Education Policy. Retrieved September 6, 2020, from https://www.mhrd.gov.in/sites/upload_files/mhrd/files/NEP_Final_English_0.pdf

The National Council of Educational Research and Training. 2005. National Curriculum Framework. Retrieved September 4, 2020, from https://ncert.nic.in/pdf/nc-framework/nf2005-english.pdf

Radhakrishnan, S. 2017. Dr. Radhakrishnan Commission Report on Higher Education. *NMIMS Journal of Economics and Public Policy*, II, 11.

Rogoff, B. 1993. Observing Sociocultural Activity on Three Planes. In *Sociocultural Studies of Mind*, ed. J. V. Wertsch, P. del Río, and A. Alvarez, 139-163. New York: Cambridge University Press.

Winch, Christopher. 1996. Constructing Worthwhile Curriculum. *Journal of Philosophy of Education* 30:1, 45-56.

REVISITING GANDHI IN OUR CONTEMPORANEOUS WORLD

Virendra Kumar

Introduction

While exploring the relevance of Gandhi in our contemporaneous world within the ambit of the given theme, 'Mahatma Gandhi Then and Now,' the question that needs to be raised at the very outset is, 'what is Gandhi?' and not just 'who is Gandhi?' 'Gandhi is dead; long live Gandhi,' as we may say in a jurisprudential discourse for providing continuity from one generation to another. Likewise, in our contextual response, Gandhi stands for a unique idea, an innovative thought, or simply a benevolent philosophy of life emanating from the model of his own conduct, his life and his thoughts and actions. This is what survives even after the exit of Gandhi from the temporal world.

For deciphering the values of Gandhi's life, which have profoundly impacted the world in ways more than one in shaping its social, economic and political thinking, I tend to turn to the limited arena of his experiment during the freedom struggle with a diehard revolutionary. This was a young man, by the name of Prithvi Singh, with a chequered history of revolutionary exploits, and carrying a heavy price on his head, who voluntarily surrendered himself to Gandhi in 1938.

The historic account of the life of Prithvi Singh is well documented in the biography written by Rahul Sankriyayan, known as the Father of Indian Travelogue literature, in Hindi under the title *Sardar Prithvi Singh* (1944).[112] This account stands

---

[112] Peoples Publishing House, Pt. Ltd., New Delhi. The first edition of 1944 was followed in quick succession by the second edition in 1946, and

updated by Prithvi Singh in his own autobiography, also in Hindi, titled *Krantipath ka Pathic* (1964)[113] with a Foreword by Dr. Hazari Prasad Dwivedi, an eminent Hindi novelist, literary historian, essayist, critic and scholar par excellence.[114] The second Hindi edition was further updated and translated into English, and published by the Bhartiya Vidya Bhavan, Bombay, with the title *Baba Prithvi Singh Azad—The Legendary Crusader* (1987).[115]

Baba Prithvi Singh Azad (1892-1989) was one of the founder members of the Gadar Party in the United States of America in 1913, who suffered incarceration during the pre-independence period, including a long term in the Cellular Jail in the Andamans. After independence, he was accorded a position of great eminence when he was chosen as the President of the All India Freedom Fighters' Organization unanimously. The grateful Nation honoured him with the award of Padma Bhushan in 1977 'for his distinct contribution to society.' In 1978, he earned the Soviet Land Nehru Award for his reminiscences (in Hindi)—*Lenin ke desh mein* (In the Land of Lenin).

This essay is an attempt to bring to light some of the basic values of life emanating from the intimate interaction between Gandhi and Prithvi Singh. And how Gandhi's philosophy of truth and non-violence tempered and moulded the life of Prithvi Singh,

---

thereafter the third edition in 1979. Rahul Sankrityayan (9 April 1893–14 April 1963) played a pivotal role in giving the travelogue a 'literature form'.

[113] The first edition was published by Pragya Prakashan, Chandigarh. The second edition published by Shivlal Aggarwal & Co., Agra, appeared in 1970.

[114] Dr. Hazari Prasad Dwivedi (19 August 1907–19 May 1979) in his Foreword has, *inter alia*, commented: 'What is special about Baba Prithvi Singh's autobiography is the evidence of great faith and self-confidence, integrity and introspection. It is remarkably free from bitterness. He does not try to prove his point of view by condemning others. There is no place in his life for obstinacy. When he surrendered himself to Gandhiji, he showed an open mind, supreme courage and commendable detachment. He has the courage to shed his pet convictions...'

[115] Hereinafter simply cited as *The Legendary Crusader* (1987).

who was steadfast in his belief anchored in violent revolution. In this dedicated discourse, what is of crucial significance is not merely the end-result of attainment of freedom from the foreign rule but, also the *means* to attaining that end. It is in this process of pursuing that ultimate goal of freedom that some ideas, thoughts or principles get crystalized, which may be typically termed as the Gandhian principles of life. In this contextual matrix, we may finally examine how, in what respect, and to what extent those crystalized Gandhian principles continue to be of any relevance in our contemporary world, which is beset with multiple challenges in education, self-reliance, social relations, environment, etc., impinging upon the lives of people both as individuals and individuals as an integral part of society.

Saga of Revolutionary Exploits of Prithvi Singh (Prior to his Voluntary Surrender to Gandhi in 1938)[116]

Prithvi Singh, at heart ever a revolutionary, left his home and hearth at the prime age of 17 with the objective of liberating the motherland from the oppressive rule of the British. He travelled to Singapore, Hong Kong, Manila, and America incognito to seek support for his mission and avoiding police detection. During his sojourn in America, he joined a group of like-minded young people in 1913, who had founded a party—the Gadar Party—vowing to uproot the foreign power from Indian soil. For accomplishing their liberation mission, a group of those young revolutionaries, called Gadarites, returned to India by ship. However, while doing so, they all were caught at Calcutta port, excepting only one member, who managed to evade detection at that time. But soon he was also caught and sent to serve a long-term imprisonment. He was Prithvi Singh.

Owing to his exemplary courageous revolutionary spirit, Prithvi Singh was implicated in the First Lahore Conspiracy

---

[116] This account has been abstracted from *The Legendary Crusader* (1987).

Case (1915), and sentenced to death. However, as if by a quirk of history, the death sentence was commuted to life imprisonment, and he was lodged in Cellular Jail in the Andamans, which was the place for keeping apart the persons who were either the most dreaded criminals, or who were considered as the deadliest enemies of colonial rule in India.

During his lodging at Cellular Jail for about seven years, Prithvi Singh was not deterred from creating a sort of revolution amongst the otherwise subdued prisoners by undertaking a fast unto death for the inhuman treatment meted out to his fellow prisoners.[117] Somehow or the other, news about the totally unacceptable beastly treatment of prisoners and the unprecedented fast unto death for five long months leaked out to the mainstream population of India. This instantly created unrest and upheaval amongst the Indians across the country, and, which, in turn, forced the British to immediately shift him from the Cellular Jail in the Andamans to a prison house somewhere else in India.

In this process of transferring and re-lodging, while being escorted to Calcutta, Prithvi Singh jumped out of the running train in order to escape the life-term imprisonment. However, he was caught again and thereby ended his devilishly earned, short-lived 'freedom'. In due course of time, this mode of escape proved to be a mere rehearsal for his second similar attempt, jumping out of a running train in 1922, and thereafter Prithvi Singh remained underground and untraced for the next 16 years. During this long period, he pursued his revolutionary mission in close proximity to leading lights such as Dr. Narayan Damodar Savarkar, the younger brother of Veer Vinayak Savarkar, Shri Ganesh Raghunath Vaishampayann and Dr. P.V. Kane. With a generous grant from Maharaja Krishan Kumar Singh of Bhavanagar, a petty state in Saurashtra, and the invaluable

---

[117] Some of them died. However, Prithvi Singh survived with forced feeding over five months.

advice and help of Col. Zoraver Singh, Advisor to the then Resident of the British Government, Prithvi Singh managed to start a *Vyayamshala* (gymnasium), known as Ganesh Krida Mandal, and established himself as a 'physical instructor' under the assumed name of Swamirao. This gave him an opportunity to meet thousands of young minds and fill them with patriotic fervour.[118] However, during all these years of underground life in disguise, Prithvi Singh carried a heavy reward on his head, dead or alive, to any person who could help the British police in tracing him!

With the launching of the Satyagraha Movement by Mahatma Gandhi in 1930s, there came about a perceptible change in the political awakening of masses in India. This changed scenario made Prithvi Singh re-think at least on two clear counts. One, to overthrow the British power in India through armed rebellion was neither feasible nor desirable. Two, and this was indeed a knotty question, what sort of critical contribution he could make to the liberation front while remaining underground under the continual shadow of death?

At this critical juncture, Prithvi Singh, by virtue of his exploits in disguise against the British rule, which were amply reflected in the look-out notices affixed at all railway stations and other prominent public places, was tracked down as a fellow revolutionary by Sardar Bhagat Singh, Chandrashekar Azad and Sukhdev. This became feasible through the agency of trusted friends in the state of Gujarat. The trio instantly persuaded him to go to Soviet Russia as a member of the Republican Army with the objective of learning the strategy that ensured the success of the Red Army in bringing about a socialist revolution in Russia. How, in what manner, and at what opportune time to reach Russia, 'the land of revolutionaries' political dream,' was left to the ingenuity of Prithvi Singh himself. However, as a token of affirmation of their faith in their fellow revolutionary, they

---

[118] *The Legendary Crusader*, pp. 122-25.

gave him fifty cartridges along with an automatic pistol that could fire 11 bullets.[119]

Prithvi Singh managed to reach Soviet Russia, and studied the strategies of bringing about revolution, which were essentially premised on the fundamental principles of communism. He stayed there in Russia for about three years. Soon thereafter he returned to India and roamed stealthily for about five years here and there in search of an opportunity to accomplish his mission of liberation. However, one thing became increasingly clear to him that it was no longer possible to remain undetected by the British police and their CID. This thought of being caught at any moment became confirmed by the flashed news about the arrest of his very close fellow revolutionary, Comrade Gurmukh Singh, due to betrayal by an acquaintance.[120] This was a sharp reminder to him of the imminent danger of his being similarly caught at the instance of a bare acquaintance, who may not be able to resist the temptation of claiming a large reward by informing the police about his whereabouts. And that would, besides his own instant elimination, also play havoc with the life and interests of all the patriotic persons who had hitherto helped him, directly or indirectly, to remain underground for 16 years.[121] This in itself was the thought that pricked the conscience of Prithvi Singh continuously.[122]

Moreover, he also clearly perceived and understood that, by the year 1938, the political climate in India had dramatically changed. There was no longer any such revolutionary activity going on that required collection of arms or running an underground press for creating the environment of armed rebellion against British rule. Weary of living an underground life under the continual shadow of death, Prithvi Singh shared

---

[119] *Id.,* p. 144.

[120] *Id.,* p. 203.

[121] *Id.,* pp. 203-204.

[122] *Id.,* p. 204.

his predicament with his 'communist comrades' and sought their counsel.[123] 'They had nothing to guide me except to approach Gandhi ji,' recalls Prithvi Singh in his autobiography.[124]

Prithvi Singh 'Approaching' Gandhi through His Soul-stirring Surrender and Its Profound Impact on the Former

Prithvi Singh, with his chequered history of revolutionary exploits against the British Rule in India, and who was also carrying a reward on his head, met Gandhi in person for the first time in 1938. The meeting was arranged through persons close to Gandhi at about 10 p.m. on May 17, 1938 as soon as Gandhi returned to the Ashram after attending a Working Committee meeting of the Congress party.[125] The moment Prithvi Singh introduced himself as a person who had remained underground for 16 years and described the life he had hitherto lived under the assumed name of Swami Rao, Gandhi became instantly interested in him as he had already heard the name of Swamirao and his constructive work amongst the youth of Gujarat.[126] Spontaneously, Gandhi asked him to write down a brief account of his life and bring that narrative to him the next day.

Prithvi Singh took temporary shelter at the residence of one of his most trusted beneficiaries, and spent the whole night writing what Gandhi wanted him to reveal about himself. After doing what he was desired to do by Gandhi, Prithvi Singh felt somewhat shaky for a moment in his resolve to surrender. Since that short candid account of himself in his own handwriting

---

[123] *Ibid.*

[124] *Ibid.*

[125] The meeting was arranged through the intervention of two prominent personalities, Pattabhai Sitaramayya and Nanabhai Bhatt. See *ibid.*

[126] Swamirao of Ganesh Krida Mandal was a house-hold name in the State of Gujarat.

constituted clear confessed evidence against himself, it merited his instant hanging by the British government. In this alarming situation, he at once wanted to consult his 'communist friends at an appointed time,' but 'they did not turn up.'[127] This 'hurt' him a lot.[128] His predicament at that moment, in his own words, was: 'Surrendering myself to the police whom I had eluded for so many years with so many hair-breadth escapes was a question of life and death to me.'[129]

Be that as it may, the next day, before daybreak, Prithvi Singh moved to the residence of one of his confidants[130] and stayed with him till sunset. At nightfall, he called on Gandhi at the appointed time and place and submitted his narrative. Gandhi read his narration with 'all seriousness,' and spontaneously 'remarked' that Prithvi Singh was 'a dangerous man to the British Government,' and that his release was 'next to impossible.'[131] However, there was still one 'more serious problem' appended to his voluntary surrender: whether the British Government would let him live? And this prompted Gandhi to add:[132]

---

[127] *The Legendary Crusader*, p. 204.

[128] *Ibid*. The feeling of 'hurt' in the situational context, it needs to be borne in mind, should not be construed in the sense of 'betrayal', for it has already been stated that the eventual decision of surrender was taken by Prithvi Singh in consultation with his close communist friends. Thus, the so-called 'hurt' was just a panic reaction when there was every danger of being caught by police even before he could surrender himself to Gandhi, the prospect that he had successfully avoided for 16 long years. Maybe those communist friends had nothing more to add to what was already known and decided, and that there was no easy mode of communicating with Prithvi Singh to that effect either. Moreover, the chances of his being caught turned out to be true by the news of Prithvi Singh's anticipated surrender to Gandhi before his actual surrender.

[129] *Ibid*.

[130] Shantilal Shah, see *ibid*.

[131] *Ibid*.

[132] *Ibid*.

> 'You had better give up the idea of self-surrender and spend the rest of your life as you did for about 16 years. This country is bound to be free sooner or later. And then you would be a free man.'

To this candid counsel of Gandhi, filled with genuine concern for the safety of his life, Prithvi Singh readily responded with equal vehemence by saying:[133]

> 'Self-surrender does not mean only my personal [physical] freedom. It is high time to come into open and play the political game and set an example to the youth of the country.'

In the light of this intense interaction, although very short and cryptic, yet revealing the profound purpose of voluntary surrender, Gandhi 'postponed the issue for the time being,' and desired that 'in the meantime we both have time to think over and decide.'[134]

However, the 'time to think over and decide' was not to be, as the news of Prithvi Singh's intended surrender leaked out.[135] This led Gandhi, who intended to correspond with the Viceroy on the issue of voluntary surrender by Prithvi Singh, to change his mind the moment he was told that his idea had leaked. Without losing any time, Gandhi penned a letter on the issue of voluntary surrender by Prithvi Singh and sent the same through his private secretary to the Commissioner of Police, Bombay. In his communication, he stated frankly, without any prevarication, that Prithvi Singh, who was a rebel against the Government and had broken out of jail more than once, had taken refuge in his Ashram, and that the Commissioner of Police was welcome to come and arrest him while in his custody. To

---

[133] *Ibid.*

[134] *Ibid.*

[135] This news was confirmed by one of the very close friends of Prithvi Singh, namely Bahuddin Usman, who immediately rushed to meet Mahadev Desai, the private secretary of Gandhi, to check the veracity of the news, and found that it was absolutely true.

this cryptic communication, Gandhi added an earnest suggestive plea that if the Police Commissioner would let Prithvi Singh stay on in his Ashram, 'it would be good of him.'[136]

Realizing the fugitive character of Prithvi Singh and the anticipated portentous fallouts of his voluntary surrender, the Police Commissioner did not desire to act on his own. Promptly he wrote to the Central Government seeking their urgent directions in the matter. Lo and behold, the Viceroy ordered him 'to arrest Prithvi Singh, who was a dangerous criminal and to do so with due care.'[137] Pursuant to this directive, the Police Commissioner rang up Gandhi to say that 'according to instructions received from above, he would reach the Ashram the following day at two o'clock to arrest Prithvi Singh,' and that 'he would be grateful if Prithvi Singh was made available then.'[138]

When the news of his impending arrest by the police was conveyed to Prithvi Singh, he felt happy, without entertaining any feeling of remorse whatsoever. At this cheerful voluntary surrender by Prithvi Singh, Gandhi 'felt gratified.'[139]

The Police Commissioner along with a CID Officer arrived at the Ashram at the stipulated time. On his arrival, he immediately dismissed the Bombay police force, which had reached earlier and surrounded the Ashram to meet any eventuality or untoward situation. While disbanding the police force, the Commissioner said that he himself would take charge of Prithvi Singh and escort him to jail. The inmates of the Ashram assembled and began to recite prayers as a token of their farewell to Prithvi Singh. Some snapshots were also taken. With their blessing, Prithvi Singh left the Ashram happily and walked out with the Police Commissioner to jail, his new abode!

The next day, the news of Prithvi Singh's surrender to the

---

[136] *Ibid.*

[137] *Ibid.*

[138] *Ibid.*

[139] *Ibid.*

police was published in the local newspapers along with the political statement by Gandhi. However, an authentic historic account of how, in what manner and under what circumstances Prithvi Singh approached Gandhi, and then how he had voluntarily surrendered to the Police, was affirmed by Gandhi editorially in his weekly, *The Harijan* (May 28, 1938) under the title, 'The Fellow Pilgrim.'

After a detailed account of how Prithvi Singh was convicted for life in the Lahore Conspiracy Case of 1915, how he spent years in Andaman Cellular Jail and other jails in Madras and Rajmahendri, and how he succeeded in escaping from police custody by jumping out of a running train in 1922, and how thereafter he remained underground for 16 long years till the date of his surrender to him on May 18, 1938, Gandhi described him as a 'great revolutionary', who 'master minded his own movement.' About how Gandhi came to take him into his Ashram, he wrote:

> My ideology has no place for any kind of secrecy and I made it clear to him the self-surrender to the police was an act of national service. He accepted my view and offered himself on May 18, and the very next day I wrote to the District Collector that I would like to talk about his release for he had offered himself to the Government. And if the Government was not prepared to permit him to stay in my Ashram, the District Collector can come to my Ashram and take Prithvi Singh away. He wrote back that he had no power to order his release. He came the next day with Superintendent of Jail and took Prithvi Singh away.
>
> I was assured that he would be treated as an 'A' Class prisoner, which status I thought he richly deserved from the account of his life which he had written down at my instance. I am still of the opinion that he had done nothing to be ashamed of... He told me that he was wholly devoting himself to the study of non-violence in all its aspects, particularly its applicability in the struggle for freedom and that other revolutionaries like him were thinking along these lines. They had no other aim in

life but freedom of their country. He put his case so seriously
and earnestly that I did not find it difficult to agree with him.
Rather, I felt happy to be in their company on our pilgrimage.

Thus began the new chapter in the life of Prithvi Singh in
prison, from which he would be released (as per the history
sheet appended to his case) in the year 1966 after serving a
life sentence. For Prithvi Singh, his past was dead on May 18
(on the day of his surrender to Gandhi), and a new birth began
on May 19 (on the first day of his prison life)—this is what he
wrote in his diary, in which he began to write his autobiography
at the instance of Gandhi.

Soon thereafter, Gandhi continued to write persistently to
the Viceroy for the release of Prithvi Singh, but all in vain. The
British Government could not afford to oblige Gandhi on this
count, for 'they were not going to put their trust in Prithvi Singh,
taking him to be the most dangerous prisoner ever held.'[140]

In prison, Prithvi Singh spent most of his time in spinning,
reading and writing his biography as advised by Gandhi. He was
also encouraged by Gandhi to write to him regularly, giving an
account of his activities. Gandhi's responses to his letters are
truly illuminating and instructive. To wit:

On August 24, 1938:[141]

I had your letters. I am glad you are having good treatment
and that you have mental peace. I know that non-violence in
thought is the most difficult of attainment. And yet without
the co-operation of thought, non-violence in word and action
does not become the all-pervading irresistible force that it
undoubtedly is. Such non-violence comes through God's
grace. And that grace descends only on those who make
ceaseless effort much greater surely than what we make to
attain material ends...'

---

[140] *Id.*, p. 212.

[141] Gandhi's letter to Prithvi Singh, placed in Appendix, *The Legendary
Crusader*, p. 318.

On October 5, 1938,[142] recognizing the importance of spinning in attaining non-violence in thought, Gandhi, *inter alia*, wrote:

> I must get hold of the new type of wool-spinning Charkha for you.

On December 21, 1938:[143]

> Though I do not want to publish your letter, as the authorities may not like its publication whilst you are still a prisoner. I am going to make judicious use of it amongst those who are still unconvinced of the matchless superiority of non-violence over violence...

On May 21, 1939, after the completion of Prithvi Singh's first year in prison, Gandhi, responding to his letters, *inter alia*, wrote:[144]

> It is satisfying to note that you have sufficient inner-experience. You would have noticed in my recent articles that I lay much importance to spinning as a means of developing a sense of non-violence. I take it as a symbol. The pleasure that one receives on working at the spinning-wheel for a long time does prevent him from getting ruffled easily at a small provocation. If the wheel is in order, one is apt to be lost in one's own thought, for the harmonious sound of the wheel helps focused thinking: one who does not possess control over spinning, cannot be called a spinner.

> I hope that in the second year of your jail life, you would acquire great skill in spinning for the development of your belief in Ahimsa. *Your experiment and experience would be very helpful, for I think that you are one of the few who are capable of*

---

[142] Gandhi's letter to Prithvi Singh, placed in Appendix, *The Legendary Crusader*, p. 319.

[143] Gandhi's letter to Prithvi Singh, placed in Appendix, *The Legendary Crusader*, p. 320.

[144] Gandhi's letter to Prithvi Singh, placed in Appendix, *The Legendary Crusader*, p. 321. See also, *id.*, p. 216-217.

understanding their mind. People are deceived more by themselves than by others [Emphasis added].

A year later, Gandhi's emissary, Mahadev Desai, his private secretary, visited Prithvi Singh in jail. In his editorial note in *The Harijan* (September 1939) under the heading, 'A Prisoner among Prisoners', he recorded that he found Prithvi Singh in absolute cheerful exposition without bothering about his early release, and that he had 'already spun eighty pounds of wool' during his sojourn in prison.[145] Gandhi felt extremely happy to learn that Prithvi Singh fully comprehended his 'ideas on spinning' and that he had 'no difficulty in understanding the working of Ahinsa.'[146]

The sudden breakout of World War II in September 1939 brought about an understanding between the Viceroy and Gandhi to cooperate with the British Government in 'emergency'. This instantly resulted in the release of Prithvi Singh on September 23, 1939. The unexpected release brought him to the Ashram of Gandhi at Sevagram in Wardha, where he saw in person how Gandhi, through the exemplary mode of his own conduct, was desperately trying to teach the principles of 'truth and non-violence' in thought and action by leading a 'simple life.'

Crystallization of Value-principles of Life from the Interactive Association between Gandhi and Prithvi Singh and their Relevance in Our Contemporaneous World

Under the mould of Gandhi, Prithvi Singh truly turned into a different human being. On the very day of his voluntary surrender to Gandhi on May 18, 1938, we may recall that Prithvi Singh himself recorded in his prison diary that his past was dead and a new life began. How has this metamorphosis come about? In

---

[145] *Id.,* p. 213.

[146] See Gandhi's letter to Prithvi Singh, placed in Appendix, *The Legendary Crusader,* p. 217.

order to find an answer to this seemingly simple question, we need to remember the first point of contact between Gandhi and Prithvi Singh, and then ask ourselves: Why did Prithvi Singh choose Gandhi and surrender himself and his fate to him? It was indeed a very difficult and dicey proposition, involving the issue of his 'life and death.'

According to the account of the unfolding story of the life of Prithvi Singh, the initiating thought was none other than the innate feeling of *Trust* or *Faith* in Gandhi and his philosophy of non-violence. This very thought with due deliberation took him to Gandhi on the night of May 17, 1938. What did Gandhi do? Did he take him instantly merely at his word? No. Instead, he asked Prithvi Singh to come the next day with a brief written account of his life.

After putting down the naked facts about his underground life of 16 years in his own handwriting, and how he was sentenced to death in the Lahore conspiracy case of 1915, and how he made a daring escape by jumping out of a running train, Prithvi Singh himself became somewhat shaky in his resolve to see Gandhi. He immediately contacted his confidant communist friends to consult them before he took that critical step of surrendering, for it was pregnant with the possibility of his instant death at the hands of the British government on the basis of his own recorded handwritten statement, requiring no more corroborative evidence. Since nobody turned up to help him as promised, Prithvi Singh, albeit unsure of his decision, met Gandhi the following night.

On reading Prithvi Singh's candid account, we may recall what Gandhi said. He stated spontaneously that he would like him to re-consider his decision of voluntary surrender, as it would be 'next to impossible' for him (Gandhi) to get Prithvi Singh released, for he was already identified as the most 'dangerous man to the British Government.' The decision on voluntary surrender was, thus, deferred for the time being.

What was the impact of this deferment? Prithvi Singh's trust in Gandhi as the saviour of the situation got confirmed and validated. Gandhi's trust in Prithvi Singh gained ascendance in his estimation, for he saw and visualised his critical role in the struggle for freedom. This made Gandhi to plan at that very moment to correspond immediately with the Viceroy about his case being treated as that of surrender by a political person and not by a fugitive. This mutuality of trust turned out to be of crucial significance: Prithvi Singh's 'hesitant' surrender became truly 'voluntary,' as it was based upon 'understanding' the intent and spirit of Gandhi; and Gandhi also felt assured in his resolve, as he perceived the possibility of transforming a 'violent' man into a person pursuing the principle of 'non-violence' in his thoughts and actions for attaining the goal of freedom.

This background of mutuality of 'trust' and 'understanding' on both sides led Prithvi Singh to enter prison life with a positive mind. And with this began a new relationship of 'teacher and taught' between Gandhi and Prithvi Singh. At the very threshold, as a first step towards comprehending the principle of 'non-violence' (Ahimsa), Gandhi exhorted Prithvi Singh to make the spinning-wheel his constant companion. Which he did decisively, without entertaining an iota of doubt. So much so that he spun about eighty pounds of wool within a short span of about eight months and proudly sent the same to Gandhi, his revered teacher, for his kind perusal!

What is the inherent linkage between non-violence and spinning? Through his several letters to Prithvi Singh in prison, Gandhi explained to him how spinning on the Charkha is a singular mode of going into meditation. Spinning requires the utmost concentration. The slightest distraction or deviation in thoughts of the spinner causes discord between the spinning thread and the wheel, resulting in a break in the thread. With ceaseless practise of spending hours at the spinning-wheel, the power of concentration increases, which, in turn, makes one's own inner thoughts pure and sublime, free from hatred and prejudices, and thereby inculcating the values of compassion, simplicity and self-sacrifice. Thus, the spinning exercise itself manifestly becomes, as Gandhi himself put it, 'a means of developing a sense of non-violence.' In Gandhi's estimate, Prithvi Singh is 'one of the few who are capable of understanding' and realizing this simple truth in their 'thought and action'.[147]

In sum, the Gandhian principle of non-violence (Ahimsa) is not just an opposite of violence (Himsa), but an all pervading, comprehensive, concept, inhering the multiple core values of life. And the teacher in Gandhi successfully taught those values to the student in Prithvi Singh. This teacher-taught relationship between Gandhi and Prithvi Singh, in our understanding, is premised on the Upanishadic principle of lore, which clearly states that one can attain enlightenment only through *faith, understanding, and realization*. This is what had happened in the life story of Prithvi Singh under the benevolent influence of Gandhi.[148] In the light of this narrative of teacher-taught relationship between Gandhi and Prithvi Singh, we may now examine its relevance in the contemporary system of education in India.

Most recently, our modern system of education stands marked by the latest new National Educational Policy (NEP) of 2020. This policy has been searchingly formulated with the emphatic objective that the purpose of education is to 'enable personal accomplishment and enlightenment, constructive public engagement, and productive contribution to society.'[149] With the formal announcement on July 29, 2020, the new NEP (2020)

---

[147] *Ibid.*

[148] The correspondence between Gandhi and Prithvi Singh, shows how the teacher in Gandhi influenced the student in Prithvi Singh, so much so in the estimate of Gandhi, Prithvi Singh was 'one of the few who are capable of understanding their mind.'

[149] The NEP (2020) took about six years to fructify since January 2015, and is premised upon nearly two lakh solid suggestions emanating from unprecedented wide range consultation that took place with 2.5 lakh Gram Panchayats, 6,600 Blocks and 676 Districts in Committees constituted under the chairmanship of former cabinet secretary T.S.R. Subramanian and eminent scientist K. Kasturirangan. In this respect, the objective of successive national

'replaces the 34-year-old National Policy on Education and is aimed at paving the way for transformational reforms in school and higher education systems to make India a global knowledge superpower,' proclaimed Prime Minister Narendra Modi.[150] He elaborated that there was a need 'to take knowledge related to agriculture and its practical application to school level,' and that under the NEP (2020) efforts are on 'to introduce Agriculture subject at middle-school level in villages.'[151] He sanguinely hoped that 'the cooperation of the agricultural universities in developing ecosystem to streamline the flow of knowledge and expertise from campus to field' would play a vital role in the reconstruction of society.[152]

Speaking at the Conclave on NEP (2020) organized by the Ministry of Education via video conference held on September 11, 2020, Prime Minister Modi spoke again on the inherent and implicit value of the new education policy. He laconically stated that hitherto in our approach to education, 'mark-sheet' has become a 'pressure sheet' for students and a 'prestige sheet' for parents.[153] Recognizing this 'marks driven' approach as a 'major drawback,' he emphatically recounted that NEP (2020) is essentially and basically focused on true 'learning' by moving 'away from high stakes tests' and 'towards self-assessment and peer assessment.'[154]

---

educational policies as reflected in University Education Commission (1948-49), Secondary Education Commission (1952-53), D.S. Kothari Commission (1964-65), and the National Policy of Education (1968) may be compared.

[150] See, *The Indian Express*, August 30, 2020: 'Need to take farm education to middle-school level.' PM Modi made this elaboration after the virtual inauguration of the College and Administration building complex of the Rani Lakshmi Bai Central Agricultural University, Jhansi (Haryana) on August 29, 2020.

[151] *Ibid*.

[152] *Ibid*.

[153] See, *The Indian Express*, September 12, 2020: 'Mark-sheet shouldn't be pressure sheet or prestige sheet.'

[154] *Ibid*.

This pragmatic perspective of NEP (2020) stood fully realized by Gandhi in his exposition of the prime principle of *truth and non-violence*. Prithvi Singh has alluded to this prime principle of Gandhi as an integral component of the daily life of an individual by observing:[155]

> Bapu had taught us to prepare compost manure but our countrymen have not yet appreciated this cheap method of doing so. It is not mere hygienic consideration, which keeps our latrines clean. It has an economic value which we should learn to understand and to carry out. On occasions, I have explained to others Bapu's point of view. But most of the Ashramites did it only to please Bapu and to earn his blessings.

The new policy of education with its central focus on 'personal accomplishment and enlightenment' of each and every individual, engaging one and all to contribute towards the gigantic task of socio-economic reconstruction by being one's own productive best, is indeed a historic step. In our own view, NEP (2020) resolutely rejects the policy of 'exclusion' premised upon the contrived processes of 'selections' through an incredibly high rate of 'rejections'. This was the colonial concept of education. It was indeed a shrewd strategy of creating an elite class out of, and amongst, the Indian masses. It created a sharp divide rather than uniting people. Gandhi vehemently opposed it. As early as during the Round Table Conference in 1931, Gandhi is reported to have said in one of his speeches:[156]

---

[155] *Legendry Crusader*, p. 220.

[156] This prophetic statement of Gandhi has been quoted by Arjun Ram Meghwal, Union Minister of State for Parliamentary Affairs and Heavy Industries & Public Enterprises, while commenting upon the new NEP (2020): *The Indian Express*, August 31, 2020: 'On education, looking ahead,' wherein he acclaimed the NEP as 'an important milestone in India's journey towards becoming a global knowledge superpower' inasmuch as it makes a significant departure from the hitherto held policy-perspective of education.

> The beautiful tree of education was cut down by you British. Therefore, today, India is far more illiterate than it was 100 years ago.

The colonial concept of education was good for them, but no good for us. Unfortunately, however, we have lingered on with their concept, perhaps unwittingly. Hitherto we have been structuring the whole range of course curricula, right from the school to the university level, which forces gullible students to prepare for the high-stake national competitive examinations. Seemingly, bearing in mind this state of our system of education, a distinguished duo of a teacher and a researcher from a reputed IIT offered their incisive comments. They were prompted to make their comments in the context of the UGC making it mandatory for all universities to hold various entrance examinations before the stipulated date of September 30, 2020 despite the persisting pandemic of Covid-19.[157] Poignantly, they pointed out:[158]

> National competitive exams such as JEE (Joint Entrance Examination), NEET (National Eligibility-cum-Entrance Test) and GATE (Graduate Aptitude Test in Engineering) *have become the de-facto standards for education. The folly of this is well-known. They adversely impact the overall development of our youth.* They encourage coaching, and intervene in the state's ability to provide doctors and engineers from the local population. They distort the meaning and practise of science. And yet their impact on students and society has not been formally measured or accepted by the MHRD. The most exceptional is the UGC-NET, the qualifying exam for college teachers [Emphasis added].

Hopefully, this new NEP (2020), which is premised upon pragmatic suggestions, emanating from wide range consultations

---

[157] See, 'UGC versus States,' by Milind Sohoni, who teaches at IIT Bombay and IIT Goa, and Oshin Dharap, a researcher at IIT Bombay, published in *The Indian Express*, August 27, 2020.

[158] *Ibid.*

with the people at the grass-root levels, is bound to be distinctly different, both in its core objectives and methods of implementation. It is people-centric in its objective, as it is expected to fulfil diverse societal needs, taking the individual as the basic unit of the social group of which he or she is an integral part. In its implementation, the teachers are desired to perceive the problems of their students meaningfully and impart basic knowledge to resolve those problems skilfully through the presentation of real-life situations. Thus, both in the objective of the NEP (2020) and its eventual realization we foresee the evolving process of individualization-cum-decentralization of the whole gamut of education. Gandhi, in our understanding of him through Prithvi Singh, did visualize the evolution of such a process in the realm of education when he strongly mooted the concept of self-sufficient and self-reliant villages functioning as a little Republic.[159] Happily, Prime Minister Modi's emphatic statement of integrating the subject of agriculture into the curriculum at middle-school level under the NEP (2020) recalls the vision of Gandhi.

Finally, the question that remains to be considered is whether Gandhi's emphasis on living the life of austerity, simplicity, cleanliness, self-sacrifice, and self-dependence is of any relevance to us today. Prithvi Singh fully realized the value of these norms in his life as a practical exposition of the profound principle of truth and non-violence. He vouched for their validity during his sojourn in Gandhi's Ashram at Wardha.

Our contemporaneous world is most conspicuously characterized by the Covid-19 phenomenon. This has caused and is still causing unprecedented disruption in the history of human existence. It is a pandemic across boundaries of nations, irrespective of their status in terms of rich or poor, high or low, developed or developing, geographical location, etc. It has

---

[159] For the exposition of this concept, see M.K. Gandhi, 'Every Village A Republic,' chapter 24, in *India of My Dreams*.

turned lives upside down. Since its breakout in early March 2020, scientists the world over, with all their super scientific knowledge and computerised-technological-advancements, are still desperately trying to meet the menace of Covid-19. However, till the vaccine was discovered, their main recommendation was the concept of LOCKDOWN, which is 'one of the very few concepts' having 'unanimous scientific backing.'[160]

Lockdown, in its functional realistic terms, means to stay put within the confines of your 'home and hearth'. This led us to a very strange situation, for it instantly impacted almost all the facets of our life. All the educational institutions, schools, colleges and universities, for instance, stood shut. Movement of all goods and services stood suspended likewise. Any national or international travel is still sanctioned most grudgingly.

A way has to be found to come out of this turmoil. One solution was the rule of 'social distancing' backed by the mandatory wearing of masks by individuals.[161] This resulted in relaxing the inexorable rule of national lockdown. This allowed successive phases of lifting of the lockdown, permitting relatively more freedom and fewer restrictions on movement of people and goods and services. But still by scrupulously observing the norms of social distancing and wearing mask.[162] Despite these measures, as well as the administration of the vaccine, Covid-19 is still with us and according to all scientific predictions, it is likely to stay with us for an indeterminate time to come.[163]

---

[160] 'India's true Covid-19 test,' *Hindustan Times*, September 7, 2020.

[161] See, *The Indian Express*, September 17, 2020: 'Protections like Wearing Masks, which proved divisive in the United States, are now widespread on the Continent.' Even the USA is falling in line, see The Indian Express, September 18, 2020: 'Masks protect better than a vaccine would: CDC director (USA).'

[162] See the editorial, 'Lonely in the crowd—India is reopening after half a year in confinement, but social distancing is taking half of the joy out of it,' *The Indian Express*, September 12, 2020.

[163] With all cautious estimates, the WHO chief Tendros Adhanom

The continuing Covid-19 phenomenon has prompted us to recognize the mantra of 'stay home, and stay safe,' almost as an integral part of our social living. The world is 'learning to live with coronavirus,' else we are destined to be bogged down by the sheer weight of 'crippled economies.'[164] The gloomy prospect of Covid-19 has, thus, led us to discover new normative rules of social living. We are now used to cooking our own meals, washing our own clothes, cleaning our own toilets and bathrooms without the availability of part-time services of maids residing in close-by colonies. We are, per force, required to maintain our own lawns and kitchen gardens without seeking the assistance of a regular gardener. With the lurking fear, turning out increasingly to be more real than imaginary, of being caught by coronavirus, we are learning to forego the pleasure of going to theatres, restaurants, excursions, et al. All this is significantly and substantially changing the pattern of our living in the matters of consumption.[165]

Aren't the new emerging patterns of life leading us to be self-contained and self-reliant to the best possible extent? Aren't we learning to live the life of simplicity by critically differentiating the essentials of life from the non-essential ones? Perhaps we might be motivated to move towards re-establishing the social order, whose foundational values rest on the genuine concern

---

Ghebreyesus, on the analogy of 1918 Spanish flu, has surmised that Covid-19 pandemic 'will last less than 2 years.' However, he added that 'in our situation now with more technology and of course with more connectedness, the virus has a better chance of spreading: it can move fast because we are more connected now.' See, *The Indian Express*, August 23, 2020.

[164] See, *The Indian Express*, September 17, 2020: 'Even as cases are on the rise, Europe is learning to live with coronavirus.' 'In the early days of the pandemic, President Emmanuel exhorted the French to wage 'war' against the coronavirus. Today, his message is to 'learn how to live with the virus.'

[165] The most recent Reserve Bank of India Report made headlines in the national press on August 26, 2020 indicating the impact of Covid-19: 'Consumption shock severe, economic recovery will take longer, poorest hit the hardest: RBI' See, *The Indian Express*, August 26, 2020

for the welfare of others, as passionately pursued by Gandhi. Maybe, with the stamp of Gandhi-Prithvi Singh's first-hand pragmatic experience, some of the new emerging norms under the shadow of Covid-19, will prove to be a blessing in disguise. Don't we feel motivated to willingly accept and adopt those so-called 'abnormal' norms as truly healthy 'normal' norms of life even after the impending danger of coronavirus is over?[166]

In sum, in all the policy programmemes moving towards making India *atmanirbhar* (self-dependent) with all such small initiatives as *Swatchhbharat abhiyan,* movement to have clean, closed toilets in villages (from *satyagrah* to *swatchhagrah*), etc., aren't we re-visiting Gandhi? Gandhi's experiment with Prithvi Singh in the exposition of the complex concept of truth and non-violence, thus, continues to be inspirational, inasmuch as it teaches us how to make our social living simple, self-contained and self-sufficient.[167] As a pragmatic example of teacher-taught relationship, we, the teachers, also need to learn and imbibe from Gandhi-Prithvi Singh's experience, how the mutuality of

---

[166] See. *The Indian Express*, August 28, 2020: 'New Normal' by Commander N.K. Singla. He has candidly stated that the public is restricting itself to the purchase of only the essentials, the utility stuff, and getting used to making do with whatever is available, the demand of luxury items like jewellery, expensive clothing, watches, shoes, etc. has evaporated. He concluded by saying that 'Corona is changing our behaviour about shopping and purpose of movement. The technological interventions may make many of these changes last.'

[167] The writer had the privilege of being the son-in-law of Baba Prithvi Singh. He got married to his distinguished daughter Dr. Pragya Prabha Prithvi Singh, who joined Punjab Civil Medical Service [PCMS] after her selection through Punjab Public Service Commission. This proximity gave him an exquisite opportunity of observing the impact of Gandhi on Prithvi Singh. To wit, Prithvi Singh was the first one to start in his native village *gobar gas plant, providing gas for cooking and lighting, manure for organic farming, and closed clean toilets, maintenance of a water tank for providing clean water for animals, and procuring a healthy Bull for improving progeny of cows and bullocks!*

trust is perhaps the most critical element in the whole process of learning and imparting education.

Besides, happily, the very name and association of Gandhi still evokes admiration and respect for him and his philosophy of truth and non-violence the world over. How else do we explain that a simple pair of spectacles once worn by Gandhi while in South Africa would fetch 260,000 pounds in an online auction![168] Herein lies the value of Gandhi not only then, but even now!

____

[168] See, *The Indian Express*, August 23, 2020: 'Spectacles 'worn by Gandhi' sets auction record.'

GANDHIJI AND MANI BHAVAN

Sandhya Mehta

1919 and Satyagraha against Rowlatt Act

1919 was a very important year for Gandhiji and India. In February 1919, the Rowlatt Bill was passed by the Imperial Legislative Council in London which curbed the liberties of Indians. The colonial government could arrest any person without a trial who was suspected to have anti-British activities and exercised strict control over the press. Gandhi felt that this Bill was a severe blow to the freedom and rights of an individual. He called for a nationwide Satyagraha or passive resistance against the Rowlatt Act or Black Act as it was known in India. Thus 'the first step that shook the mighty British Empire was taken here' (*Gandhiji and Mani Bhavan*).

Gandhi gave a call that 6th April 1919 should be observed as Satyagraha Day against the Rowlatt Act. It was a day of national humiliation and mourning. He urged people to keep a fast and take the pledge of Civil Disobedience on that day. The day was known as Black Sunday. 'On 4th April 1919, the poster of the 'Black Sunday' appeared in The Bombay Chronicle. Directions (and the poster both presumably drafted by Gandhi) were also given to the demonstrators to observe 6th April as 'a day of humiliation and prayer and also of mourning by reason of the Delhi tragedy' (Thakkar and Mehta 2017, 36).

Early morning of 6th April, Gandhiji walked from Mani Bhavan to Chowpatty to observe Black Sunday by taking a bath in the sea, offering prayers and observing the fast. He was the first to arrive on the scene. To defy the Rowlatt Act, 'Gandhi as the President of the Satyagraha Sabha and D. D. Sathye, Umar Sobani and Shankerlal Banker as its secretaries, had appealed to people to make copies of the prohibited literature themselves and make them freely available to the people' (Thakkar and Mehta 2017, 39).

On 7th April, the day after 'Black Sunday', Gandhi published a newspaper, *Satyagrahi*, in defiance against the Indian Press Act. It was published from Mani Bhavan. The paper was the size of half a sheet. The Editor was Mohandas Karamchand Gandhi and the address given was Laburnum Road, Gamdevi, Bombay. The price of the paper was one pice. On top of the paper was written: 'Please read, copy and circulate among friends; and also request them to copy and circulate further'. On the same day, from Mani Bhavan Gandhiji sent a copy of *Satyagrahi* with a note to Mr. F. C. Griffith, the Commissioner of Police, Bombay, 'Dear Mr. Griffith, May I send you a copy of the unregistered newspaper issued today by me as its Editor? Yours sincerely, M. K. GANDHI' (Gandhi 1915-1917).

The enthusiastic support from the people of Bombay made this *hartal* a complete success.

It was during his stay in Mani Bhavan in 1919 that he took over *Young Indian* and *Navajivan* weeklies in English and Gujarati respectively (*Gandhiji and Mani Bhavan*, 15).

Non-Cooperation Movement

In 1920 Gandhiji decided to start the Non-Cooperation Movement against the British Government. He asked all Indians to relinquish their titles, resign from government jobs, asked parents to withdraw their children from government schools, boycott foreign clothes, councils and courts as a mark of protest. To put into action the scheme of non-cooperation, Gandhiji returned the Kaiser-i-Hind gold medal granted to him for his humanitarian work in South Africa. 'In his letter dated 22nd June 1920 to the Viceroy, written from Mani Bhavan, Gandhi stated that the Muslims and the Hindus as a whole had lost 'faith in British justice and honour'. Under the circumstances, non-cooperation was the only dignified and constitutional way' (Thakkar and Mehta 2017, 77).

On 1st August 1920, the Non-Cooperation Movement was to start with *hartals* and fasts. On the same day, Bal Gangadhar Tilak died in Bombay. From Mani Bhavan Gandhi wrote in *Young India*, 'Lokamanya Bal Gangadhar Tilak is no more. It is difficult to believe that he is dead. He was so much part of the people. No man of our times had the hold on the masses that Mr. Tilak had. The devotion that he commanded from thousands of his countrymen was extraordinary. He was unquestionably the idol of his people. His word was a law among thousands. A giant among men has fallen. The voice of the lion is hushed' (Gandhi 1918). Gandhiji announced the collection of Rs. 1 crore towards Tilak Swaraj Fund within a year.

The Prince of Wales was to arrive in India in 1921. To further the Non-cooperation movement, the Congress Working Committee meeting passed a resolution that, 'on the day of the landing of His Royal Highness the Prince of Wales, there should be a general *hartal* throughout India; and as to the effective boycott of any public welcome to His Royal Highness during his visit to the different cities, the Working Committee leaves the arrangements in the hands of respective Provincial Congress Committee' (*Gandhiji and Mani Bhavan*, 15). The Prince of Wales arrived in Bombay on 17th November 1921. People were asked to observe complete *hartal* that day by boycotting the functions held in honour of the Prince of Wales and attend the public meeting at a bonfire of foreign clothes at Elphinstone Mills compound.

On the morning of 17th November, Gandhiji addressed the public meeting at the bonfire of foreign clothes at Elphinstone Mills compound. He appealed to the people to be peaceful and follow swadeshi to win Swaraj and then lit the bonfire of foreign clothes. This was the third bonfire, the previous two being held on 31st July and 9th October respectively. The meeting was peaceful but in other parts of the city riots broke out. Gandhiji was aggrieved. He issued an appeal to the people to maintain peace. Realizing that the riots were not going to end soon, Gandhiji undertook an indefinite fast till the people from the different communities in the city made peace with one another and normal conditions in the city prevailed. When he was assured that the riots had subsided and peace had been restored in the city, Gandhiji broke the fast on 22nd November 1921 in Mani Bhavan along with the representatives from different communities who were invited to partake of the refreshments.

The Congress Working Committee Meeting, 1931

Mani Bhavan remained an important venue for the Congress Working Committee meetings. National leaders like Sardar Patel, Jawaharlal Nehru, Maulana Abul Kalam, Sarojini Naidu, Pattabhi Sitaramayya, Rajendra Prasad, Pandit Madan Mohan Malviya, Rajagopalachari and Abdul Gaffar Khan came to here to attend the meetings or to confer with Gandhiji.

On 9th June 1931 the Congress Working Committee met in Mani Bhavan to discuss the general situation in the country. Gandhi was against proceeding to London to attend the Second Round Table Conference unless the Hindu-Muslim question was resolved in India. (The First Round Table Conference convened in London on 12th November 1930 was inconclusive, as neither the Congress nor Gandhi was a party to it). He felt that if the conference became entangled in the communal issue right at the beginning, the real political and economic issues would not get adequate consideration. The Working Committee decided that if other conditions were favourable, Gandhi should represent the Congress at the Round Table Conference. He accepted the verdict but took the public into his confidence (Thakkar and Mehta 2017, 175). The talks between Gandhi and the Congress on one hand and with the government on the other continued. Following the talk between Lord Willingdon and Gandhi at Simla, a communiqué, sometimes called the 'Second Settlement' was published on 28th August. It provided that the Congress would be solely represented at the Round Table Conference by Gandhi. The document was signed on 27th August. A special train from Simla to Kalka was arranged to enable Gandhi to reach Bombay in time to sail on the S.S. Rajputana. The Commissioner of Police, Bombay, received a telegram from Simla on 27th August. 'Gandhi will arrive at Bombay on Saturday morning to catch the mail steamer leaving for England that day. He has no passport. Will you kindly arrange that he has no difficulty in getting one—Home.' A special passport was issued to Gandhi in twenty-four hours. A noteworthy feature of this passport was that a wrong birth-year was entered in it on account of the hurry involved. Gandhi wrote from Mani Bhavan before his departure, 'I must go to London with God as my only guide...The horizon is as black as it possibly could be. There is every chance of my returning empty-handed' (Thakkar and Mehta 2017, 180).

Return from London

Gandhi returned from London on December 28th, 1931. As Gandhiji disembarked from S. S. Pilsna, he was greeted by Kasturba, Vallabhbhai Patel, C. Rajgopalachari, Abbas Tyebji, Pattabi Sitaramayya, Subhash Bose, K. M. Munshi, Revd. Elwin, Mrs. Perin Captain and other leaders. The *Bombay Chronicle* gives a vivid description of the reception accorded to Gandhiji at the pier: 'holding a bunch of red roses in his hand and wearing a benevolent smile, Mahatma Gandhi passed through seething masses of humans' through his way to Mani Bhavan. 'The car bearing Mahatmaji passed swiftly through the city streets, reaching 'Mani Bhuvan' in less than 15 minutes...At Mani Bhuvan crowds thronged to have a *darshan* of Mahatmaji throughout the day, necessitating Gandhiji to appear on the balcony to acknowledge the people's greetings' (*Bombay Chronicle* 1931).

On 30th December 1931, the Congress Working Committee met in Mani Bhavan. It was attended by Subhash Chandra Bose, C. Rajgopalachari, Govind Vallabh Pant, Pattabi Sitaramayya,

Vallabhbhai J. Patel, M. K. Gandhi, Dr. M. A. Ansari, Abul Kalam Azad, Babu Rajendra Prasad, Madhavrao S. Aney, Dr. Mohamed Alam, Dr. Syed Mahmood, K. F. Nariman, Jamnalal Bajaj, Prabhashankar Pattani and Jairamdas Daulatram Alimchandani. In the meeting, Gandhiji gave a detailed account of his work in London.

The Round Table Conference was not successful. Gandhiji had returned home with empty hands. Though he received a grand ovation upon his return, he was heartbroken.

Just before his arrest on 4th January, Gandhiji wrote to Tagore from Mani Bhavan expressing his anguish, 'Dear Gurudev, I am just stretching my tired limbs on the mattress and as I try to steal a wink of sleep I think of you. I want you to give your best to the sacrificial fire that is being lighted. With love, M.K. Gandhi. January 3rd, 1932' (Gandhi 1929-30).

Arrest in 1932 from the terrace of Mani Bhavan

Gandhiji was arrested from the terrace of Mani Bhavan in the early hours of 4th January 1932, 'He emerged from Mani Bhavan, walked arm in arm with Devdas to the police car, and quickly took his seat. He was cheered by the large crowd which by then had gathered outside Mani Bhavan' (Gopalaswami 1969, 532).

Verrier Elwin, the renowned anthropologist and tribal activist, was invited by Gandhiji to stay with him. He wrote an eloquent description of Gandhiji's arrest from the terrace of Mani Bhavan:

> Gandhi was staying in a house called Mani Bhuvan and he invited us to stay with him there. There was great excitement in the city; the Viceroy had finally rejected the Congress offer of peace; Nehru was already in jail, and arrest of other national leaders was expected at any moment. But when we reached Mani Bhuvan and climbed to the roof, we found a great serenity in astonishing contrast to the crowds and turmoil outside. The roof was a very pleasant place. Low tents had

been erected, and there were palms and plants; at least 300 people could gather there. It was cool and you could see the stars. Bapu was sitting at the wheel quietly spinning. He had already begun his weekly silence. I carried on a one-sided conversation with him, and he wrote down his questions and replied on a scrap of paper which I still have. I must have begun by asking if there was anything I could do...Then Shamrao and I retired to the smaller tent and Bapu lay down about three yards from us, while some thirty others lay on the roof under the canvas shelter. Mrs. Gandhi and Miraben gave us a surprisingly satisfying supper of dates, nuts and fruit. But I could not sleep...At last I lay down between Shamrao and Bernard on my hastily improvised bed on the floor, just beside Bapu, and fell into a deep sleep, when suddenly like the coming of a dream there was a stir and a whisper: 'The police have come.' We started up and I saw what I shall never forget—a fully uniformed Commissioner of Police at the foot of Bapu's bed, and Bapu just waking, a little bewildered, looking old, fragile and rather pathetic with the mists of sleep still on his face. 'Mr. Gandhi, it is my duty to arrest you.' A beautiful smile of welcome broke out on Bapu's face and now he looked young, strong and confident. He made signs to show that he was keeping silent. The Commissioner smiled and with great courtesy said, 'I should like you to be ready in half an hour's time.' It was five minutes past three. Bapu looked at his watch and the Commissioner said, 'Ah, the famous watch!' and they both laughed heartily. Bapu took a pencil and wrote, 'I will be ready to come with you in half an hour.' The Commissioner laid his hand on Bapu's shoulder with a gesture so full of affection that I thought it was an embrace, until I realized that it was the formal token of arrest. Bapu then cleaned his teeth and retired for a moment. The door was guarded, and all of us who were on the roof sat round in a circle. I looked out onto the road where some had been keeping an all-night vigil and where a small crowd, very quiet and orderly, had gathered, but there were no special police precautions. When he was ready, Bapu sat in the midst of us for the prayers and we sang together the song of the true *Vaishnava*. Then

Bapu took a pencil and paper and wrote a few messages, some last instructions to his followers and a letter to Sardar Vallabhbhai...He then wrote a short note and gave it to me... Then Bapu stood up to bid farewell. It was a strange sight: the police at the door, Miraben and Devdas bustling to and from with the baggage which was already packed, Bapu surrounded by his friends, many of them weeping. Mrs. Gandhi with tears running down her cheeks said, 'Can't you take me with you?' Everyone in turn touched his feet, and when I said goodbye he pulled my ear with a smile. He was in very good spirits: he might have been going to a festival rather than a jail. Then, followed by the whole company, he went downstairs. Shamrao and I watched from the roof. The tiny figure got into the car and the crowd surged around it. It was a wonderful tribute to India's non-violence that there were only a few policemen and they were able to be in the midst of the crowd without fear of danger. Just at that moment, a message came to say that Sardar Vallabhbhai, the Congress President had also been arrested. And then the crowd scattered as the car bearing the very soul of India drove away through the dark and deserted streets (Gandhi 1930).

1934: Gandhiji's Last Stay in Mani Bhavan

'Congress Parliamentary Board met in Mani Bhavan on 15th and 16th June 1934. Prominent leaders who attended the meeting were M.K. Gandhi, Pandit Madan Mohan Malaviya, Sarojini Naidu, K. F. Nariman, Bhulabhai Desai, Bidhan Roy, K. M. Munshi, S. Satyamurti, Asaf Ali, Maulana Abul Kalam Azad, M. S. Aney, Govind Vallabh Pant and C. Gopalachari.' (*Bombay Chronicle* 1934). Again on 17th and 18th June 1934, Congress Working Committee met at Mani Bhavan, and 'passed a resolution on the Communal Award without accepting or rejecting it' (Gandhi 1932-1933).

While the Congress Working Committee meeting was in progress in Mani Bhavan, 'the crowds of people had gathered in front of Mani Bhavan throughout the day and clamoured for his *darshan*. The large throngs outside repeatedly raised cheers of cries of 'Mahatma Gandhi ki Jai' and on one or two occasions the demand for *darshan* was so insistent that Gandhiji appeared on the balcony and addressed few words to the gathering advising them to help the Harijan Cause both by action and by funds. Gandhiji performed his prayers in the open compound of Mani Bhavan instead of the terrace at the end of which he collected money for Harijan fund' (*Bombay Chronicle* 1934).

This was probably Gandhiji's last stay in Mani Bhavan.

Letters Written from Mani Bhavan

Gandhiji was a prolific letter writer. The following are glimpses of some of the letters which he wrote from Mani Bhavan or which mention it, which give us an insight into Gandhiji's life. It is interesting to note that Gandhiji signed the letters endearingly to his close associates: for Charles Andrews he was Mohan, to Sarojini Naidu he signed as Spinner, to Sardar Patel he was Mohandas and to Nehru a simple Bapu. The letters reproduced here are taken from *The Collected Works of Mahatma Gandhi*, with corresponding dates and volume numbers.

Bal Gangadhar Tilak had written to Gandhiji inquiring about his health. Gandhiji replied to him on 25th August 1918:

'I am thankful for your sympathies. It is natural that you are worried about my health. By the grace of God I am now better. But for some days I shall not be able to leave my bed. The pain was severe. Now it has subsided. I do not intend to attend the Congress session. Also I do not intend to attend the Moderates' Conference. I know that my view differs from those of both—Mohandas' (Gandhi 1918-1919, 204).

To Devdas, Gandhiji mentions having dinner with Rabindranath Tagore in Mani Bhavan:

'CHI. DEVDAS, (15th April 1920) I arrived in the Ashram today, Thursday. I completed the two-day fast in Bombay. I got the letter which you wrote after your return from Patna.

Sarladevi and Panditji are in Bombay. They will arrive here on the 19th, leaving Bombay for Godhra on the 16th. I saw a good deal of the poet (Rabindranath Tagore) in Bombay, too. I also had him once for dinner at Revashankerbhai's. The collection in Bombay should be considered good, though of course, it fell below my expectations. Blessings from BAPU' (Gandhi 1920, 209).

To the Editor, the *Times of India*:

'DEAR SIR STANLEY REED, (April 30th, 1919) I enclose herewith the form of the swadeshi pledge. I am anxious, if I can, to secure English supporters. I am the more so at the present moment in order to emphasize in a concrete manner the fact that swadeshi is being taken up not in any spirit of antagonism or retaliation, but that it is being taken up as a matter of necessity for the well-being of India. I would be delighted if you could see your way to sign the pledge, and if you approve of it, I would like you to secure further English signatures. M. K. G.' (Gandhi 1918-1919, 461).

To Lady Tata:

'DEAR LADY TATA, (August 21st, 1919) No apology was necessary regarding the spinning-wheel. I am sorry you remained without one for so long. If you would send your car about noon (Friday), I shall send one machine and some dressed cotton with Govind Baboo who will be able to give you a few tips about spinning and keeping the machine in order, if you could give him a little time. I shall treasure that story about the Governor. It is too good to be hawked about. You need not therefore fear publicity. God willing, your prophecy shall come true. Yours sincerely, M. K. GANDHI' (Gandhi 1919, 308).

To Patel:

'BHAI SHRI VALLABHBHAI, (On or after July 15th, 1921) Please settle the matter of the grant (to schools) to Anusuyabehn (Anusuyaben Sarabhai). Go and see her and give her a cheque or as much as she wants.

Tell Maniben or Dahyabhai that I had again a long talk with Vithalbhai. I think he understands the importance of the spinning wheel a little better now. I do feel that his proper field is the Councils. He cannot go among the people, mix with them and serve them. It is not as if he did not want to serve. Only he has not trained himself to do so. He has trained himself for other work. It seems to me that the two kinds of work require different aptitudes. I have come across no one in Bombay who speaks ill of Vithalbhai. Vandemataram from MOHANDAS' (Gandhi 1921, 432).

To C.F. Andrews:

'MY DEAR CHARLIE, (July 18th 1921) I am neglecting you if not writing to you can be called a neglect of duty. You are ever with me in spirit. I had thought you were in Simla. I have not seen Stokes' open letter. But this week's Y.I. (*Young India*) will have a leading article on *begar* and on the position of women. I have dealt with your message to Bengal in the matter. Do please get well. Give my love to Gurudev and tell me how he is keeping in health. With love, Yours, MOHAN' (Gandhi 1921, 453).

To Sarojini Naidu (August 7th, 1929):

'MY DEAR PEACE-MAKER, I have your letter giving me all the information about dogs and daughters. I suppose you put the dogs first because they are less troublesome. I shall be in Bombay on 11th by the Gujarat Mail, not the Kathiawar Mail which comes an hour later. I dare not stay at the Taj. I must go to Laburnum Road (Mani Bhavan). Nothing will be required at Mr. Jinnah's house as I shall have taken horse's food at Laburnum Road. You will please send me back the same day. Lovingly yours, MATTER-OF-FACT (NOT MYSTIC) SPINNER' (Gandhi 1929, 354).

To Nehru:

'MY DEAR JAWAHAR, (January 2nd, 1932) I was delighted to receive your letter. You have no cause to envy us poor folk outside. But we do envy you for getting all the glory and leaving the drudgery to the outsiders. But we are plotting vengeance. I hope you are allowed to get some newspapers. In all I am doing you are constantly before my mind's eye. I saw Kamala the other day. She does need plenty of rest. I shall try to see her once more and insist upon her not leaving her room till she is thoroughly restored. I hope you will approve of the action taken regarding Dr. Mahmud. I am sure that the promise to pay the assessment on Anand Bhawan should be paid [sic]. Love to you both. BAPU' (Gandhi 1931-1932, 352).

Mani Bhavan—A Place of Pilgrimage

Mani Bhavan was the nerve centre of Gandhiji's activities and movements from 1917 to 1934. Whenever Gandhiji was in Mani Bhavan a large number of men and women would gather outside the entrance to get a glimpse of Gandhiji and sing patriotic songs. This house played host to prominent national leaders, Congress workers, businessmen, foreign delegates, journalists and well-wishers—who would call on Gandhiji for meetings, discussions or consultations.

Today it stands as a memorial to Gandhiji's life and teachings. This house continues to inspire people from all walks of life. The distinguished leaders and dignitaries from India and around the world come here to pay rich tributes to their hero, Mahatma Gandhi.

References

Bombay Chronicle December 29, 1931.

Bombay Chronicle, June 16, 1934.

Bombay Chronicle, June 15, 1934

Gandhi, M.K. 1940 *An Autobiography: The Story of My Experiments with Truth* accessed on January 5, 2021 https://www.mkgandhi.org/autobio/autobio.htm

1915-1917 (May 21, 1915-Aug 31, 1917)*The Collected Works on Mahatma Gandhi (CWMG)* Vol 15. Accessed on August 19, 2021. https://www. gandhiashramsevagram.org/gandhi-literature/mahatma-gandhi-collected-works-volume-15.pdf

1917-1918 (Sept 1, 1917-April 23, 1918) *The Collected Works on Mahatma Gandhi (CWMG)* Vol 16. Accessed on February 8, 2021. https://www.gandhiashramsevagram.org/gandhi-literature/mahatma-gandhi-collected-works-volume-16.pdf

1918-1919 (April 26, 1918-Apr 1919) *The Collected Works on Mahatma Gandhi (CWMG)* Vol 17. Accessed on February 9, 2021. https://www.gandhiashramsevagram.org/gandhi-literature/mahatma-gandhi-collected-works-volume-17.pdf

1919 (May 1, 1919- Sept 28, 1919) *The Collected Works on Mahatma Gandhi (CWMG)* Vol 18. Accessed on January 26, 2021. https://www.gandhiashramsevagram.org/gandhi-literature/mahatma-gandhi-collected-works-volume-18.pdf

1920 (March 25 1920- June 30, 1920) *The Collected Works on Mahatma Gandhi (CWMG)* Vol 20. Accessed on January 26, 2021. https://www.gandhiashramsevagram.org/gandhi-literature/mahatma-gandhi-collected-works-volume-20.pdf

1921 (April 6, 1921-July 21, 1921) *The Collected Works on Mahatma Gandhi (CWMG)* Vol 23. Accessed on February 2, 2021. https://www.gandhiashramsevagram.org/gandhi-literature/mahatma-gandhi-collected-works-volume-23.pdf

1921-1922 (Oct 27, 1921- Jan 22, 1922) *The Collected Works on Mahatma Gandhi (CWMG)* Vol 25. Accessed on March 26, 2021. https://www.gandhiashramsevagram.org/gandhi-literature/mahatma-gandhi-collected-works-volume-25.pdf

1929 (May 12, 1929-Aug 31, 1929) *The Collected Works on Mahatma Gandhi (CWMG)* Vol 46. Accessed on March 28, 2021. https://www.gandhiashramsevagram.org/gandhi-literature/mahatma-gandhi-collected-works-volume-46.pdf

1929-1930 (Nov 21, 1929- April 2, 1930) *The Collected Works on Mahatma Gandhi (CWMG)* Vol 48. Accessed on February 22, 2021. https://www.gandhiashramsevagram.org/gandhi-literature/mahatma-gandhi-collected-works-volume-48.pdf

1930 (April 3, 1930- August 22, 1930) *The Collected Works on Mahatma Gandhi (CWMG)* Vol 49. Accessed on April 8, 2021. https://www.gandhiashramsevagram.org/gandhi-literature/mahatma-gandhi-collected-works-volume-49.pdf

1931-1932 (Oct 13, 1931-February 8, 1932) *The Collected Works on Mahatma Gandhi (CWMG)* Vol 54. Accessed on April 8, 2021. https://www.

gandhiashramsevagram.org/gandhi-literature/mahatma-gandhi-collected-works-volume-54.pdf

1932-1933 (Nov 16, 1932- Jan 12, 1933) *The Collected Works on Mahatma Gandhi (CWMG)* Vol 58. Accessed on May 30, 2021. https://www.gandhiashramsevagram.org/gandhi-literature/mahatma-gandhi-collected-works-volume-58.pdf

1946 (Aug 9, 1946-Nov 6, 1946) *The Collected Works on Mahatma Gandhi (CWMG)* Vol 92. Accessed on May 30, 2021. https://www.gandhiashramsevagram.org/gandhi-literature/mahatma-gandhi-collected-works-volume-92.pdf

*Gandhiji and Mani Bhavan:1917-1934-*1959 New Delhi: Gandhi Smarak Nidhi

Gopalaswami, K. 1969. *Gandhi and Bombay.*Bombay: Gandhi Smarak Nidhi & Bhartiya Vidya Bhavan.

Thakkar, Usha & Sandhya Mehta. 2017. *Gandhi in Bombay: Towards Swaraj.* New Delhi: Oxford University Press.

AFTERWORD

Gandhi's Legacy: Satyagraha as Solidarity

Neera Chandhoke

I. A Fine Sentiment Called Solidarity

'[However] selfish a man may be supposed, there are evidently some principles in his nature, which interest him in the fortune of others, and render their happiness necessary to him, though he derives nothing from it except the pleasure of seeing it... [Emotion], like all the other original passions of human nature, is by no means confined to the virtuous and the humane...The greatest ruffian, the most hardened violator of the laws of society is not altogether without it' (Smith, 9). This is the opening sentence of the eighteenth-century Scottish moralist Adam Smith's magnificently crafted *The Theory of Moral Sentiments*. Though Smith is better known for his theory of self-interested action, in this work he focussed on the capacity of human beings for an 'original passion' he called sympathy. Sympathy is more than fellow-feeling. Persons are able to feel another's pain and grieve for their calamities because they possess imagination. We can experience the torture our brother suffers on the rack through our imagination. We can forge bonds of sympathy with people we may never meet. We can be happy together and mourn together. Sympathy breeds a fine virtue called solidarity.

A political community which is based on solidarity establishes a truth that is often overlooked by legal jurists. A society cannot be held together only by the dry bones of law. Legal ties prove brittle, laws are subverted, corrupted and ignored. Law inhabits a cold hard place. Political communities should be able to reach out to vulnerable sections of society, and to connect with each other. We should be capable of sympathy and solidarity. Otherwise we will continue to live in the Hobbesian pre-political state of potential war against others.

It was precisely solidarity that motivated the Russian poet Anna Akhmatova's famous poem 'Requiem without a hero'. In the 1930s, thousands of Russians were rounded up and sent to the Gulag. Anna spent 17 months waiting in long queues outside a jail in Leningrad to find out what had happened to her son. She began the Requiem with these heart-rending lines: 'No, not under a foreign sky/ Nor in the shelter of a foreign wing/ With my people there stood I/With them in their suffering.' How many of us stand with our own people when their rights are violated? If we do not do so, are we not diminished as human beings?

In recent years the notion of solidarity has gone missing from the Indian political scene. Religion has been politicised, and fashioned into a weapon to divide a democratic political community, and we see the deepening of fault lines in society. History, however, teaches us that where there is power there will also be resistance.

On 9 December 2019 the government introduced the Citizenship Amendment Bill (CAA) in the lower house of Parliament. At the heart of the Bill lies the dangerous idea that citizenship is dependent on the religion people belong to. Cleared by the cabinet in the previous week the (CAA), which was passed by Parliament on 11 December 2019, grants citizenship to non-Muslim refugees who seek to escape religious persecution in Pakistan, Bangladesh and Afghanistan, three countries in which Islam is the official religion (The Citizenship Amendment Act, 2019). The link between citizenship and religion violates the Constitution of India. It is inherently discriminatory. If religion is introduced into the concept of citizenship, the proposed National Population Register and the National Register of Citizens will be based on religious criterion. Who was to speak up for the minorities and for those of us who saw the Bill as discriminatory? Civil society has been pulverised, the media has knelt before power, judicial decisions have become predictable, and contentious laws are rushed through Parliament without discussion or debate.

And then the political miracle happened. On 15 December 2019 students belonging to the University Jamia Milia Islamia came out in large numbers to protest against the CAA. They demanded withdrawal of the legislation that connected citizenship rights with religion. This was India's civil society moment.

Civil society protests are however no longer acceptable to the current government. The police attacked the procession. Students were subjected to violence and the campus was ransacked. This sparked off chains of protests led by university students in the rest of the country against police brutality and against the imminent disenfranchisement of minorities. Indians marched in protest, holding the national flag in one hand and copies of the Constitution in the other. They assembled against the background of the national flag and portraits of Bhagat Singh, Gandhi and Ambedkar. They sang the national anthem and read out the Preamble of the Constitution that promises liberty, equality justice and fraternity. The Constitution was transformed into a public, accessible, and democratic document. The constitution, the protests established, is the anchor of our identity, the protector of our rights, our legacy and our culture. The occupation of public spaces, sit-downs on public roads, and the coinage of innovative slogans proclaimed and enacted popular sovereignty. The objective was simple, to reclaim the constitutional rights that had been granted to all citizens of India (Anti-CAA Protests, 2021).

The protestors highlighted one factor that is of enormous import. Citizens of a political community owe each other obligations of justice and solidarity against state repression. Citizenship, our young people reminded us, is not only about our status as a holder of rights, it is about membership of a political community. It is a relational concept because it establishes a bond between us. The bond is not based on blood but on belonging to a civic community defined by a Constitution. Citizenship is solidarity. And it is precisely solidarity that large sections of Indians expressed towards the minorities when they supported the latter's protest against potential disenfranchisement (Chandhoke, 2021b).

The onset of a social movement inaugurates a new phase of politics in a different mode. People come together, occupy public spaces, and through sheer togetherness demonstrate the power of alternative forms of politics. They reinvent the notion of popular sovereignty. In December 2020, thousands of farmers assembled on the borders of the capital city to demand the withdrawal of laws that were bound to harm the agriculturalist. Alongside, they asked the government to protect their livelihoods through other means. The visual and the political impact of the assembly was extraordinary.

So was the scale of the movement, led initially by farmers from Punjab, Haryana and Uttar Pradesh (Mashal et al, 2021). Within a short period of time farmers from other states joined in to create one of the most spectacular struggles for wellbeing, state protection, and the right of people to protest. The occupation of public spaces reiterated the basic right of citizens to protest against palpable unjust laws. We witnessed the recovery of agency in times of authoritarianism. The movement demonstrated that ordinary people possess the political competence to evaluate laws, and to judge an elected government. Politics is too important to be left to crafty politicians. In a democracy, the people have the ability as well as the right to participate in decision-making processes. In a democracy, the government is obliged to heed popular opinion. If it does not do so, citizens have the right to protest through a variety of means. The occupation of public land is one of these means.

The moment protestors occupy public land, space is transformed into a site of struggle. Movements imprint onto space the fundamental understanding that politics is contestation. They act against a form of politics that attempts to dominate and subjugate. They fight for a different sort of politics, a more caring politics, and a politics that is sensitive to the needs and the travails of vulnerable sections of society. They act, and in the process, they acquire agency that tells us who we are and what our rights are. This is intrinsic to the right to assemble peacefully. When citizens enter the public arena physically, they have to justify the stand they take. The act of entering the public sphere declares: This is who I am, this is what I stand for.

The process of justifying our stand makes individuals a part of a community. They understand that they are related to others because they believe in the same cause. Alternatively, they bring critical perspectives onto the issue at hand and thereby engage in processes of rethinking and reorganising. From a random collection of individuals the 'people' become a collective. That is why we witnessed the forging of a rare virtue called solidarity among different sections of the farming class, and between the farmers and other Indians. We noted with surprise and delight the development of a massive support system that clustered around the movement. Many demonstrators in the movement were not agriculturalists. But they were ready to defy the power of the Indian government; a government, elected in 2014 and re-elected in 2019, that is not precisely known for tolerating dissent. Numerous individuals and groups set up *langars*, provided tents, health facilities and small shopping areas for everyday needs. They played and sang the music of protest. Farmers planted flowers on their side of barbed-wire barricades erected by the police, others recorded day-to-day activities; some drafted petitions and demands, and answered questions of journalists, others strategized.

All of them bore stoically the infamies that were heaped on their heads by the cheer leaders of the ruling party. Protestors braved epithets, slogans that denigrated them, and allegations that they were nothing but instruments of separatism and terrorism. They saw their comrades brutally run over and killed by SUVs allegedly driven by functionaries of the ruling class in Lakhimpur

Kheri in Uttar Pradesh. They collectively mourned the death of their own. They withstood the blazing heat of Delhi summers, the crippling cold of winters, and torrential rains that reduced the site of struggle to slush. But they persisted. The scale and the intensity of political protest stirred imaginations and energized other people here and abroad.

Earlier, in the 1980s and 1990s, the Narmada Bachao Andolan had involved the same scale of mobilization and excitement. Issues ranging from the illegitimacy of forcible displacement, to the rights of Adivasis to land, to the harmful effects of big dams, to the disastrous consequences of the generic notion of development, compensation, and protection of the environment were catapulted onto political agendas. The movement generated a wide-ranging and exhilarating debate on these and related issues across the country and abroad. Engineers, architects, development experts, activists, academics, and journalists discussed, debated and disagreed on the advantages versus the disadvantages of large dams, and the right of forest dwellers to their habitat. The scale of mobilization was inspiring; the scale of debate over the ambiguous notion of development even more so. Research scholars completed doctorates on these issues, books were written on the theme, and internationally the movement attracted attention. The no-dam stance of its leaders dovetailed into an incisive critique of development by the global community of non-governmental organizations.

The movement perfected the art of non-violent struggles. Medha Patkar stood in the swirling waters of the Narmada river for days to protest against raising the height of the dam, because that would displace even more Adivasis. Participants went on hunger strikes, demonstrated in front the World Bank that had given a loan to the Indian government to build the dam, and as the farmers' movement would do many years later, stoically bore the most virulent of criticism. The farmers' struggle similarly catapulted an informed debate on the rights of agriculturalists to be protected by the state. The Narmada Bachao

Andolan lost its case before the Supreme Court, but activists continue to fight for the right of forest communities not to be displaced. The farmers' struggle won, in a manner of speaking. The Prime Minister, Narendra Modi, agreed to withdraw the three laws that corporatized agriculture, but the leaders of the movement rightfully want the government to deal with other pressing issues that threaten most sections of the community (Chandhoke 2021b).

Social movements might lose out against the power of the almighty state, or they might win. In any case they leave powerful imprints on the political consciousness of society. Every social movement inspires and instructs. And each movement throws up a number of questions that attract the attention of scholars and social activists. What inspires women and men to leave their homes and their workplaces and occupy public spaces for months on end? Perhaps protestors understand that the politics of assembling in public spaces carries a more powerful message than occasional soap-box activity or online petitions. Demonstrators observe silence together, they sing in tandem, they give and listen to speeches, they clarify issues that have impelled them to come out of their homes and occupy public land. In the process they clarify what they stand for, and from where they speak.

This is not surprising when we recollect that we are the legatees of Gandhi's Satyagraha, a mode of peaceful resistance that not only appeals to higher standards of political ethics to judge a law, but that also intends to conquer fear. So let us turn to Gandhi and his legacy of peaceful resistance and of the conquest of fear. We need to reinvent Gandhi as not the Mahatma who stood above politics, but as a political philosopher who can help us to negotiate our political predicaments and show us the way forward.

II. Our Political Predicament

We know by now that members of a given plural society are likely to disagree not only on what the precise nature of substantive justice is, but also on what the governing norms which can arbitrate between competing notions of substantive justice are. The recognition poses a rather intractable problem for political theory, because it enables us to recognise that a society may not be able to balance diversity of conceptions of the good with allegiance to a wider political community (Chandhoke 2010). Now that the assumption that the public sphere is neutral towards competing notions of the good has been exposed as one of the vanities of political modernity in society after society, the carefully constructed, but rather precarious, boundary between the public and the private has become even more unstable, even prone to collapse. Along with this debacle, the belief that people can fashion and pursue their projects according to their notions of the good, *provided* these projects conform to certain shared norms in the public sphere, has taken a hard knock. India's plural society is a deeply divided society, divided not only over issues of what constitutes a political community but also on the norms that can referee competing conceptions of good. The first tension, that is conflict between different conceptions of the good, can be resolved. The resolution might well consume time, and extract patience, energy, imagination and political innovation, but it can be done. The second issue is considerably more inflexible and resists resolution, simply because the status of the norm as one that is morally binding, and one that is a constitutive feature of our political community, is disputed.

There are two ways in which these obdurate tensions can be addressed. One, the state can establish through law what the governing norms of justice are, prevent further debate and contestation, and thereby proclaim an end to the matter. But attempts to reduce democratic politics to administration constitutes bad political judgment. It also shows lack of common sense. For politics refuses to accept banishment and erupts as a social movement but also as violence. Moreover, a foreclosure on debate and contestation contributes nothing towards the establishment of the morally binding status of the norm. It remains disputed. The other, and perhaps the only politically viable alternative, is to institutionalise procedures which enable dialogue among different groups on specific policies, as well as on the appropriate normative structures that should regulate a good society.

Dialogue on what the governing norms of a polity should be can aid the establishment of the moral status of these norms, and, thereby, render them binding, for one main reason. The process reassures participants and/or aspirant participants that they have 'voice' in the forging of these norms, or at least that they have the right to such 'voice'. And we can hardly dismiss norms as *not* morally binding if we have a say, or at least have the right to have a say, in the processes whereby these norms are forged. Dialogue appears particularly appropriate for divided societies like ours which is marked not only by a variety of perspectives, belief systems and values, but is also stamped by deep disagreements on the norms that can arbitrate between competing conceptions of the good. But there is a rather inflexible problem that we can locate precisely here. Theorists tend to assume the following preconditions for dialogue: equality, freedom, openness, publicity, readiness to give and accept reasonable arguments, and an equal willingness to modify original positions through debate and deliberation. But plural societies tend to be deeply divided and fractious. For this very reason the assertion and counter-assertion of truth claims are regarded by other groups as representing partisan points of view, and as self-regarding.

This closes off the very possibility of dialogue, foments the politics of distrust, leads to constructions of 'otherness', fragments civil society, proclaims an end to inter-group solidarity, and gives to the state immense freedom to manoeuvre between competing claims. None of these consequences are particularly favourable for upholding the norm which arbitrates between competing conceptions of the good and which can be regarded as the foundational principle of the body politic.

How do we establish the pre-conditions for debate and deliberation among participants who see each other as either the 'unknown', perhaps the 'unknowable', and often as the 'adversary'; in short, as the 'other' with whom there can be neither truck nor transaction? How do people who wish to put forth a particular point of view establish their credibility: that their reflection and their proposed courses of action are in the public interest, and not in the pursuit of some selfish private gain? How can communication among agents be enabled at all insofar as these agents can be persuaded to modify or moderate their original position in and through the process of dialogue?

Arguably, we have historical precedents that help us to address these questions: mainly, the Gandhian philosophy of satyagraha. Consider that Gandhi managed to accomplish precisely the onerous task identified above—that of instituting dialogue in India in the early years of the twentieth century, against great odds. In 1920 Gandhi set out to forge a mass movement in the country against British imperialism. He proceeded to transform the Indian National Congress from an elitist to a popular organization. By the time Gandhi embarked on this venture, colonial policies of enumeration and separate electorates, and the politics of religious organizations which had appeared on the political horizon to push their own separatist agendas, had propelled and consolidated divisive tendencies among the people. If on the one hand, communal riots among Hindus and Muslims had scarred the body politic with particularly vicious modes of violence, on the other, caste discrimination proscribed the 'coming together' of members of the Hindu community, as well as those of other communities, in any shared struggle. Undeterred by these somewhat formidable impediments to dialogue, Gandhi set about forging massive coalitions of religious groups, castes and classes, and thereby instituting dialogue. And dialogue requires people to be connected to each other through sympathy and solidarity. The process of dialogue allows us to understand the pain of fellow-citizens and enables solidarity.

Gandhi did not succeed completely in this endeavour because the country *was* partitioned on religious grounds in 1947. Yet he did not fail either, because millions of people across caste, creeds and class did 'come together' in and through the struggle against colonialism. The issue of 'untouchability' was raised in the public sphere by Gandhi and more effectively by Ambedkar. And the mainstream national movement led by the Indian National Congress did try to address the communal problem and commit to state neutrality and minority rights. The seeds of sympathy and solidarity had been sown.

There is more to the notion of Satyagraha which provides the philosophical foundation for civil disobedience against the state.

The Philosophy of Satyagraha

Gandhi defined the concept of satyagraha as '[t]ruth is soul or spirit. It is, therefore, known as soul-force'(1966c, 466)[169]. Distinguishing satyagraha from passive resistance and other forms of civil disobedience, Gandhi suggested that the philosophy is not a weapon of the weak.[170] On the other hand, it demands tremendous moral strength and fortitude, because satyagraha involves a relentless *search* for truth with steadfastness,

---

[169] Gandhi's doctrine of Satyagraha was derived from many sources; from the 'Sermon of the Mount' as much as from the sacred text the Bhagavad Gita, from Tolstoy as much as from Thoreau, whose works on civil disobedience he had become familiar with when he launched the civil disobedience campaign in South Africa.

[170] For Gandhi, passive resistance avoids violence but it does not exclude the use of violence; it is therefore a weapon of the weak. Civil disobedience is a civil breach of unmoral statutory enactments and accepting punishment, therefore, it is a weapon of the strong (Gandhi 1966c, 466).

commitment, fearlessness and willingness to accept punishment (Gandhi 1966c, 466). The philosophy of satyagraha enlightens the mind, but more importantly, gives to us a theory of action. In other words, if satyagraha gives us a theory of knowledge, it also guides us towards the right path. For Gandhi knowledge is action, and action should mirror knowledge.[171] The launch of satyagraha accordingly demands adherence to rather stringent requirements: agents must engage in processes of moral reasoning and moral judgment that allows them to single out an issue as a moral one, assess the issue in light of several competing moral considerations, and identify it as one that demands collective action. For Gandhi these processes are infinitely facilitated *if* satyagrahis subject themselves to rigorous codes of self-discipline. For instance, any satyagrahi who embarks upon civil disobedience must practise fasting, refrain from the pursuit of material interests and adopt celibacy.[172]

Agents have to undergo this rigorous training in self-discipline because both the body and the mind have to be completely at rest, and this is only possible if the agent is detached from worldly consideration. Detachment is an indispensable precondition of selfless action, inner strength and the capacity to bear suffering. Satyagraha is not meant only to challenge laws that in our considered opinion are unjust; this mode of activism also conquers fear. The conquest of fear through self-discipline

---

[171] Gandhian philosophy forms part of a general concept of *karmakand* or that the search for truth is an inescapable feature of action. Knowledge-howsoever provisional this knowledge may be-of what the agent is required to do, is the philosophy that bequeathed by the Bhagvad Gita enjoins action. This philosophy overlaps with, and yet is quite distinct from the philosophy of *gyanakand* or the attainment of knowledge, and *bhaktikand* or knowledge through worship. Gandhi's satyagrahi is a *karmayogi* who acts selflessly for the sake of truth. I wish to express my gratitude to my former student Rajesh Kumar for having pointed this out to me.

[172] In the Hindu and the Buddhist spiritual tradition, the search for truth involves deep reflection; therefore, all factors which may conceivably distract the agent from the pursuit of truth have to be laid aside.

helps to purify the mind of negative thoughts, haste, hatred and ill will to others. For Gandhi, these sentiments not only cloud perception, and thus thwart the making of choices that are indisputably moral, they are also indicative of a tendency to violence. And violence is the greatest betrayer of dialogue, because it subverts the very possibility of a shared search for truth.

How do agents go about establishing their moral credentials? How do they demonstrate to the political public that the issue that they seek to foreground in the discursive community is in the public interest, and not in the pursuit of some private benefit? Gandhi's advice to agents who wish to initiate a dialogue on the nature of justice is the following: prepare yourself for the original struggle; that of convincing other agents that the agenda of action you want to set forth has been arrived at through processes that are indisputably moral.

Processes of moral reasoning, moral judgment and self-discipline might well contribute to the prospect of establishing and reproducing the conditions of dialogue. This is because these processes help to establish the credentials of the agents who invite other moral agents to a dialogue as (a) selfless beings who are committed to the search for truth, in the public interest, and in a non-violent manner, (b) that the cause for which satyagraha has been initiated is a moral one, (c) that agents have undertaken satyagraha in full consciousness of what the penalties are, and (d) that they are willing to bear the costs. And it is possible to establish this, because not only dialogue but the *preconditions* of dialogue have to be both public and transparent.

Gandhi, as suggested by Rudolph and Rudolph, transgresses what are for Habermas 'foundational dichotomies', or the division between the private and the public. Gandhi's ashrams were public places, accessible to all, because these provided the sites for training in satyagraha (Rudolf and Rudolf 2006, 153). In other words, the moment the agent begins the preparation for satyagraha through moral reasoning, moral judgment, and self-discipline, these processes should be as transparent and accessible as the process of dialogue. The lesson is that agents must think through carefully the ideas which they bring to the dialogical public sphere. Or that positions that are taken in the dialogical space should reflect moral processes which are *prior* to the dialogue itself. This is the only way in which participants can be persuaded that the moral standing of the agent is beyond suspicion.

III. Gandhi's Truth

Theorists of dialogue tell us that participants must be ready to listen to, respect and accept other points of view as equally valid. Gandhi, I think, articulates compelling reasons *why* participants should be ready to respect the truth claims of others, and why they should be willing to modify their own claims to truth. One, satyagrahis cannot assert that their claims are based upon the discovery of absolute truths and are, therefore, non-negotiable, simply because, for Gandhi, no one can discover the full truth. We can only strive towards the attainment of truth. This carries the process of dialogue further, because the conviction that we are capable of knowing but the *partial* truth, serves to discipline the self, teaches us to modest about our own pretensions, and compels us to be accommodative about the claims of others.

Gandhi's truth pre-empts the use of violence in any form in the dialogical space. Violence for Gandhi symbolizes arrogance; or the conviction that since we know better than others what the truth is, our views should be given precedence in the dialogical sphere. Such a stance kills the very possibility of any meaningful exchange of arguments, because it admits of no other version of the truth but ours. The imposition of our truth upon others is to do violence to their truths. But for Gandhi, since human beings are not capable of knowing the absolute truth, they do not have the competence to punish other people through violent words, deeds or even thoughts (Gandhi 1966c, 466).

The nature of Gandhi's truth establishes equality in the dialogical space. The readiness to accept that our truth can be modified by the truth claims of others, and that their truth can further be mediated by yet others, and so on, does much to establish that there is no single privileged truth which can arbitrate between other notions, and which puts the owner of this truth in a privileged position. All known truths are partial; therefore, all truths are equally valid and deserving of respect. In sum, the partial nature of known truth acts as a powerful moral imperative to regard other participants as equal.

Thereon, the possibility of dialogue is greatly improved, because other parties are not constructed as the adversary, as the enemy, or as the 'other', but as partners in a shared search for the truth. This contributes much to validate the standing of other people as beings who have something worthwhile to contribute to the elaboration of an idea or a worldview. In other words, when we invite others to share in the quest for truth, or justice, on the basis of equal respect, we recognize the other person as someone who matters. We connect, we sympathise with the predicament of others, and we establish solidarity. This institutionalises mutual respect, prohibits the construction of 'otherness', and neutralises conflict which arises out of non-recognition in divided societies. The search for truth is inescapably social.

Contrary to popular belief in Hindu and Buddhist spiritual thought, that truth can be found only when the searcher seeking refuge from all distractions retreats to the forest or to the cave, as Gautam Buddha did, for Gandhi truth cannot be comprehended in and through the processes of solitary reflection or meditation. The real location of his truth is found in the plurality and the unity of life. 'If I could persuade myself that I should find Him [God] in a Himalayan cave', writes Gandhi, 'I would proceed there immediately. But I know I cannot find Him apart from humanity' (Gandhi 1976, 240). It is precisely this conviction that provides the philosophical underpinnings of theories of dialogue which emphasise the interconnectedness of human beings.

Gandhi's theory of Satyagraha contributes much to the reproduction of the dialogical process over time. Substantive rules of justice cannot be produced once and for all. Democratic politics is not a matter of reproducing that which has already been produced. There is, in Gandhian thought, no notion of an original Hobbesian social contract which binds citizens in perpetuity. The terms of the contract have to be constantly renegotiated, even as new insights on what justice is, and what truth is, emerge onto political horizons. Is the right to private property just, or should it be balanced by social wellbeing? Should a democratic system promote the rights of cultural communities to maintain and replicate their distinct practises because this is just and fair? Is it fair to discriminate against the minorities? Does the majority have the absolute power to rule?

For Gandhi the quest for truth is more significant than a final arrival, or the discovery of the ultimate truth. It is more important that people continue to speak to each other, rather than proclaim a closure on dialogue because they have arrived at a definitive truth. It may sound paradoxical but truth is always subject to re-negotiation. This is particularly relevant for divided societies. People should be allowed to come together and keep the conversation going. And this by itself might contribute to the ironing out of senseless conflicts that arise out of the lack of communication in such societies.

IV. Gandhi's Theory of Non-Violence and Imperfect Knowledge

Central to Gandhi's philosophy of Satyagraha that inspires many social movements in India today is his theory of non-violence and of imperfect knowledge. Gandhi begins his critique of violence in *Hind Swaraj* (2006 edition) by unsparingly condemning the culture of violence embraced by revolutionary terrorist groups in India and in London. This was in response to the 'reader's' suggestion that India could win independence by random acts of violence. Isolated and indiscriminate acts of violence would likely precipitate a freedom struggle. A quarter of a million men may be lost, but the land would be regained. The partner to the dialogue, the 'editor' (who but lip syncs Gandhi's words and beliefs) responds with outrage: '[D]o you not tremble to think of freeing India by assassination?'(Gandhi 2006, 60).

Gandhi's justification for non-violence, can be summed up in three interconnected propositions (Chandhoke 2021a, 213-223). One, the violence of colonialism is likely to precipitate violence as resistance, but history shows us that the second category simply does not work. In 1920, Gandhi at a public meeting in Calcutta asked the audience to ponder on the history of British rule in India. Did this, he demanded, not demonstrate that Indians have never been able to either resist, or counter violence with violence? 'Whilst therefore I say that rather have the yoke of a Government that has so emasculated us, I would welcome violence, I would urge with all the emphasis that I can command that India would never be able to regain her own by methods of violence' (Gandhi 1966a). But this is not practical, because Indians would never be able to arm on the same scale as the coloniser. To adopt violence in such circumstances would be to commit political harakiri.

But even if this were to happen, even if India could be freed at the cost of torn feet and bloodied hands, her people would never be able to realise what is rightfully theirs, or come into 'their own'. The phrase 'their own', which indicates that something is historically due to India, was related to his core concept of swaraj, and his belief in the unique civilisation of India that made the realisation of substantive freedom possible. His negation of violence lies at the intersection of the concept of swaraj and what to him was the historical legacy of the country.

When violence becomes the architect of history, Gandhi suggests, it can only replace one sort of oppression with another sort of oppression. Those who rise to power by murder, he said, will certainly not make the nation happy. When the political finger, whether colonial or nationalist, writes the alphabet of power in blood and gore and moves on, the script is ineffaceable and the imprint it leaves on the body politic, indelible. Violence leaves stigmata much like the murder of Duncan left blood on Lady Macbeth's hands: 'What, will these hands ne'er be clean?'. Gandhi understood the attraction that violence holds for a people frustrated and exhausted by the depredations of colonialism. But he also believed that it was possible to negate violence. If only we knew, Gandhi seemed to suggest, what violence is about, we would willingly forswear it.

He warns us that the power of violence over human beings must not be underrated. It is not a weapon that we can pick up and discard at will. It can best be likened to a quagmire that relentlessly sucks people into its murky depths. From here there is no escape. In other words, when violence holds individuals and groups in thrall, moral disintegration follows. For we cannot control violence; violence controls us. Referring to the killing of Lord Curzon Wylie by Madanlal Dhingra in July 1909 in London, Dhingra Gandhi suggested that, 'in my view Dhingra was innocent. The murder was committed in a state of intoxication. It is not merely wine or bhang that makes one drunk; a mad idea can do so. That was the case with Dhingra.'[173]

It follows that even if independence is won through violence, people remain in the grip of violence, and those who have committed violent acts become the rulers. Nothing changes, and nothing ever could change when violence is used to craft historical transitions from colonialism to freedom. If 'we' followed the logic that brute force should be used to get what we want, because the English used this sort of force to get what they wanted, then we 'can get only the same thing that they got'.[174] That he did not think much of British rule, which was based on greed and protected by armed force, was made clear

---

[173] Cited in Dutta, 1978, p. 72.

[174] M.K Gandhi, *Hind Swaraj*, op cit, p. 61.

in this stinging critique of western civilisation in *Hind Swaraj*. It was simply not a model that was worth emulating. Moreover, nothing will change unless people change their hearts and minds that have been enslaved by western civilisation. All that we shall see is more of the same, the reproduction of the rule of western civilisation in new forms and by new people.

More significantly, Gandhi seems to suggest that though spectacular acts of political violence may appear courageous and praiseworthy, they belong to the realm of illusion. The masses might admire and acclaim the terrorists for personal bravery, but they will remain untouched and steeped in passivity. Acts of violence are isolated from political movements. They reduce the people to an audience. No agent has invited them into history, and called upon them to make their own history. The people are condemned to remain spectators of actions performed by others, condemned to live out their lives as subjects, not agents.

If the colonial state after the 1857 revolt had tried to browbeat Indians into submission through efforts to create compliant subjects, revolutionary terrorists had converted them into spectators. These enervating effects on popular energies had to be neutralised, and people brought to realisation that the attainment of swaraj requires an enormous amount of hard work, courage, commitment to the truth, steadfastness and, above all, a system of public ethics. It is only then that millions could be motivated to struggle together for freedom, and reinvent both themselves and society. Swaraj, for Gandhi, cannot be won by the actions of a few; it demands collective efforts and transformation. It demands satyagraha.

Interestingly, Gandhi's rejection of violence runs along Marxist lines. The prime precondition of revolutionary transformation is political mobilisation. It is not as if a subject people do not have the capacity to struggle and speak back to a history not of their own making. But isolated struggles have to be brought together, energies have to be pooled, and political imaginations sparked through an ideology that gives them both a vision and an objective. This task has to be undertaken by a cadre of committed people, who have taken care to prepare themselves for the task of readying others for struggle. Having undergone rigorous training, the activist proceeds to inspire people and transform individual consciousness. There is a reciprocal relationship, between collective action and individual sensibilities, that of awareness of the issues involved and that of the need to transform oneself or radicalise oneself in and through the process of struggle. Struggle educates, motivates and transforms. No person, once he or she has been radicalised, can ever be the same. And no society, once it has been radicalised, can ever be the same.

Gandhi's rejection of irresponsible acts of violence as a catalyst for change was based on the same lines because the cadres he sent out to politicise people had to abide by the basic principles of Satyagraha. 'The small body of men and women who had prepared themselves for satyagraha through rigorous training must first mobilise public opinion against the evil which he was out to eradicate by means of a wide and intensive agitation...the success of the satyagrahi's efforts must necessarily depend not merely on the appeal to his own conscience *but even more on the awakening of the slumbering conscience of a large number of people'* (1973, 286).[175] Much like the vanguardist party, the satyagrahi has to tap and mobilise public opinion through clarifying the issues at stake, emphasising that injustice is a violation of what human beings are owed, and highlighting the need for struggle. And much like the vanguardist party that is expected to have studied history, sociology, political economy, psychology, crowd behaviour, collective action and strategy, the satyagrahi prepares himself or herself through rigorous training.

But precisely at this point, Gandhi departs from ideologies of revolution. Iyer writes that in his appeal to public opinion, and to the concept of truth and non-violence, the satyagrahi

---

[175] Italics mine

differs from methods of violent action, by emphasising self-suffering. We have to go, Gandhi suggested, beyond reason to appeal to people who have settled views. Their eyes are opened not by rational argument but by the suffering of the satyagrahi through fasting, and willing acceptance of consequences of their action or civil disobedience. The satyagrahi as a moral exemplar awakens collective conscience first through rational argument and persuasion, and then by appealing to emotions. As people begin to reflect on and analyse the injustice to which they have been subjected and that needs to be battled, they also come to think about the methods that should be used to battle these injustices. In the process, they are politicised and motivated to act. And this Gandhi felt was revolutionary because public opinion becomes a vital force and develops the real sanction which is satyagraha.

Much as the philosopher Plato in ancient Greece theorised, Gandhi sees society as the individual writ large. A free society is an essential precondition for living a life that we consider worthwhile, but unless we strive towards the realisation of personal freedom by trying to conquer ignoble and base passions, such a society cannot possibly come into existence. Connecting his rejection of violence with the need to go beyond the concept of mere independence, which will in all probability turn out empty and devoid of any further possibility, Gandhi suggested that violence can only befuddle the mind and obscure issues at stake. It is only non-violence that illumines our minds and our sentiments. For this the pitfalls of political violence need to be spelled out. Because it is only then that people will be transformed from being spectators to being participants in the struggle for swaraj.

Gandhi rejects violence for a second reason. Great historical injustices have been committed because agents of violence are convinced that their truth, as the only truth, has to prevail over rival versions of the truth. Battles over religion were grounded in flawed notions because of the very idea that we and only we know the truth, that truth is synonymous with knowledge and wisdom but goes beyond both these concepts to be identified with the ultimate meaning of life. This, however, is a mistaken belief.

Socrates had elaborated precisely this perspective in Plato's *Apology*, which Gandhi had translated into Gujarati. According to Chaerephon, Socrates at the trial before which he stood as an accused, had asked the Oracle at Delphi whether anyone was wiser than Socrates. The Oracle's reply was in the negative. 'When I heard the answer,' Socrates continued, 'I was puzzled because I knew that I have no wisdom, small or great. The only way of establishing that my knowledge was far less than the knowledge possessed by other men was to find someone who knew more than I did, then I might go to the god with a refutation in my hand. But when I began to speak with men who had a reputation for knowledge, I realised that I was wiser than them only because these knowledgeable men did not even know that they lacked knowledge. 'I am better off than he is, for he knows nothing and thinks he knows, I neither know nor think that I know. In this latter particular, then, I seem to have slightly the advantage of him' (Plato 1952, 205).

Gandhi comes to the same conclusion when he begins to examine the nature of truth. I, he was to write, have been striving to serve the truth and have the courage to jump from the Himalayas for its sake. At the same time, he confessed, I know I am still very far from that truth. As I advance towards it, I perceive my weakness ever more clearly and the knowledge makes me humble. Evoking the parable of the seven blind men who had only limited access to knowledge about the elephant they were asked to describe, Gandhi suggests that since human beings are in the position of these seven men, we must therefore be content with believing the truth as it appears to us.

But this does not mean that we stop searching for the truth, because truth, or in Hindi, *sat*, means a state of being. Our status is connected to our knowledge of the truth. Nothing is or exists in reality except truth. Where there is no truth, there can be no true knowledge. Yet, different sorts of truths can only approximate the ultimate truth. What appears as the truth to one person often appears as untruth to another person. But that need not worry the seeker, because different truths are like different leaves of the same tree. There is nothing wrong in human beings following their own truth, provided Gandhi warns again and again that we be certain that we know only the partial truth. We are all seekers after the truth.

There is a third and a stronger argument that Gandhi makes for negating violence. The western tradition sees individuals as moral beings but as discrete and as separate and separable from each other. We owe each other because each of us possesses a moral status and this status entitles us or them to be treated with respect. Gandhi eschews the idea that the other is distinct from us or is separable. Steeped in the Hindu doctrine of *advaita* or non-dualism, Gandhi argued that those who hurt others assault their *own* integrity, or that we harm a part of ourselves when we harm others because they are 'ourselves in a different form. If others represent us in a different form, then their welfare is bound up intrinsically with ours. I believe in *advaita* [monism or non-dualism]. I believe in the essential unity of man and for that matter all that lives. Therefore, I believe that if one man gains spiritually, the whole world gains with him and, if one man falls, the whole world falls to that extent' (Gandhi 1967, 390).

In most of his writings on violence and non-violence, Gandhi argues that we are not individuals who sit atop a mountain all by ourselves, nor do we arrive at a notion of what is of value and what is not. We are a part of society and this society gives us knowledge about ethics. Not only is the construction of divisions between human beings, or the forging of notions of 'us' and 'them', highly arbitrary, this construction is also harmful for us. This becomes clear the moment we begin to wonder what harming another person does to our own moral personalities. Gandhi's rejection of violence and the defence of non-violence tells us how people should see each other, as ourselves in a different form.

Gandhi's rejection of violence moves to a negation of violence and then a transcendence of violence and the embrace of non-violence. Gandhi negated violence because he saw it as incapable of bringing about substantive freedom, because it presupposes a flawed conception of the truth, and because it ultimately harms the perpetrator. The alternative to violence is, therefore, non-violence, which is a companion concept to Gandhi's theory of the truth and swaraj. For Gandhi non-violence is a default principle. It is not as if individuals are naturally drawn to non-violence. But they can be guided towards this end by the satyagrahi who as we have seen is a model of ethical conduct, and who by setting an example motivates people to seriously think about the problems with violence and the advantages of non-violence. This is something the individual who adopts violence to hammer in his ideology, whether the domination of the majority religion or the superiority of his caste, cannot do. The use of violence for domination closes minds and denudes psyches. Not only are the aims of those who adopt violence narrow, and their commitment to this mode of domination unthinking, they can only diminish society. Random acts of violence achieve nothing except a diminution of the human spirit.

Lessons of Satyagraha for Social Movements

The nature of Gandhi's truth enjoins all moral beings to seek to discover the truth along with others, in and through dialogical interaction. Dialogue, sympathy and solidarity is inbuilt into the philosophy of satyagraha, for satyagraha means nothing less than a shared search for the truth. The other political postulate generated by the philosophy of satyagraha is that of toleration. The moment persons realise that not just their religion, but all religions yield principles of morality, they also realise that all religions are equally valid. Truth can be found in great religions because each of these religions shares the same moral core: respecting the dignity of persons, and understanding the best life as one that moves beyond hatred or necessity and aims at non-violence and morality. 'The rules of morality laid down in the world's greatest religions,' writes Gandhi, 'are largely the same...if morality is destroyed, religion which is built on it comes crashing down' (Gandhi 1986, 62). It follows that all the principal religions are equally valid and deserving of respect (Gandhi 1974, 353).[176] This particular recognition was to define the proposition of *sarva dharma sambhava* or the equality of all religions, which was the unique Gandhian contribution to the concept of secularism in India.

The argument for toleration is deceptively simple. If persons have the moral capacity to know the truth, but not the entire truth, then no one person or group can claim superiority over another on the ground that their truth is the ultimate truth, and that other truths are false or travesties of the real thing. On the contrary, we should realise that just as our truth is dear to us, others' truths are bound to be dear to them. There is, therefore, neither any point in comparing religions nor in grading them. 'If we had attained the full vision of the Truth,' Gandhi was to write, 'we would no longer be mere seekers, but become one with God, for Truth is God. But being only seekers, we prosecute our quest and are conscious of our imperfection. And if we are imperfect ourselves, religion as conceived by us must also be imperfect... [and] is subject to a process of evolution and reinterpretation... And if all faiths outlined by men are imperfect, the question of comparative merit does not arise' (Gandhi 1932, 55).

This realisation leads slowly but surely towards respect for plurality of beliefs and *toleration*. In sum, Gandhi's theory of toleration is anchored in his theory of knowledge. It is of some

---

[176] Gandhi further validated this position by referring to the unique nature of Hinduism as a religion in which 'there is room for the worship of all the prophets of the world. It is not a missionary religion in the ordinary sense of term. It has absorbed many tribes in its fold but this absorption has been of an evolutionary imperceptible character. Hinduism tells everyone to worship God according to his own faith or Dharma, and so it lives in peace with all the religions' (Gandhi, 1966, 250).

interest to note that Gandhi's theory of knowledge provides the conceptual basis for his theory of toleration, exactly in the same way as John Locke's theory of knowledge inexorably leads to his theory of toleration. The parallel is not surprising when we recollect that Gandhi's theory of knowledge was fashioned exactly in the same context as the one in which John Locke wrote his famous essay on toleration: that of immense religious strife. Parekh suggests that Gandhi's notion of non-violence is conceptually located in a 'novel epistemological argument' that violence rests on false epistemological foundations (Parekh 1989, 173). But before Gandhi, Locke had arrived at exactly the same conclusion, through different modes of reasoning.

We do not know whether Gandhi read Locke's 'Essay on Toleration', though he was perfectly familiar with all variants of western thought: liberal, romantic, anarchic, and anti-modern, but there are certainly strong overlaps between the two theories, perhaps because the political contexts of these theories were similar. Notably, many of the enduring and authoritative arguments for toleration in seventeenth-century Europe arose in the middle of religious strife, the adoption of one religion by states as the state religion, suppression of minority religious groups and forcible conversions. Conflict over religion engulfed most of the continent in rampant civil war, posed a direct threat to social cohesion and political stability.

Locke's celebrated 'Letter Concerning Toleration', written in 1667, and his *Epistola de Tolerentia*, written in 1689 (Locke 1968), grappled with the very real problem that confronted English society in that period, and his position was developed on the basis of a specific theory of knowledge. Therefore, although Locke could argue that the origins of discontent could be traced to merger of the state and the church, official disregard of other religions and persecution of minorities, he also theorized *why* people had to be tolerant of other religions. All four drafts of the essay declared that all men had a right to their beliefs, or that all 'speculative opinions and divine worship' had a 'clear title to universal toleration', an 'absolute and universal right to toleration', and a perfect and 'uncontrollable liberty', because of the very nature of knowledge.

There is a vital difference, suggested Locke, between knowledge that flows from the comprehensions of propositions that relate to the experiential and the concrete, and knowledge based upon faith. The former genre of knowledge is verifiable; the latter is not since it emanates from revelation. Each human being has to, through certain justificatory procedures which involve reasoning, personal convictions, conscience and relevance, validate his or her faith. For this reason, *no one* other than the person concerned can ever understand why people believe the way they do. And if persons have determined their own faith because they have tested it against their own understanding and reason, they must allow others to so decide their own faith. There is no Archimedean point from which we can referee another's faith and find it wanting, because faith is purely subjective, and subject to only internal reasoning of the believer. Locke's theory of knowledge moves therefore in the direction of toleration.[177]

Gandhi's theory of toleration and proscription of violence is based on roughly the same context: violence between religious communities that had become the norm during the second decade of the twentieth century. Gandhi wished to negate this violence for three reasons—of which one reason was pragmatic, and the other two embedded in his philosophy. One, conflict between religious communities made the task of forging a mass movement impossible; a way out of this pointless violence had to be found. This he found in the precept of equality of all religions. Secondly, the employment of violence in the pursuit of goals dictated by 'this' or 'that' religion went against his felt conviction that no religion can ever provide a reason for, or legitimize, violence. Thirdly, toleration is inbuilt into the philosophy of satyagraha in general, and the nature of knowledge in particular.

But notably, toleration in Gandhian theory is not passive;

---

[177] On this, see Chandhoke, 1999, 96-101

it does not amount to the proposition that you remain content with your version of the truth, and I remain content with mine. In this sense Gandhi goes further than Locke, simply because he decrees that uncertainty about knowledge of truth should propel a shared search for the truth. And it is precisely this shared quest that establishes connections in and through processes of dialogue, and through action. The final expression of Gandhi's truth is not knowledge for the sake of knowledge, but knowledge for the sake of moral action.

Conclusion

Satyagraha can therefore be conceptualized as a form of dialogue in which agents seek to discover truth in and through processes of political engagement with other persons. It is difficult to know whose version of the truth is more valid. Truth can only be realized in and through dialogue, through giving of reasons which have been morally arrived at for our considered convictions, a willingness to accept other belief systems as valid, and an equal willingness to move forward with others in the search for truth. This is possible only when participants recognize that it is not their reputation as persons of integrity, or as possessors of truth, which is at stake. *At stake is the conception of truth itself.* Therefore, even though we enter the discursive arena of politics with considered convictions, and acquire thereby a certain moral standing, and proceed to engage with others on the nature of these convictions and on the nature of other such convictions, we do so in full comprehension of the limits of our own knowledge. Satyagraha thus involves connecting with others, developing sympathy with the political predicament of others, solidarity, and collective action in full knowledge that all of us are partners in a shared search for the truth. This is the spirit that motivates social movements in contemporary India and it is this spirit that guides knowledge of how people who belong to different commitments can live together in some degree of harmony.

References

'Anti-CAA protests gather fresh steam' 2021, *The Hindu*, 22 November, accessed on 7 July 2022 https://www.thehindu

Chandhoke, Neera. 1999. *Beyond Secularism: The Rights of Religious Minorities,* New Delhi: Oxford University Press.

2010 'The Quest for Justice: Evoking Gandhi' in Aakash Singh and Silika Mohapatra edited *Indian Political Thought: A Reader,* 39-50. London: Routledge

2021a *The Violence In Our Bones: Mapping the Deadly Fault Lines Within Our Society,* New Delhi: Aleph

2021b 'Re-Appropriating 'We Are the People' from Politicians Who Only Want Control', *The Wire,* 3 December https://www. thewire.com

Dutta, V.N. 1978 *Madanlal Dhingra and the Revolutionary Movement,* New Delhi: Vikas Publishers

Gandhi, M.K. 1932. *From Yeravada Mandir,* Ahmedabad: Navjivan Press.

1966a 'Speech on Non-Cooperation', Calcutta, 22 December 1920 in *The Collected Works of Mahatma Gandhi,* Vol XIX, 102-103 New Delhi, Government of India, Publications Division

1966b 'Hinduism' in *The Collected Works of Mahatma Gandhi* vol XXI, 245-250 New Delhi, Government of India, Publications Division.

1966c 'Satyagraha, Civil Disobedience, Passive Resistance, Non-Co-Operation' in *The Collected Works of Mahatma Gandhi,* Vol XIX, 465-467 New Delhi, Government of India, Publications Division.

1967 'Not Even Half Mast', 4 November 1924, in *The Collected Works of Mahatma Gandhi,* Vol XXV, 389-392, New Delhi, Government of India, Publications Division.

1974 'Notes: How Do You Pray?' in *The Collected Works of Mahatma Gandhi,* Vol LVII, 353-354. New Delhi, Government of India, Publications Division.

1976 'A Discussion with Maurice Frydman' in *The Collected Works of Mahatma Gandhi,* Vol LXIII, 240-241. New Delhi, Government of India, Publications Division.

1986 'Ethical Religions' in Raghavan Iyer edited *The Moral and Political Writings of Mahatma Gandhi: Truth and Non-violence* Volume II, 50-69. Oxford: Clarendon Press

2006 *Hind Swaraj or Indian Home Rule.* Ahmedabad: Navjivan Publishing House

Iyer, Raghavan. 1973. *The Moral and Political Thought of Mahatma Gandhi,* New Delhi: Oxford University Press

Locke, John. 1968. *A Letter on Toleration* (Latin Text, *Epistola de Tolerentia*), edited by Raymond Klibansky, translated into English by J. W. Gough Oxford: Clarendon Press

Lloyd I. Rudolph and Susanne Hoeber Rudolph. 2006. 'The Coffee House and the Ashram Revisited: How Gandhi Democratised Habermas's Public Space' in *Postmodern Gandhi and Other Essays*, edited Lloyd I. Rudolph and Susanne Hoeber Rudolph, 140-176 New Delhi: Oxford University Press.

Mashal, Mujib, Emily Schmall, Russel Goldman. 2021. 'Why India's Farmers are Protesting' *The New York Times* accessed on 7 July 2022 https://www.nytimes.com

Parekh, Bhiku 1989 *Colonialism, Tradition And Reform: An Analysis of Gandhi's Political Discourse*, New Delhi: Sage Publications

Plato 1952 'The Apology' *The Dialogues of Plato*, Translated by Benjamin Jowett, 200-211 Chicago, William Benton, Encyclopedia Britannica, reprinted by Oxford: Oxford University Press

Smith, Adam. 1976. *The Theory of Moral Sentiments.* Oxford: Clarendon

The Citizenship (Amendment) Act 2019, 12 December accessed on 7 July 2022 http:// www.egazette.nic.in

ABOUT THE CONTRIBUTORS

Akeel Bilgrami is Sidney Morgenbesser Professor of Philosophy, and Professor, Committee on Global Thought at Columbia University. He is a secularist and an atheist who advocates an understanding of the community-oriented dimension of religion. He possesses a degree in English literature from Bombay University (1970), Bachelor's degree in Philosophy, Politics, and Economics from Oxford University (1974) and a Ph.D., from the University of Chicago (1983). Professor Bilgrami has two relatively independent sets of intellectual interests—in the Philosophy of Mind and Language, and in Political Philosophy and Moral Psychology especially as they surface in politics, political economy, history, and culture. In the domain of Philosophy of Mind and Language, he has published a book in 1992 called *Belief and Meaning* (Blackwell) and another book published in 2006 called *Self Knowledge and Resentment* (Harvard University Press). His book *Secularism, Identity, and Enchantment* was published by Harvard University Press in 2014. He is also the editor of the books, *Democratic Culture* (2011), *Who's Afraid of Academic Freedom?*—with Jonathan Cole (2014), *Marx, Gandhi, and Modernity* (2014), and *Beyond the Secular West* (2016). He teaches courses and seminars regularly on the Philosophy of Mind and Language as well as Moral Psychology, Meta-Ethics, and Political Philosophy; he also teaches seminars in the Committee on Global Thought, the Religion Department, and in Political Science, on politics and rationality as well as on a range of issues from questions of secularism and identity to the effects of globalization on politics and political thought. His areas of research interest are Philosophy of Mind, Philosophy of Language, political philosophy, moral philosophy and moral psychology.

Neera Chandhoke is distinguished Fellow at the Center for Equity Studies, New Delhi. She was formerly Professor of Political Science and the Director of Developing Countries Research Centre at the University of Delhi. She has held several fellowships abroad and has authored many research papers and books. Some of her recent books include *Violence in Our Bones* (2021), *Rethinking Pluralism, Secularism, Tolerance: Anxieties of Co-Existence* (2019), *Democracy and Revolutionary Politics* (2015) and *Contested Secessions* (2012). She routinely writes essays and columns in mainstream media publications such as *The Hindu, The Wire, The Indian Express* and *The Tribune.*

Saurabh Chaturvedi: holds an LLB, LLM and Doctorate in Law from CCS University, Meerut, India, and PGDHRM from Indira Gandhi National Open University, India. Before joining academia, Saurabh served corporates including Reliance Industries, KJMC Merchant Bankers and Electra (India) Ltd. for more than 9 years at various levels and was deputed in various countries in Southeast Asia and Europe. Saurabh has taught at National Law Universities at Jodhpur and Patna in India, Ethiopian Civil Services College, Addis Ababa (Ethiopia), University of Iringa (Tanzania) and Queensland State University, Brisbane (Australia). Saurabh took many academic sessions with Southampton and Aberdeen Universities in the UK and Ghent University in Belgium. Saurabh has authored two books, *Child Jurisprudence* and *International Trade Law*, published in international ISI /Scopus and ERA Indexed Journals, and attended various conferences/ seminars organized by international bodies in France, Sweden and India. Saurabh supervises Ph.D scholars and guides LLM/M.Phil. students in the areas of Cyber Law, Human Rights and Jurisprudence.

Rajendrakumar Dabee is lecturer of Indian Philosophy in the Department of Philosophy, School of Indological Studies at the Mahatma Gandhi Institute located at Moka in Mauritius. He is currently Head of the Department of Indology. He has been in the teaching profession since 1991. Dabee holds a B.A (Hon) in Indian Philosophy with Education from the University of Mauritius and a PGCE in Hinduism from the Mauritius Institute of Education. He also possesses a Diploma in Sanskrit from the Mahatma Gandhi Institute. He did his Masters in Philosophy from Bharathidasan University, Trichy, and completed his Ph.D from Dr. Radhakrishnan Centre for Advanced Study in Indian Philosophy, Madras University, India. His thesis was on *Dynamism and Development of Māyā-avidyā in the Tradition of Advaita.* As an academic, Dabee has contributed several papers related to Indian Philosophy and Sanskrit language and has attended as well as read papers at conferences and seminars. He was also awarded Best Local Writer (English) in 2017 for his play *The Visitor* during the National Drama Festival. He is also a Certified Trainer of Facilitators for Ethics Education for Children by Arigatou International, Geneva and participates actively in Interfaith Dialogue, Peace and Nation Building projects under the aegis of the Council of Religions, Mauritius. He is the proud father of three daughters.

Anita Patil Deshmukh is a USA-trained faculty neonatologist by profession, self-taught social scientist by passion and developmental researcher by preference. Dr. Anita Patil-Deshmukh is the executive director of Partners for Urban Knowledge Action and Research (PUKAR). Anita received her master's degree in Public Health from Harvard and worked as a faculty neonatologist in a teaching institute in Chicago for over 25 years where she was the director of the Ambulatory Pediatric Residency programme for 9 years and Director of Continuous Medical Education (CME) department for 25 years. She played a major leadership role within India Development Service (IDS), a pioneering Chicago-based organization supporting developmental projects in India. During her voluntary tenure of 15 long years in IDS, she visited 44 Integrated Rural Development Projects in 12 states of India and learnt about the developmental issues from grass root activists and practitioners. She relocated to India in 2005 to contribute to the developmental sector and joined PUKAR. Her research interests are urban poverty, social determinants of health and urban knowledge production through the lens of marginalized youth. She has built successful collaborations with major global academic institutions like Harvard, Columbia, University of Chicago, Berkeley, and the Max Planck Institute in Germany, to name a few. For her pioneering work with Barefoot Researchers in slums, she was awarded the Innovator of the Year Award from the Harvard School of Public Health in 2012 and an honorary Ph.D from Bradford University in 2019. Recently she was invited by the UN Foundation to speak about the digital divide as a part of her work with the World Benchmark Alliance of which she is a member.

Karen Gabriel heads the English Department at St. Stephen's College, University of Delhi. She is also Founder-Director, Center for Gender, Culture and Social Processes at St Stephen's College. She has published extensively on issues of gender, sexuality, cinema, representation, melodrama and the nation-state, which are her core research interests. Her publications include *Melodrama and the Nation: Sexual Economies of Bombay Cinema 1970-2000*, and the edited volume, *Gendered Nation*. She is currently working on a book on dystopia, and one on homosociality. Her international fellowships and awards include the Digital Fellowship (2021), World Society Foundation and the Council for European Studies (CES-WSF) at Columbia University, the European Union's International Incoming Marie Curie Fellowship, Scholar in Residence at the College of William and Mary (USA), the Leverhulme Fellowship at the UK, Post-doctoral Fellowships for Gender Excellence at the Centre for Gender Excellence, Linköping University, Sweden, and the Government of Netherlands fellowship for her doctoral research.

Faraz Khan is a concept composer, singer and music director, Raag Gandhi. He is a registered Ghazal Artist at the cultural ministry, government of Madhya Pradesh. He has been awarded a production designer award at Reels Festival Los Angeles for the Art Film, *Road to Sangam*. He is also awarded by the government-recognized Yayawar group in Uttar Pradesh for work in the field of classical music. He does playback and background music in Ramdhari Singh Dinkar's Rashmirathi poetic *Mahabharat* light and sound drama. He has composed ghazals and songs for 4 live albums.

Suchita Krishnaprasad served as faculty in the department of Economics at Elphinstone College from 1984 to 2019 till she retired. She has also worked at S.P. Jain Institute of Management, Mumbai for a brief period. Her areas of interest are labour and development economics and industrial relations. She is a life member of the Indian Society of Labour Economics, and has presented and published several research papers at various annual national conferences held by the Society, besides a similar contribution in various international conferences. Papers written by her have been published in edited volumes dedicated to themes like globalization and industrial relations. She is closely associated with the Ambedkar Institute of Labour Studies (AILS) and has consistently worked as a resource person for the training programmes jointly organized by AILS and FES to empower trade union leaders with ideas for future strategies. Besides contributing as a chairperson for several University Grants Commission sponsored workshops, she has worked as a consultant and an external collaborator on two projects by the International Labour Organization (ILO). Presently she is working on another project for ILO.

Virendra Kumar joined the department of law in Punjab University as a Lecturer in 1967. In 1969 he proceeded for his doctoral studies at the University of Toronto, Canada and was conferred the Degree of Juridical Sciences (SJD) in 1973. Dr. Kumar joined as Professor of Law at Punjabi University Patiala in 1979 and later joined the parent Punjab University (PU) Chandigarh as Professor in 1981. Thereafter he was Dean, Faculty of Law from 1984-87, Chief Editor, *Punjab University Law Review* (1982-85) and Fellow (nominated), PU. In 1988, he was invited to be a member of the UGC Curriculum Development Centre in Law which produced the report of the Curriculum Development Centre in law (UGC, New Delhi, 1990)—a comprehensive report on legal education in India in order to promote excellence in teaching and research. He was awarded UGC Emeritus Fellow in Law (200-2004) and in 2004, and invited to contribute an article on Hindu Law to *The Oxford International Encyclopaedia of Legal History* (Oxford University Press, USA), published in 2009. He has to his credit 85 published papers, and his critique of judicial decisions of the High Courts and the Supreme Court (mostly in the area of Election Law, since the year 1984), is published every year in the Annual Survey of Indian Law. He has been founding Director (Academics), Chandigarh Judicial Academy (2009-12) and member of the committee constituted by the Chief Justice of India for examining the functioning of the National Law School University, Bangalore (2008-2009).

Vinay Lal is Professor of History and Asian American Studies at the University of California, Los Angeles (UCLA). He writes widely on Indian history, historiography, the Indian diaspora, colonialism, the architecture of nonviolence, Gandhi, American politics, contemporary culture, and the global politics of knowledge systems. His 18 books include the two-volume *Oxford Anthology of the Modern Indian City* (2013); *The Future of Knowledge and Culture: A Dictionary for the Twenty first Century*, co-edited with Ashis Nandy (Viking Penguin, 2005); *Of Cricket, Guinness and Gandhi: Essays on Indian History and Culture* (Penguin, 2005); *The History of History: Politics and Scholarship in Modern India* (Oxford, 2003); *Empire of Knowledge: Culture and Plurality in* *the Global Economy* (Pluto Press, 2002); and, most recently, *India and Civilizational Futures: Backwaters Collective on Metaphysics and Politics II* (Oxford, 2019) and (co-edited) *A Passionate Life: Writing by and on Kamaladevi Chattopadhyay* (Zubaan Books, 2017). *The Fury of Covid-19: The Passions, Histories, and Unrequited Love of the Coronavirus* was published by Pan Macmillan in October 2020. He blogs at vinaylal. wordpress.com and maintains an academic YouTube channel at youtube.com/user/dillichalo which has two million views. He also blogs at abplive.in

Sandhya Mehta is an independent researcher and a social media coordinator of Mani Bhavan, Gandhi Sangrahalaya Mumbai. Her publications include *Gandhiji's Views on Religious Conversion* and *Gandhi in Bombay: Towards Swaraj*, co-authored with Dr. Usha Thakkar. She holds a degree in history from the University of Delhi.

Zubin Mulla is a Professor at the School of Management and Labour Studies at the Tata Institute of Social Sciences (TISS), Mumbai. He has a degree in mechanical engineering, followed by a post-graduate diploma in business management and a doctorate in management from Xavier School of Management (XLRI), Jamshedpur. Prior to joining academics in 2005, he worked for seven years in engineering design and management consulting. As a management consultant, he coordinated large scale change management efforts in manufacturing and service organizations. His research interests include transformational leadership, values, Indian philosophy, careers, and evidence-based management. His research involves use of content analysis, survey methods, laboratory experiments, and field experiments. His pioneering contribution has been in conceptualizing and validating the construct of Karma-Yoga in management literature.

Ravi Narayanan holds a postgraduate degree in Social Psychology from Mumbai University. Ravi is Deputy General Manager, Sales Planning at Tata Motors and has been with the company for the past 22 years. With a flair for poetry in four languages, in 2016, along with Shital, he published a tri-lingual book which is a compilation of their poems titled *Do Kavitayein*. He is also passionate about music, being a percussionist himself. He finds it most fulfilling working with children in workshops. When he is not doing anything, he either listens to music or cooks for his family and friends. Knowing it is time to give back to society, Ravi co-founded the Saaraakassh Trust in 2015 with Shital.

Fauziya Patel is a lecturer at the Department of Economics, Shankar Narayan College of Arts, Commerce & Professional Courses, Bhayandar, Thane. She is also a visiting faculty at various other institutions. She is a writer of ghazals and poems in Urdu and Hindi. She is pursuing her Ph.D in International Trade at the University of Mumbai.

Nandini Patel is Associate Professor in Political Science at the Catholic University of Malawi. She is also involved in teaching the master's programmeme in Public Administration at Chancellor College, University of Malawi. Patel has over 30 years of teaching experience in India and Malawi. Her research focus is mainly on democratic institutions with particular focus on elections. She has conducted a number of studies on democracy and elections in the Southern African region. She is currently working on an edited volume on Malawi's 2019 tripartite elections focusing on the institutional consolidation of Malawi's democracy. She was a guest researcher at the Centre for Development and the Environment (SUM) at the University of Oslo, Norway in the year 2011, and the University of Fribourg, Switzerland in the year 2006. She was a member of the UN Peacekeeping Mission to Cambodia in 1993. She has participated in a number of International Election Observer missions in Africa. Dr. Patel is a board member of EISA—Electoral Institute for Sustainable Democracy in Africa. She was a commissioner with the Special Law Commission on Electoral Reforms from 2016-2017. She is Chairperson of the Institute for Policy Interaction (IPI), a governance think tank established in 2001.

Aparna Phadke is Assistant Professor in the Department of Geography, University of Mumbai. She has been engaged closely in innovative methods of learning to Jilla Parishad School children. She is also engaged in the wetland protection movement in the capacity of an expert. Currently she is working on a research project sponsored by the Indian Council of Social Science Research (ICSSR), New Delhi, IMPRESS on 'Urban Liveability'. Her research work has been published in peer-reviewed national and international journals. She has also participated in national and international conferences.

Niharika Ravi is a second year student of the BA.LL. B (hons) course at NMIMS, Navi Mumbai. She is a dog lover, an aspiring writer and a passionate student of Bharatanatyam. Niharika has invested in learning about history, international polity, feminist ideas and environmental issues. She is always on the hunt for the next opportunity to write more about these, but meanwhile, she is often found reading a tome in the campus library.

Shital Ravi is Co-Founder of Disha Counselling Center, and holds a postgraduate degree in Counselling Psychology from Mumbai University. She has also completed a certificate course in peace studies from the Mahatma Gandhi Peace Center (MGPC), University of Mumbai. In the last 22 years of her counselling practise, she has worked extensively with children, adolescents and adults. A seasoned classical danseuse, Shital holds a Nritya Alamkar in Bharatanatyam from the Akhil Bharatiya Gandharva Mahavidyalaya. She has won National titles like 'Singar Mani' and 'Natyamayuri', is a graded artiste of Doordarshan, and the recipient of the prestigious Central Government Scholarship awarded by the Department of Cultural Affairs, Govt. of India. A prolific writer, Shital has featured as a weekly columnist in *Daily News Analysis* (DNA) and as a fortnightly columnist in *Yuva Sakal*, supplement of *Sakal*. Some of her short stories were published in dailies like the *Hindustan Times*, *Dombivli Kalyan Plus*, the *Times of India*, etc. She is a poet who writes in 4 languages. Her English poems were published in magazines such as *Life Positive*, while some of her Hindi and Marathi compositions have been presented as dance pieces. In 2016, along with Ravi, she published a tri-lingual book which is a compilation of their poems titled *Do Kavitayein*. Knowing it is time to give back to the society, Shital with Ravi co-founded the Saaraakassh Trust in 2015.

Sybil Thomas is Professor at the Department of Education, University of Mumbai and has been in the field of teacher education for over 20 years, with a short stint of administrative experience as Principal of the St. Xavier's Institute of Education. She began her career in Higher Education by working with the Department of Adult and Continuing Education and Extension, University of Mumbai. Then she worked with K.J. Somaiya College of Education Training and Research for 9 years and then joined the Department of Education, University of Mumbai, in 2009. She is passionate about seeing how teacher education evolves to fulfil the objectives of Higher Education. Using mixed methods as an approach to research, she would like to see how teachers and students alike take part in the process of knowledge generation for the service and transformation of society. Her recent research project is *Understanding the Concept of Teaching and Learning in Teacher Education Institutions in Mumbai* as a co-investigator with a faculty from TISS funded by the Azim Premji Foundation University.

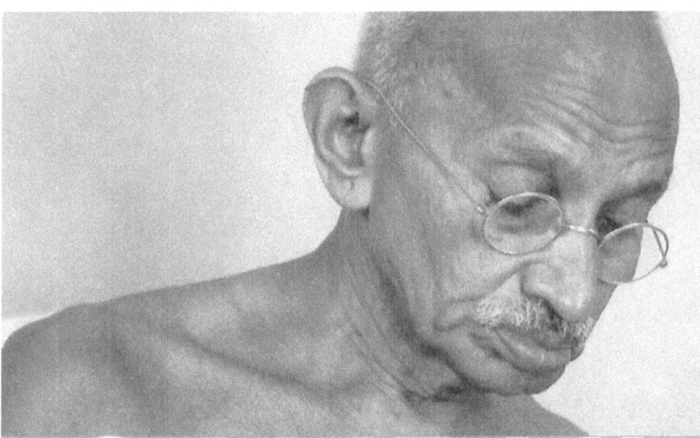

GANDHI
Then and Now

Autobiographies and Conversations

Edited by

Satishchandra Kumar,
Kanchana Mahadevan,
Meher Bhoot
and Rajesh Kharat

Foreword by **Bhikhu Parekh**